This Is Eric Sevareid

Books by Eric Sevareid

This Is Eric Sevareid

Not So Wild a Dream

In One Ear

Small Sounds in the Night

THIS
IS
ERIC
SEVAREID

BY ERIC SEVAREID

McGraw-Hill Book Company

New York   Toronto   London

This Is Eric Sevareid

FIRST EDITION

56338

Certain portions of this book have appeared in article form
in the following magazines:

"Warning to Young Men": *The Saturday Evening Post.* Copy-
        right © 1959 by The Curtis Publishing Company.

"You Can Go Home Again": *Collier's.* Copyright 1956 by The
        Crowell-Collier Publishing Company.

"Mano a Mano": *Esquire.* Copyright © 1959 by Esquire, Inc.

"Take Heaven, Take Peace, Take Joy": *Redbook Magazine.*
        Copyright © 1962 by McCall Corporation.

"A Harsh Word for TV Critics": *The Reporter.* Copyright ©
        1958 by The Reporter Magazine Company.

"Why the Aspens Quake": *Saturday Review.* Copyright © 1962
        by Saturday Review, Inc.

"What Makes America Great": *McCall's.* Copyright © 1961 by
        McCall Corporation.

Certain other portions were first broadcast over the CBS radio
and television networks and a number of other selections first
appeared in Mr. Sevareid's regular column, which is distributed
to newspapers by The Hall Syndicate.

For Scotty

Acknowledgments

The publisher wishes to thank the following magazines for granting permission to reprint articles by Mr. Sevareid which originally appeared in their pages: *Esquire, McCall's, Redbook, The Reporter, The Saturday Evening Post,* and *Saturday Review.*

Thanks are also due to CBS News, for which Mr. Sevareid is a correspondent, for permission to include many of his broadcasts, and to The Hall Syndicate, Inc., which granted permission to reprint Mr. Sevareid's columns.

Contents

This Is Eric Sevareid

Introduction

The twentieth century has now run more than
half its course, with its brilliant and blinding
discoveries, its terrible exactions in human suffering, its destruction of old verities and the
meanings of words. The author of the assorted
pieces in this volume has been writing, almost
daily, on the affairs of men, mostly their "public" affairs, for a third of a century. I am hard
put now to know if the forces of disorder on this
crowded planet, in this jostling American country are not overmastering the human instinct for
order; and, as I look over the contents of this
book, I am hard put to know if they represent
any philosophical order or not. If they do not,
then perhaps they reflect the events of recent
years with the only fidelity there can be.

A general journalist is jack-of-all-trades and
master of none, save the trade of being jack-of-
all. It means, I think, that he knows just enough
about almost everything to know when something hitherto unknown comes along. Others
wield the cutting edge of history, but he lives at
the growing points of society. Since he works

within the institutions and requirements of an essentially middle-. class society his work is bound to be essentially middle-brow work. He makes many mistakes but none is ever so serious as the mistakes of the specialist, as his discoveries are never so important. His daily work can be satisfying, his total professional fate rarely so. He is perpetually at school and conducts his education in public, which is often hard on others and embarrassing to him.

It is true that someone must do it, but it is also probably true that too many do it now. The modern means of instantaneous communication have made news of the doings of the most remote African tribe, and to feed this master's maw, the journalistic populace, the number of "communicators," to use one of the new words that offend my old-fashioned self, has doubled and tripled in my own time. I doubt that this represents progress, but then this is one of those bends in the historic cycle when men doubt the reality of progress in general; I freely admit that in the years since the last Great War I have often felt this doubt.

In any case, this is the age of the journalist, more than the age of the artist, the teacher, the pastor. It is the age of "nonfiction" because imagination cannot keep up with the fantastic daily realities. Like my colleagues, I am a creature of my times; all that we can do is to try to put down our daily nonfiction with some effort at locating its historical context, with some tenderness toward the flavor and integrity of words, and, in our moments of higher wisdom, with awareness of the eternal fate of man, a creature "trapped between earth and a glimpse of heaven." Without this saving grace falling upon us from time to time, without these reminders that this, too, shall pass, that men will do even more marvelous and awful things tomorrow and affairs will look quite different next year—without this, we should be proper candidates for the asylum.

In this troubling period since the Great War I have drifted all unsuspectingly into middle age, and perhaps because of this combination of periods, the world's and mine, I have found my own views changing; they are not as consistent as I think they once were. This has bothered me. It bothers me most acutely when I find myself with political liberals with whom I was once of consistent like-mind, people who have carried not only their thirst for but total faith in human betterment, straight from those exalting New Deal days, through the war and through this cold war. I know how comfortable they are and how snugly comfortable I once was. (I very nearly struck the adjoining typewriter key and made it "smugly.")

Long ago I accepted the whole formula. Conservatives were essentially reactionary, and what was not liberal was not only wrong but evil. Upper-class flesh did not feel pain as did lower-class flesh. Environment, chiefly poverty, was totally responsible for crime and vice. Colonialism had nothing at all good in it; all peoples instinctively preferred democracy to directed government and would make it work, given half the chance. What was morally wrong for a person was morally wrong for a government, even when dealing with a government like the Soviet Union which operates under totally different moral rules.

I am not so sure on any point, any more. I think now that a civilized man with a respect for the realities is both progressive and conservative, one who cherishes tradition and works ceaselessly for change where change is due. Nationalism may be the world's ultimate undoing, yet I know it is not possible for any but saints to love strangers as themselves and that a man who does not love his own country, and deeply, is maimed in his personality. I have acquired a more careful respect for man's genes and the animal instincts he has carried all this way from his jungle beginnings, and I tend to place more credit and blame for his behavior on his anthropological history, and less on his economic and political past.

I think, though others disagree, that one may be a cultural conservative and a political liberal. I do not know that education for the generality of children must penalize the gifted, that urban redevelopment must cost us our few lovely buildings, that air and space for the deprived must destroy our wild places. I know what Lenin meant when he spoke of the "idiocy of rural life," but it seems to me that life in New York, our cultural headquarters, to which the aspiring young still flock, is becoming an idiocy. I am aware of the "rising expectations" in so many poor lands, but I see too little evidence that it is a rise toward happiness or even contentment.

I may well be an example of intellectual schizophrenia, as one or two critics have suggested; if so, I hope I find the cure one day. For the present I find myself divided, not only between political liberalism and cultural conservatism, but I find myself politically liberal on domestic affairs and increasingly conservative on foreign affairs. This may be a genuine split in my marrow that no arguments of mine can bandage over. In the opinion of some men for whom I have a great admiration, I am just wrong in this. I have tried hard to see this and to make repairs, but so far I have failed.

I cannot get over the feeling, painfully acquired by travels of inquiry in Europe, Africa, and Latin America, that many of the best-hearted American—and British—liberals have misjudged the postwar era in consequential respects. In the realm of the political cold war they have been as essentially wrong as they were essentially right in the prewar era of Fascism's rise. Their intense self-consciousness about the faults of their own societies obscured their vision of Communist method and purpose and often caused them to equate East and West, in specific crises, when equation was false. The Cuban missile crisis was a prime example. They have not understood that, save in the vaguest of long runs, this is not a "battle for men's minds," that communism is not so much an alternative way of life as a political technique for seizing power.

In the realm of the transactions between rich nations and poor they have again tended to blame themselves, have not—until recently, perhaps—understood that economic rehabilitation as so remarkably performed in the Marshall Plan is profoundly different from economic development of backward societies; that the latter must be the work of generations, not of ten-year crash programs. They had not accurately measured the severe limitations upon one society's capacity to alter the nature of an alien society, or even to comprehend what is in the true interest of an alien society.

My recent travels taught me a cautious conservatism about American efforts to fulfill the "expectations" of foreign peoples. This mood settled slowly upon me; given my previous assumptions, I wore this mood awkwardly. I had entered a strange room, as it were; my eyes were not quickly adjusted to this half-light of dawning realities, and I frequently stumbled over the unfamiliar furniture. But I knew I was in the right place. It was a reassurance later to come upon a measure of corroboration in some words written by that perceptive diplomat, George Kennan.

We should, he said, "have the modesty to admit that our own national interest is all that we are really capable of knowing and understanding, and the courage to recognize that if our purposes and undertakings here at home are decent ones, unsullied by arrogance or hostility toward other people or delusions of

4

superiority, then the pursuit of our national interest can never fail to be conducive to a better world ... to many it may seem to smack of cynicism and reaction. I cannot share these doubts. Whatever is realistic in concept, and founded in an endeavor to see both ourselves and others as we really are, cannot be illiberal."

In June of 1961 I stopped in New York after two months in Latin America. The Bay of Pigs tragedy had happened. The American press and airways were still full of the cries of masochistic liberals who abhorred the invasion attempt, not because it was bungled, but because it had ever been conceived. They were righteously certain that the effort to help free men to free their imprisoned countrymen was not only against American tradition, but immoral. (Were Cuba under a Fascist, not a Communist, dictatorship, how differently they would have spoken!) They all fell back upon the argument that the real way to stop Castroism was to lift the burden of poverty from Latin America's two hundred million people. This was a preposterous argument, because poverty is only one of many elements—and not always the most important one—that ripens a society for a Communist seizure, and because ending or even sharply reducing poverty in most of that immense region is not within the powers of this generation. They did not understand that the Communists were lighting very short fuses.

My own pent-up feelings came to a sudden head of steam in a column written in pure anger, the one printed on page 162 of this volume. Like most things written in heat, it was melodramatic, in part overdrawn, but it produced a startling effect; no one was more startled than I. These words were reprinted all over the country and abroad. Liberal friends attacked me vigorously. Some of the most reactionary and isolationist of American politicians saw in me, they thought, a convert and ally.

However overdrawn, the article had a good effect. By reason of the fact that I was known as a liberal journalist and by reason of its fortuitous timing, it served as an intellectual catalyst. Responsible American writers and political figures began debating whether, after all, there was such a thing as "world opinion." The supposed virtues of the neutral nations were examined afresh. For the first time an intimation that Castro could, and might, try to hold the United States hostage to serious physical damage entered people's minds. (This was nearly a year and a half before the missile crisis.) The article helped set in motion a new and critical look by liberals and middle-of-the-roaders at our easy premises

5

concerning "foreign aid," its promise and its limitations. It increased the general but vague awareness—a burning conviction with me—that a showdown must come and must be won, if we were ever to get off the defensive in the cold war. It came, of course, when Khrushchev put the missiles into Cuba and this country, by the uncommon courage of President Kennedy, supplied what had always been the missing ingredient in the worldwide contest: the credibility of the American deterrent.

I was accused of advocating preventive war, which was far from my mind. I was accused of profound immorality in implying that the one sin history would never forgive us for would be the loss of this struggle, and was told that if we resorted to rough measures victory would be worthless, because we would have corrupted ourselves and the meaning of America. I do not believe this; I think American history disputes the notion. In any case, we were standing in more danger of purity preceding paralysis than of pride preceding a fall. One does not become a Machiavellian advocate of treachery or cruelty by saying that the moral concepts that should govern individual relationships cannot automatically be applied to the relationships of nation-states. The end *can* justify the means where matters of finality are concerned. Corruption sets in at the point when the means *become* the ends; I cannot believe America is going to arrive at that point, or anywhere near it. I remain uneasy when liberalism melts into purism, and I fidget when I hear statesmen say that so long as one American Negro is deprived of his rights, we have no license to be concerned about injustice in other lands. The first foreign policy this attitude would wreck is that of the moralists themselves.

Pressure and power are not everything, as De Gaulle seems to believe, but without national power there is little effective power to do international good. America cannot become cynical; it can only be itself. It is a good self because, almost alone among great nations, it still believes that men can be happy. If we cease to believe this, the world will turn gray. But how much happier we would be ourselves, if only we could remember that our moral duty to do good to others cannot exceed our practical capacity to do so!

It seems to me now, in 1964, that in the cold war between the United States and the Soviet Union things have taken a better turn. If cold war means a condition in which the big powers talk as if they were at war without actually going to war, then perhaps we are entering a period of "cold peace" with

Russia—a condition in which the powers talk as if they were at peace without actually ratifying the peace. That would be progress; but if it has come about, it has done so not because we have trusted Russia, but because we have firmly opposed her. The successful showdown over the Cuban missiles and the break between China and Russia have made a difference. It has been political events of this magnitude that have governed the changes, not our propaganda efforts, our Peace Corps, or our foreign aid, valuable as these enterprises are within their limited spheres. There is, between the two big powers, a kind of balance; the pax atomica is a scary peace, but it is the one we have. I do not see its replacement in my time. The danger remains, not of another 1939 with direct aggression between great powers, but another 1914 with the eruption of smaller powers involving the big ones.

So, life goes on. The ordinary affairs of men proceed if they do not always progress, and the traveler come home directs his attention more and more to the life of his homeland. The internal American revolution continues and never ceases to fascinate, to inspire, and to appall. The instincts of youth are still working in this country, as if by habit; yet there is a crosscurrent of the cautious second thoughts of middle age in the American stream. We do not automatically equate size with strength so much any more, or motion with progress. John Kennedy was the first of recent Presidents to directly concern himself with the qualities in American life, rather than with the quantities alone.

Not in a long time, I think, have Americans been so aware of the elements of venality, vulgarity, and meretriciousness in this society, as well as the elements of goodness. We may be breaking out of our obsessions with moneymaking and concrete-spreading. We are taking a harder look at what we have done to our systems of education, to our minorities, to our once-lovely landscape, and to our great cities, now becoming compartmentalized, faceless, losing their flavor and spirit. We now really, publicly, ask ourselves if Chamber of Commerce concepts of progress may not be our ruination.

America has always been told what it was *going* to be, as if the future alone was real. Now, it is becoming aware that there is no such thing as tomorrow, there is only today, and America wants to know what it *is*. Deep in its heart it yearns for an order, a form, and it is frightened in the thought that the hour may be too late for a high civilization, distinctly American, that our raw, youthful notions of progress, driven on by the mighty engine

7

of affluence at the top, may have lost the chance forever. We are frightened to think that the very rich grow richer, the very poor poorer, the dark-skinned more violent, our cities simultaneously more crowded and more desolate, our countryside more ugly.

Of course, the clichés we have lived by seem meaningless, "conservative" and "liberal" among them, in many contexts. The old apposition of "government interference" and "free enterprise" now makes only the most limited sense. It has become harder to believe that if only the people are given the truth, they will do the right thing, that some kind of folk instinct is better than expertise and aristocracy of wisdom and taste. It may be that without acceptance of intellectual and esthetic élites there can be no high order at all, only disorder; it is an ancient argument. What is immediately disturbing is that the contrast between the enormous amount of discussion and the small amount of sensible action is growing. Our traditional agencies and institutions for effecting even popular will are barely working, so remote have they become, so paralyzed are they by the infinitude of counter pressures. It is not that "the people don't take enough interest in public affairs"; it is that their interests so conflict that they cannot agree to give public authority the power to make and enforce decisions. We talk grandly of renovating the society of Brazil or Tanganyika while no American city has been able to solve its own traffic problem. Heretofore, we have "solved" many of our problems simply by using up more of our generous elbow room, in space and resources. The elbow room is about gone. America has reached a turning point; it must now begin to act as smaller, older European societies have had to act for many years. If we cannot now learn in our bones the meaning of the verbs "to refrain" and "to conserve," we are heading for the Age of American Disorder, and doctrinarians of democracy must not tell us how healthy all this will be. It will be approximately as healthy as the thrashings of a desperate man in a straitjacket. In mid-century, America is in search of its bearings, not only in terms of power and affluence, but in terms of the best sense of the word "civilization."

The present author, half sentimental and nostalgic and half hardboiled and apprehensive—that is, middle-aged in mid-century—feels sure of more questions than answers. That, perhaps, suggests the real function of the daily and weekly journalist. He is a prod, and there is little comfort in him. Mr. Walter Lippmann, who can stand as mentor to all in this trade, if anyone can, once said that the commentator's efforts are not to be taken and are not intended to be taken as final documents, but as notes made by puzzled men.

This volume consists of notations—partial, diverse, occasionally contradictory—made on the margin of time.

1

The Landscape
of Our Lives

Far more columns of correspondence have described the President's shrewd political ploy with his proposed new cabinet-rank department of urban affairs than the structure and power of the post and its relationship to existing agencies dealing with these problems now. It can be argued in this case, as in the case of his request for radically new tariff-cutting powers, that the people have not been educated in advance, that he is acting first and explaining later.

Whether, in terms of administrative efficiency, this new department is justified or not, I do not know, and those who fear the growth of federal government cannot be lightly dismissed, but the education of all of us in this matter ought to begin with an overall grasp of what is happening to our country and our life together.

America is not a city-state in the Greek sense, but it is rapidly becoming a state of cities. Two-thirds of us are now essentially city dwellers, whether we reside in the suburbs or the "loop." Through the vast coastal sprawl from Boston to Washington, D.C., the highways are not roads in the old sense, but super side streets to move the traffic through a 400-mile urban area. The number of farmers declines in absolute figures as well as proportionately; the small towns become satellites of the nearest big town, and the big town of the nearest metropolis.

Our national pattern of governing ourselves was founded not only on political principles concerning distributed and balanced power, but on the existence of distance and diversity. Along with distance, diversity is vanishing. Nearly everywhere the problems tend to be identical.

Living this close together produces the opposite of "togetherness"; it accelerates the rate of human alienation, man from man. The difference between urban and rural Americans, in their sense of comfort and security, their needs and their fears, their chance to be self-reliant, is now a chasm producing two separate classes of human beings more importantly different than the rich and the poor.

When we talk of the "youth problem" we are mostly talking of an urban problem. It is the same when we talk of the housing, medical, social security, school and, to a large degree, the civil rights and racial problems. It is becoming increasingly difficult, as this new pattern of American life fastens upon our soil, to think in terms of local answers for problems that are not really local. Our communities are producing more social history than they can consume locally.

Political conservatism of the old school becomes increasingly identified with the old, small-town pattern of American life, an ever narrowing field in spatial and numerical terms. This brand of politics narrows also, therefore, in terms of common sense. Big government in our country is perhaps less to be feared than to be deplored for its inevitable inefficiency and waste, but these faults in the innumerable conflicting and obsolescent parochial units of government are not inconsiderable when viewed in their totality; and in the last generation, at least, the corruptibility of state and local officialdom has been notoriously worse than that of federal officialdom.

To continue to think of social planning as "un-American" *per se* is to be blind to the nature of America. From planning itself there is no escape, and we have learned the bitter way that an ounce of preventive planning is worth a pound of curative planning. The lack of controlled plans turned our cities into traffic nightmares, which must now be straightened out by rigorous governmental control. The lack of planning stripped away the trees and topsoil for the new suburbias of crackerbox houses and let new industries build and operate where and as they wished. Now, Draconian measures of planning and enforcement —"government interference"—are required to slow the drop in the water level and freshen our polluted rivers.

These and many other powerful trends of this last generation were foreseeable and, indeed, foreseen. Not by any underground railroad did millions of southern Negroes move to a few centers of concentration such as New York's Harlem, south Chicago, Detroit and Los Angeles. They followed their friends and relatives, as have the Puerto Ricans who now throng uptown Manhattan. Tragedies and terrible tensions have been the inevitable result of these concentrations. Yet it was never beyond the abilities of federal, state and urban authorities, working and planning together, to redirect much of this human flow on a voluntary basis to other areas, with housing, employment and educational arrangements made in advance.

Under the terms by which modern industrial society must exist, it may be laid down as a ruling principle that for virtually any massive change in the pattern of life—none of which come as a surprise save to the blind and the deaf—there must be a measure of "government interference," *i.e.*, planning and controls, at the start of the process, or there will be an immeasurable degree of it later on.

We ought to be as much concerned with the timing of government action as with the size of government structure. In a rapidly expanding society, no one can know objectively at precisely what point government grows too big; it is far easier to know when it moves too slowly. To be concerned that it may move too rapidly is to worry about the exception that illustrates the rule.

One way to go quietly insane is to think hard about the concept of eternity. Another way, for anyone living in a megalopolis like New York, is to think hard about "progress."

The eerie sensation comes over one that true progress reached the end of its cable some years ago and is now recoiling upon us, an unstoppable juggernaut smashing masses of human beings back toward medieval conditions of life.

The streets are littered with cigarette and cigar butts, paper wrappings, particles of food and dog droppings. How long before they become indistinguishable from the gutters of medieval towns when slop pails were emptied from the second-story windows?

Thousands of New York women no longer attend evening services in their churches. They fear assault as they walk the few steps from bus or subway station to their apartment houses. The era of the medieval footpad has returned, and, as in the dark ages, the cry for help brings no assistance, for even grown men know they would be cut down before the police could arrive.

A thousand years ago in Europe acres of houses and shops were demolished and their inhabitants forced elsewhere so that great cathedrals could be built. For decades the building process soaked up all available skilled labor; for decades the townspeople stepped around pits in the streets, clambered over ropes and piles of timber, breathed mortar dust and slept and woke to the crashing noise of construction. The cathedrals, when finished, stood half-empty six days a week, but most of them at least had beauty. Today the ugly office skyscrapers go up, shops and graceful homes are obliterated, their inhabitants forced away and year after year New Yorkers step around the pits, stumble through the wooden catwalks, breathe the fine mist of dust, absorb the hammering noise night and day and telephone in vain for carpenter or plumber. And the skyscrapers stand empty two days and seven nights a week. This is progress.

At the rush hour men outrun old women for the available cab; the strong bodily crush back the weak for a place to stand in suffocating bus or subway car, no less destructive of human dignity than a cattle wagon in the time of Peter the Great. When the buses and subway cars began they represented progress.

Great parking garages are built, immediately filled with cars; the traffic remains as before, and that is progress. The renowned New York constructionist, Robert Moses, builds hundreds of miles of access highways, and they are at once crammed bumper to bumper with automobiles as long as locomotives carrying an average of about two human beings apiece. Parkinson's general law applies here too, for vehicles will always increase in direct proportion to the increase in spaces to hold them. So skyscrapers and boxlike apartment houses will increase as the money to build them increases. So footpads will increase as the number of possible victims increases. But it's progress.

I am not surprised that the English writer, Mervyn Jones,

concludes after traveling throughout Russia and the United States that ordinary Americans and ordinary Russians are remarkably alike in at least two respects—in the sheer physical misery they are forced to endure in their cities and in the sheer ugliness of jumbled signs and billboards being spread across their once fair countryside.

They are alike in a third respect. As Jones writes in *Horizon* magazine, both peoples complain remarkably little. Russians don't complain because they don't expect government authorities to listen. American dwellers in our megalopolises don't complain because they have long since abandoned hope. Their authorities may listen, but they know their authorities are helpless. A city like New York is ungovernable.

The secret, terrible fact is that progress, in all measurable terms of human effort, grace and self-respect ended some years ago in the great ant-hill cities. The juggernaut of time and effort has turned around and is now destroying the recent progressive past.

The proper study of mankind supposedly is man, but we remain uninstructed in the processes that end in the death of a human city while we know precisely how a termite colony expires.

The termitary begins to die when the queen ant, deep within its recesses, herself dies or is removed. With her mysterious life force gone the worker and soldier ants mill about in disarray; discipline ends, there is no purpose anymore. All the ants, which are like corpuscles in a unified body, themselves vanish and die. The mud encasement of the ant city, which may have stood for decades, is suddenly and mysteriously permeable to water and begins to fall apart.

I never expect to discover who done it in the celebrated case of Cock Robin, but I would give a great deal to know why and when the queen ant that provided the soul, the life force, for the human termitary called New York City was taken away. For surely it is gone. The workers and soldiers and feeders march through their normal drill as if by habit, but, conscious creatures though they be, they no longer know why.

Why is New York now loud but not exciting, glassy but no longer shining? We know why its comfort vanished and then its

15

safety, but what happened to its glamor? The special and wonderful feeling that New York alone possessed and gave, when and why did this seep away?

I haven't, myself, a firm idea—an admission that should get me expelled from the columnists' club. The soul of New York seems to have died, compartment by compartment, like the organs of a body. Wall Street was power, but power is only nostalgia now among those canyons. Greenwich Village was youth and dreams of glory in the time of Edna St. Vincent Millay; it is a tarnished carbon copy now. Broadway was glory and glamor not so long ago; it is a human junkyard now and a bawling stockyard on New Year's Eve, idiot's delight. One could lie on the grass of Central Park at evening and watch the marvelous webbings of light come on, strand after strand in quick succession; now evening brings the odor of crime and fear from that once friendly earth.

Remember when there was conversation at the Algonquin, when admittance to the Twenty One Club was a triumph, when it was important to be seen at the Stork Club, when appearance on the cover of *Time* "made" a personality, when you had to read *The New Yorker*, when people bought the morning papers at midnight to read Winchell under the street lamp? The Broadway columnist died when Broadway died, or maybe when gossip moved to page one and became events.

What did it—the movement to country and suburbs by "the" people because of the city's sheer physical discomfort? Was it the deluge of affluence, so that the white-on-white boys with their expense accounts and cigars took over the glamorous places with their talk of money and contracts and deals? Or was it the simple saturation of concentrated, commercialized imitation glamor in magazines, press, radio and TV, louder and louder, shriller and shriller, until the imitation became the real thing because it was the only thing left?

Or it could be just me—and middle age. But I think not, because I have asked around among so many friends, including youthful friends, and the echoes they return confirm my suspicion that the queen ant is dead, even though the walls of this termitary remain impermeable and, indeed, mount even higher.

What has happened to New York seems to be what happened to San Francisco long ago, what happened to Chicago when Sandburg and Hecht and the old *Daily News* crowd moved on, what happened to Los Angeles when Hollywood's spirit was broken, financially and otherwise. New York, too, can become "a cluster of suburbs in search of a city." I very much doubt that the new civic or cultural centers, Grecian and gleaming though they are, will restore the mystique, whether in Los Angeles, New York or San Francisco. They are much too much like monumental, antiseptic real estate developments. They are the stuff of picture postcards and advertising copy, not of writing and art.

I had thought it was the War and that alone which dissipated the essence of Vienna. But maybe not. Maybe, in our speeding time, city essences, like innocence or fashions, simply possess a much shorter life span than they used to enjoy. Perhaps it is not really death at all, but a process of metamorphosis the queen is going through, and we will feel her life force again, act and think to the directions of quite different wave lengths. It could be that city souls are to be reborn, with new forces as strange and different as the new forms already apparent in the casing of the hives. If this is not ordained, then—dark thought—city souls are gone forever, and some of us are going to miss them.

There is no causative relationship in the fact that Congressmen are getting out of town just as the Daughters of the American Revolution are arriving *in* town, nor in the fact that Congress' spring vacation coincides with the opening of the trout season. No, it is pure coincidence and we would be the last to cast an aspersion, save, of course, in midsummer, when they are sulking under the rocks and a well-cast aspersion, weighted with small shot, is the only thing that will reach them. Anybody who will use an aspersion *before* then is a worm fisherman or common scold at heart.

Our sense of simple duty demands that as these reluctant dragonflies leave town, briefcases heavy with unfinished business and extra tackle, they take with them the benefit of our research on the issue before the House, currently designated as a parliamentary inquiry, to wit: (A) Why do fish bite, and (B) Not bite. At the outset of our labors we had applied to a private foundation for a research grant, but all their funds available to journalists were being used to count the words in the page-two headlines of the anti-Whig press in the territories between the years 1847 to 1859 inclusive. We next applied for one of the Eisenhower Fellowships, but Defense Secretary Wilson's edict against pure research had had its effect. Unless we could postulate a practical result in advance our project would be regarded as coming under his ban, informally known in the Pentagon as the Who-Cares-Why-Fried-Potatoes-Turn-Brown Prohibition, and therefore as a threat to The Team Spirit. So, slightly miffed by this, we sold some of Mr. Humphrey's low-interest bonds, bought some of Mr. Summerfield's underpriced stamps and did the whole thing by private correspondence.

Working forward from the fragmentary references to Pisciculture in the Dead Sea Scrolls, up to and including all cross references to fish in the Library of Congress beginning with Martin, Barton and ____, and ending with the Abercrombie and Fitch catalogue for the piscal year 1957, we made a number of discoveries above and beyond the true scientific definition of the dry fly, which is a wet fly which is not yet wet. We were able to distinguish five separate theories as to the biting and non-biting motivations of fish. These are: the solar theory; the lunar theory; the water-temperature theory; the psychic theory; and the morning-and-evening-rise theory, vulgarly expressed in the remark, "It don't take no damn-fool eddication to know fish bite when they get hungry."

The solar theory establishes that fish will bite or refrain from biting depending upon the angle of the sun's rays, compensating for an average 20-degree refraction under water and bifurcated obliquely from the extremity of the shadow cast by the tallest tree on the shoreline—if the tree is deciduous, of course. Otherwise, subtract.

This procedure also holds for the lunar theory, except that one substitutes moon for sun and figures countercockwise from the high- and low-tide maximums of the nearest landlocked sea water; if these statistics are not handily available, a flashlight or lantern will do, except of course on all streams where riparian rights are in dispute and *west* of the Rappahannock in counties of more than five thousand people.

The water-temperature theory has established that fish tend to seek the bottom when the surface temperature is above 60 degrees, except for the wall-eyed pike in winter waters north of the 45th Parallel, a fish whose tendency to bump its head on the ice is believed by some scholars to have given it its popular name.

Most Congressmen are not philologically equipped to follow the psychic theory which equates the biting motivations of hate and love with the compulsive eating neurosis, so we won't go into it. (See Appendix.)

In conclusion, to any Congressman failing to benefit by the above discoveries we can only suggest he find the fishing resort for which the late Stephen Leacock once wrote publicity blurbs. The place, said Leacock, "where the pickerel, chickerel and bass take the bait in their mouths and gratefully swim to shore."

I don't know whom you envy, but I envy the hunting and fishing writers for the big papers and the outdoor magazines. I stand in dumb struck awe of those fellows, not only because they write so well, but because of what they write about. They are the last of the sensible men. They stay healthier, they live longer, they have fun every week and they get paid for it. They also collect a lot of trout, quail, pheasant and ruffed grouse, though to read them you'd think they were bumbling amateurs who never connect. I suspect they write that way because if they boasted of their catch or bag, all other frustrated, city-bound fishermen and hunters would learn to hate them. They would get anonymous calls in the middle of the night and maybe plastic bombs at their doorstep—and this city-bound reporter would be the first to join the saboteurs. But let me tell you, now that the leaves are full enough to tangle the line in anybody's fly-casting backswing, about *my* triumphs on waters still and waters rapid.

I am fundamentally the anticipatory and retrospective type fisherman. That is, I manage to spend ten times the number of hours indoors, fussing with my tackle and dreaming about streams and lakes than I do actually fishing the streams and lakes. I dream in advance, and then, after my rare excursion into actuality, I dream in retrospect and find out exactly what I *should* have done. Golfers are the same.

When I was sixteen I worked a time as a so-called fishing guide on a Minnesota lake. All I did was row the visitor over near the cattails and lily pads. The bass were supposed to hang around there. The visitors never found many bass but they lost a lot of plugs and spoons, tangled in the underwater underbrush. But it's not like being a golf caddy; you can't sneak back later and find the lost equipment in order to sell it.

I suppose I caught a few good fish. I do remember pulling in two bass that had struck my plug simultaneously, each one neatly picking out a different hook; that was a thrill, but it was the day before the bass season opened and I had to throw them back. Those were the most co-operative fish I ever met.

Two years ago I whipped miles and miles of the Thurso River in northernmost Scotland, watching hundreds of great salmon leaping. They leaped right over my artfully maneuvered fly. I never touched one. A sixty-year-old lady moving ahead of me every other day caught several. I never learned her name; I never cared to. I broke all the laws of Scotland and sneaked a worm on the hook when nobody was around. The salmon ignored the worm, too. It is the same sensation, I suppose, as breaking into a bank in the middle of the night and finding the safe empty. You end up with a bad conscience and no profit.

Five years ago I was in Aspen, Colorado. Bob Craig, the great mountaineer, one of the men on the dramatic K-2 expedition in the Himalayas, led me up to a little captive lake, about 10,000-feet high—me and Scotty Reston of *The New York Times* and Reston's little boy, Tommy. Like proud and honorable men, we adults fished with flies. I generously handed my spinning outfit to little Tommy. The trout refused our flies for a half hour, then Tommy shrieked aloud. On my spinner he had caught a 3-pound rainbow. I patted his back and went on fly fishing. Little Tommy shrieked again. He had caught another 3-pound rainbow. There ensued a brief struggle between me and my conscience. I won. I firmly took the spinning gear from little Tommy's hands and began casting. I cast for over an hour and touched nothing while the boy sat on the bank and looked at me with large, wondering eyes.

Finally, as the others stood waiting, ready for the down-mountain hike, I made the absolutely last cast of the day and came up with a 3½-pound rainbow, the biggest trout I ever caught in my ill-spent life.

My desperate efforts had delayed us so long that Craig decided on a short cut down. We plunged bravely through the brush and forest. Darkness came on, and we got thoroughly lost, right in Craig's back yard. Little Tommy's bare legs were cut by briars, and we carried him in turns. We finally got out and down; Reston and I showed up fearfully late at a dinner for the British ambassador, given by the lady who more or less owned the town. I don't know if she has ever forgiven us. I don't know if little Tommy has ever regained his faith in grown-up men. I don't know if Craig ever regained his self-confidence as a mountaineer—but, I *did* catch a 3½-pound rainbow.

For a newsman I can be pretty slow; I miss some big ones, sometimes. I've just missed the most important story of the summer, but I couldn't help it. I was tucked away in a valley in Colorado, 8,000 feet up, in dry sunshine, and I had no idea it was raining in North Dakota. When it really rains in my native state, strange things are likely to happen; and this time, they happened to my home town of Velva, a word that may remind you of shaving lotion, but that reminds me of the nicest town on the prairies, a town lying in the Mouse River valley, with a lot of trees and shade which are more important than you know unless you've gone through a Dakota summer. Most of the time the people in Velva are delighted to be living in that shallow valley, but not the other week when the rains came.

Well, I got back to my house in New York from the Colorado vacation the other night and in the pile of mail on the hall table there was a rolled up newspaper; the sticker showed that it came from Bill Francis, the retired editor of the *Velva Journal.* The *Journal* is printed these days on Main Street, in the building, as I recall it, where the harness shop used to be. Bill owns the red brick building further south on Main Street, near the underpass where you drive under the Soo Line rail tracks to get to U.S. Highway 52 and turn right to get to Minot, the Magic City on the Mouse, 20 miles northwest. Bill Francis sits in an office in that brick building, writes a little insurance these days, but mostly goes over newspapers from everywhere.

Anyway, I noticed the roll of papers he had sent me wasn't the *Journal,* but the *Minot Daily News,* and I knew before I unwrapped them that something big was up. It was big all right. The headlines were black and awful and the pictures were worse. The worst flood in the history of my home town had hit the place around supper time. Not without warning, though. Mrs. John Wagner, who lives on a farm 10 miles southwest of town, had telephoned Velva to warn that a terrific flood was coming. Maybe you don't get the significance of this; she lives to the *southwest,* but the river is to the *north,* right on the north edge of town. In nearly all normal floods it's the river that floods, and the flood waters run *out* of the river. Not in my town. These flood waters ran *into* the river. It's all those ravines, we call them coulees, running down from the south hill range. They filled up with rain water, and the water, a *wall* of water, several feet high, just ran down the coulees, gathered together on the highway (which must have wrecked John Kramer's Texaco station at the intersection) and plunged through the railroad underpass and

21

roared straight down Main Street, to the river at the north side of town.

You can imagine what happened, or *I* can. You take the barber shop. It's downstairs, with a street entrance, and it must have filled up as high as the shelves where everybody's individual shaving mug used to sit in rows. The drug store must have got it, Emil Selberg's cafe, both grocery stores, the bank on the corner where my father used to have his office; the lumber yard must have been flooded and I hope it wasn't stacked with too much green timber when that water came in. I hate to think of the Oak Valley Lutheran Church. They have a brand new church there, on North Main Street, and the church, of course, like all buildings out there, has a big basement; that's where ladies aid suppers are served and the young people's Lutheran League meets once a week. I suppose those new basement rooms were just wrecked.

And the Johnson house, next to the river. It was a low-lying house and yard, below the street level; the water must have been as high as the front porch. I remember when the river flooded a little, about forty years ago, that yard was completely under water; it even covered that boulder, the one that landed there when they were dynamiting for the new north bridge.

Even off Main Street it was bad. There's a trailer camp off to the west, you know, near the woods where we used to build wigwams and play Sioux uprising; some of those trailers, where miners from the Truax coal mine now live, were just turned over on their side. Bernie Robinson, who's fifteen, waded through the water to help those people and he told the Minot paper that he could feel the electricity in the water, on his bare legs, from the wires that were down.

Of course, a stretch along Highway 52 was a mess, with water 4 and 5 feet deep and over your head in the ditches; that's where a couple of tourists were drowned. Cars were just floated along by that wall of water for hundreds of yards and some upended, of course.

The farmers beyond North Hill and South Hill had it easier, but they did get hail which ruined some crops and even some small twisters like tornadoes.

When nature goes on a rampage up there in North Dakota, it doesn't do things by halves. I can remember droughts and dust storms and plagues of grasshoppers that darkened the sky, but nothing like this, a river down Main Street. I suppose people there will be talking about this for the next forty years and forget all about the blizzard of 1919, I think it was, when the school doors weren't opened for three days because nobody could find them.

September 17, 1962

There is in this country a diffident, quiet-eyed woman who is about to demonstrate, if advance portents and premonitions be well founded, the truth of the remark that nothing is more powerful than an idea whose time has come.

The woman is Miss Rachel Carson, biologist, author of *The Sea Around Us,* poet and reverential scholar of nature. The idea, which is not hers alone but one that has been gathering force and adherents in a swelling wave of concern, is that man has forgotten he is a child of nature—or God—has come to believe that he can "conquer" nature and in his attempts is very likely to destroy his own place in nature and, thus, himself.

He may do more than that; he may write "finis" to the whole story of creation. It was Dr. Albert Schweitzer who said, "Man has lost the capacity to foresee and to forestall. He will end by destroying the earth." It is with this quotation that Miss Carson begins *Silent Spring,* a little book so explosive on every page that it can hardly fail to startle and frighten all laymen who read it, convulse the chemical industry and possibly create a whole new political issue, crossing all party and sectional lines.

She does not deal with the possibility of racial suicide through atomic war; she has little to say about radiation and its ultimate effects; she leaves to others the disturbing question of the new "miracle" drugs and what their cumulative effect may be in the human liver, nervous system and reproductive processes. Her own salient of attack and exposure is the now almost universal use of chemicals, both inorganic and the new organic, synthetic chemicals sprayed wholesale upon our croplands, forests, mosquito swamps and tree-lined city streets.

I will not try to reproduce here the graphic revelations of the immense harm already done to man's environment, the incalculable harm the future may unfold, the self-defeating nature of many past and present attempts to eliminate injurious insects, or Miss Carson's outline of the new avenues through which men may control enemy insects without disorganizing nature's balance and the built-in balance of his own body. The book must be read, and then the counterattack of the chemical companies, which have been in a fever of preparation for weeks, must be followed if Americans generally are to comprehend the problem and then act upon the consensus that surely must emerge from an argument so vital to human well-being.

It is entirely possible that Miss Carson overstates her case in some respects, obsessed as she is with the new, unplotted and mysterious dangers we insist upon creating all around us, in the air we breathe, the food we eat, the waters we drink; but surely it is past time for responsible and informed minds to become obsessed. All reformers, political, economic and scientific, have initially sounded like fanatics to the bulk of us, comfortable in our ignorance, prone to seek compromise, feeling in our bones that somehow "things will turn out all right" because things have usually done so in the past.

But three propositions remain incontrovertible: this generation's manipulation of the basic elements of nature, in drugs, in pesticides, in radiation is not under control, either between governments or within private industry; the total consequences to human life from the wholesale release of the new substances into the scheme of nature is not only unknown, but hardly guessable; we have reached the point where, if it is not already too late, the benefit of the doubt concerning every proposed action or substance absolutely must be given to the side of caution.

It is not being "alarmist"—it is only repeating the private and public thoughts of a growing body of scientists and philosophers to say that the hour is later than most of us know. There are those unshakably persuaded that all the past dangers and crises of man in all known history were minor, because transitory, compared to the irreparable injuries we are now doing and are preparing to do in increasing frequency and extent. It is quite wrong for us to assume that in atomic war lies the only danger of "setting back civilization a thousand years." In some areas of the globe sheer overpopulation, resulting from the well-intended efforts of preventive medicine, appears to be doing this already; and Miss Carson warns that the insects themselves, earth's inhabitants eons before man, infinitely more durable than man, have the capacity to overwhelm us in a retaliatory avalanche because of our tinkering with their natural balance.

Such dire prophecies were once the exclusive province of science fiction, but we should have learned from the realm of space exploration that what is fiction today is fact tomorrow, because human imagination is the prisoner of natural reality and what can be imagined can be done. Men have imagined the destruction of life on this planet; therefore, men can do it. In the sum total of uncounted, uncontrolled, often unseen little actions, men are steadily proceeding toward that goal now and will reach it unless they stop themselves by other acts. If these actions spring from reason, so much the better; if they spring from fear, so be it.

The new religion of the scientist-philosopher, like the old-time religion, invokes the sanction of hell-fire and damnation—but with proof.

Aspen, Colorado

The road around Red Mountain to the trout stretches in Hunter Creek is "jeepable," as the Army's maps in the last war defined such pathways—jeepable and barely that. Robert Anderson, the New Mexico rancher and banker, who is easy and authentic in blue jeans and Stetson, had the bucking jeep under control. But it was rough on the rib joints, and that engaging young lady, Mrs. Ethel Kennedy, probably spoke the natural sentiment of a New Frontierswoman when she gasped from her precarious perch in the back, "Don't you think the government ought to come in here and make a good road?"

Instantly and instinctively both Anderson and I said, "No!"

Improve that road and that's the end of the trout fishing in Hunter Creek, the end of one more secret joy in life, of one more dream for the winter nights in the Eastern cities, the finish of one more jeweled valley where the mule deer come out to drink and the ruffed grouse make the hollow logs boom in the mornings of spring. Maybe it will soon be finished, anyway; a private combine from the West Coast is trying to buy it up and raze the aspen and the pine for rows of little houses. This is happening in the high, narrow valleys all through the Rockies, our last frontier of serenity and space, the ultimate Holy Grail, the spirit of the West. The Rockies will be its burial place unless we learn, as the English have learned, that "progress" has to be defined to mean preserving and cherishing as well as changing and "improving," and I hope I'm dead and buried, too, when the West is gone.

I mean it. A form of madness comes over me when I think of what is happening to the Great American West and what can happen. The Bob Andersons and the Stewart Udalls are my heroes these days and to hell with all the would-be Zeckendorfs now building all over the West. If the laws won't stop this or regulate it with implacable severity, I'm for anarchy and vigilantism and would happily go to jail with those entirely respectable citizens of Aspen who obey a higher law and have been known to sneak out of their picture-window houses at night and saw down billboards.

(This is what those desperate Easterners, the cottagers on Fire Island, are going to have to do, mark my words. They are going to have to lie down in front of Robert Moses's bulldozers when he starts that doubly damnable double highway the length and breadth of that precious, irreplaceable sandpit. But I won't join them; no man should join them. Moses would run right over the men. There is a chance he might stop short of sobbing women and little children, down on their knees in the sand.)

What is the American West, after all? It is space; and if the spaciousness goes, the West is gone and something is gone out of America, out of the American tradition and dream, out of our "image" of ourselves that can never come again. We will become, I swear, a different people, a diminished people.

I know I will be told by return mail that there is no such thing as the "spirit of the West," that Westerners are just as bad and good, as unhappy and happy, as lazy and energetic, as selfish and generous as Americans in the Bronx or Boston and no more or less than Americans in Boston or the Bronx. I've been told this before, by experts, by historians and sociologists and psychologists, and they don't know what they're talking about. They almost know, but not quite.

They know all about comparable rates, West and East, of mental illness, crime, divorce, alcoholism and general human faults and flaws. I make no counterclaims. They can take apart Professor Turner's famous history lecture of 1893 and make a strong argument that the development of the free lands did not breed any noticeably rugged independence of character in Westerners, who bullyragged Uncle Sam for more handouts and privileges in one form or another from the Homestead Act on.

They make a case, all right, but if they had seen what I saw in my childhood—years and years of Dakota farmers fighting drought and locusts and dust storms and blizzards with damn little immediate help from anybody but neighbors, just to hang on to those free land gifts and improve them—maybe they would debunk a little more cautiously. I don't claim it was tougher than growing up among the pushcarts of the Lower East Side of New

York, but it was different, and in that difference lies the whole point about the West and what it means to those who know it and why their feeling about it in their bones is not false or phony.

You grew up in the West with a sense of change, of growth and improvement that even a kid could see and feel all the time. You had a sense of anticipation, of freshness, as your town developed, as the new gravel road connected your town with the nearest city, as the new bank went up, the little college began upstairs in the Opera House, the new shipment of books arrived for the town library in the back room of the bank. The future seemed as wide as the horizon. Maybe a youngster growing up in an old New England town or in the Old South had similar sensations, but I just don't believe they could have been quite the same.

Turner, as I recollect him, had the theory that the West of the moving frontier was the "typical America" and that America couldn't be understood unless the West was understood. I would be wary of designating any part of this immense and varied country as typical, and surely a New Englander or a Southerner must resent this notion about the West. America is the sum of its parts at the least reckoning.

But the Western communities grew in a way those in the Atlantic states didn't grow, or hadn't grown for so many generations as not to count for our time. It always seemed to me that Turner was right when he described each frontier community developing from scratch, from birch-bark canoe and moccasin or from sod hut and hand plow. That's the way it happened in my town from the time when August Peterson, I think it was, walked overland from the Devil's Lake region and built his shack among the oaks in our little river valley. No prefab shipment of European or Eastern culture, institutions and amenities could be brought or sent for. It all came later, bit by bit, and so a Westerner grew up as his own culture grew up. I just don't see how anybody growing to manhood in an old and settled community, whether in the American East or in Europe, just inheriting what others had created long before, can have the same sensations of participation, the same keen sense of shortcomings, but also the same keen sense of accomplishment and pride. In the West you grew up not only with an electric feeling about the future, but a sober sense of the past, because both past and future seemed so close at hand.

I suspect a lot of "typical" American traits—inventiveness,

a pragmatic faith in what works and the absence of theory and doctrine, respect for the practical man who could get things done, neighborliness, an implicit belief in progress and the solvability of problems—much of the built-in nature of our people that foreigners, at least, regard as "typically American," must have come out of that whole process, and unless I am blindly prejudiced I still feel this spirit the moment I get back to the region of the mountains and the great plains.

I know it's changing, but then it has always been changing. Turner described three distinct evolvements—the drifting squatter who grew a few necessities, then drifted on; the good farmer who put in roads and fences and permanent buildings; then the developer who brought in railroads and industries and parks. You see the third stage in operation now everywhere in the West, with the developers adding mass housing or buying up the good but small farms and ranches for amalgamation and corporate operation. Those eighteen separate farms that immediately surrounded my small town in North Dakota are now six separate farms. In the mountains uncounted numbers of Hunter Creek valleys with their cluster of one-family ranch houses are going to housing developments or resorts or corporate farming.

The spaciousness of the West will remain, in mountains or plains, as seen from a plane or a peak, but will it feel spacious when you're on the ground? It isn't any pressure of sheer population that is changing the West this side of the Pacific Coast because, actually, most of the essentially rural counties are losing population to the already big cities. It's the pressure for different *uses* of the space that can make it harder and harder for Americans to enjoy the space. Federal legislation can't save it all, and the efforts of Aspen citizens to encourage, by tax-deductible trust arrangements, the withholding of valley land for campsites and fishing and hunting grounds, ought to be a pattern for a thousand potential Shangri-las in the Great West.

Space is the key to it all; I think most Americans are slowly suffocating for want of space whether they're aware of it or not. Our genes haven't had time to adjust to the neat, tidy, orderly little life of a Britain or a Denmark; millions of us just don't thrive, in our spirits or in our flesh, in the big city. There is a craving in us for space, and the big boom in boating, in hunting and fishing proves our quiet desperation.

I stroll along the half-empty, dusty streets of Aspen as I could stroll through any small Western town, and I feel different. I feel the way I used to feel. The man strolling toward me is different. I can *see* him, his clothes, his gait, his whole nature, and he can see me. If I slow down, he will slow down; he'll know I want to talk and he will want to talk. You think it's just leisure that does this, the absence of pressures on a couple of fellows enjoying their annual vacations? It's that, but it's more than that —it's space. I'm sure that space is more important to the well-being of the human creature than leisure. In ten years, maybe, Aspen's summer population will be tripled; the streets will be crowded, and we'll walk and stop walking when and where the signs say we can. Then all will be changed; I won't see that man anymore and he won't see me, and we certainly won't stop and talk, unless we bump each other, in which case we'll exchange a few nasty remarks.

You think empty space diminishes the individual, makes him feel lost and little? Any individual who feels that way in the mountains or on the prairies has felt lost and little all his life. It's crowds and close quarters that make most of us feel lost and little; you can't increase the density of human beings without increasing the individual sense of anonymity, in a street, an apartment house, or an organization.

I'm a displaced person, and a sentimental fool perhaps, but I have a notion that I have a lot of company in this country. There must be millions of us who can't sit still for an hour in the city, even on a holiday, even in the park, without getting jumpy, but who can sit beside a Hunter Creek unaware of minutes or hours until the evening chill catches us by surprise.

When I dream of spaciousness now I dream of the West; it is destined to be our last repository of space, the final chalice hoarding the old spirit of America, or the part of that spirit that made this country something different, unmatchable and unreplaceable.

Dear God, dear Congressman, dear people, don't let the West be destroyed, not till I'm gone, anyway. If you can manage it, not till my children are gone. Otherwise, they'll think all those stories I read to them, all those youthful exploits I bragged about were phony. They ceased to believe in the Lone Ranger and Dodge City long ago, but leave them *something!*

Chestertown, Maryland

We spend our fretting lives, most of us, feeling east or west of Eden, but never in it. Its identity depends upon our particular obsession and concern, and mine, increasing with the years, is for the land and waters of America. They are wasted and soiled by crowding and greed and heedless habits until one despairs of his children's inheritance. But here, for the moment, along the shores of Chesapeake Bay, I am in Eden's blessed center, worth a notice before the creeping poison penetrates this far.

The Eastern Shore of the Bay has been off the beaten, ravaged path of the automobile hordes and the gaseous factories. In summer these lowlands of field and wood and marsh are stilled, bees drone in the hot sunlight and the odor of honeysuckle hangs in the air. Life and men move as slowly as they must have done before the Civil War.

Right now the maples and the red oak provide the color as the fields turn gray and brown. The air is sharp. The small boats and the nets are busy and refrigerators are filling up with Chincoteague oysters and softshell crabs. The great autumn run of the striped bass from Nantucket and Long Island is finished and they have taken winter quarters here in this bay of a thousand creeks and inlets.

But it was the geese and the ducks that brought me here in the company of taciturn Lee Wulff, the master sportsman, and Joe Linduska, scientist and lover of all things wild. To them I am indebted for sparing me a life bereft of one, unmatchable vision, a sight of magical beauty and power that will remain forever on the retina of the mind's recollection.

The hunting season was to start precisely at noon. I was vaguely aware that hundreds of men in canvas clothing were crouched in blinds, lying in rows of cornstalks, floating in camouflaged boats for miles about. They knew what was about to happen. What astonished me was that the geese knew—everything but the day and the hour. I ran out of my quarters as a clamor began to fill the air. It was high noon. Everywhere— north, south, east and west—dark clusters of Canada geese were rising above the tree lines. In minutes the entire sky was streaked and mottled with patches and skeins of geese, wheeling and gathering, signaling to one another in a tremendous din of honking.

Tens of thousands of geese around and above one is an almost terrifying sight, a natural phenomenon of Biblical proportions, stunning beyond my most exaggerated preconceptions. They gathered in armadas, flotillas and squadrons in one general direction where lay the sanctuary maintained by the Remington Arms Company for the preservation of this marvelous species. There they wheeled in, occasional shafts of sunlight reflected from the white bodies of the few snow geese among them. From there they traded back and forth all day, keeping altitude now, and it was a rarity to see one fall as the guns faintly popped in the distance. At sunset the shooting ceased—and the geese knew they were entirely safe, for now each phalanx drummed straight ahead without flaring, almost within touching distance as we stood in the cornfield.

It was a sight to enthrall and to humble and to make one consider the future of this American land and its natural inhabitants. The geese may endure, for the shooting is severely restricted and they nest in the wet muskeg regions of northern Canada. For ducks the shooting is also severely limited, but drought in the north has currently depleted their hordes—drought and an insane contradiction in government policies. Hunters' organizations and conservationists struggle and pay great sums, private and public, for more refuges, while other government agencies pay public money to farmers of the north central states to drain their marshes and sloughs in order to grow more of the crops already in embarrassing surplus.

It is not hunting and fishing—activities far bigger economically, than all the spectator sports, movies and concert halls put together—that are threatening our natural inheritance of wild life in this country. Indeed, in this generation it has been the hunters and their conservationist allies who have brought back such marvelous creatures as the antelope and the wild turkey, and saved the ducks and geese. It is the spreading of concrete over the land, the growth of "clean" farming, greedy commercialization of mountain valleys, the poisoning of rivers by city sewage and industrial wastes that are sickening and scarring the American land.

If all this is not checked and regulated as severely as hunting and fishing are limited now, our grandchildren will read about an America where the geese once filled the sky over Chesapeake Bay, as we read about the America of the great buffalo herds. But they will never see it.

March 18, 1963

This is a sort of "position paper" for the President's eyes about his imminent move from the Glen Ora estate in Virginia to his new house, acres and pond on Rattlesnake Mountain nearby. I should have gotten this off to him earlier, but I kept thinking that David Lawrence or James Reston would step in to advise Mr. Kennedy about his new home place, as we would call it in that back country.

Reston probably figured that since his place has a run, not a pond, and is away over near Hume, he couldn't advise with authority; and while Lawrence's acres near Centreville are within line-of-sight of Rattlesnake, the President's record of following Lawrence's advice is thin, which probably discouraged Mr. Lawrence. So, since I know both Glen Ora and Rattlesnake, and my cabin and pond are not far off, the duty obviously falls to me.

To begin with—of course you know, Mr. President, that you got stung on the acreage price, but we all do the first time we try to haggle with country slickers. Ten years from now you'll laugh about it.

Now, about the dam—the county agent over at Culpeper will advise on the construction and figure the drainage area. He won't charge you anything, even if he drives over on his day off. For goodness' sake, don't try to build the dam yourself. Ed Murrow did, and it went out in the first flash flood—gave him an extra furrow in his forehead. You'll want a dock. Make it oak or locust, the pilings well creosoted. Get hold of a fellow named Stanley Brown; he can build anything and he's very reasonable.

Time magazine must be wrong about your putting perch in the pond. Keep it to large-mouth bass and bluegills, and don't even dream about trout in that mud bottom. For an acre-and-a-half pond, I'd figure, say, 150 bass fingerlings to 1,000 bluegills. You can get application forms from the Interior Department and they will send the fish in milk cans from the hatchery on the West Virginia side of the Blue Ridge. It won't cost you a cent, because the government in Washington wants us to impound more waters against erosion, and encourage protein feed supplies for poultry. There's a manual you can get free from the Agriculture Department which proves you can harvest more pounds of food per acre of water than of soil.

In a year or two start fishing the pond hard or you'll have nothing but stunted fish from overpopulation and will have to drain the pond and begin all over again. When the bass are lunker size—you may as well face this—you'll never catch them except, with luck, on live frogs. Up to about June 15th the bluegills take dry or wet flies well. (I don't mean to intrude on family affairs, but if Mrs. Ethel Kennedy wants to practice, better lend her a knockabout fly reel. She used my Hardy reel last summer in Colorado and it's been frozen since.)

Be careful about live bait. True minnows are okay, but any rough fish like baby catfish will wreck the pond if they get loose and breed. A snapping turtle or two will keep the pond free of dead fish, but it occurs to me that Miss Caroline may want to keep ducks. In that case no snappers.

About the garden—you'll probably have to spray out the honeysuckle, although I know Miss Rachel Carson won't like this. Don't confuse it with Virginia creeper. I expect you won't want the formal gardens they have at Glen Ora. Roses and wild azaleas are naturals in that soil on Rattlesnake. Mrs. K. might want to begin with laurel; she can transplant the wild bushes which she will find on the north slopes in the shade. She should look for the kind that flowers.

If you like quail around, here's a tip—when the Rural Electrification people come along to cut out the trees and brush under the power line, see that they replant the scar with bird food and cover like lespedeza and red-top. Check Fish and Wildlife Service on this; actually, you ought to subscribe to the monthly magazine of the Virginia Conservation Department.

I almost forgot—you won't need a county license to fish on your own property, but if you do put in federal fish, any taxpayer is legally entitled to fish your pond. You will meet some pretty nice back-country folks this way, and if you drop a polite hint, they won't leave empty beer cans on the dam.

It won't take you long to get to know the best places to do your trading. Of course, for any heavy stuff like tractors, you'll want to start off right. Fred Wayland, on the Warrenton by-pass, is always reliable and can arrange terms.

If Miss Caroline and Mrs. K. keep horses up there, I think any copperheads around will soon disappear; still, if Caroline runs around in the high grass, I'd see that she wore boots, at least for a time.

Next to honeysuckle your greatest problem will be groundhogs and what they may do to your stone fences and outbuildings. I guess you'll just have to find out about that as you go along; one of the real rewards of the back country is learning as you live.

One thing, though—no matter how long you live there, you will never master the whippoorwill problem. On hot nights when you can't shut the windows they're just going to cost you your sleep, that's all, unless you can use those earplug things. I find them too uncomfortable, and just doze, reminding myself that auto horns and sirens are worse evils, anytime, than the call of the whippoorwill.

Aspen, Colorado

An *auslander* from the steaming cities and the baking plains is a little startled when old-time residents in this 8,000-foot-high valley say, "Hot enough for you?" as the mercury barely creeps past 80. In this dry climate nobody sweats and at night one hears the thermostat-controlled heat go on and reaches for an extra blanket.

Aspen is one of many American Shangri-las, above not only the sweltering of summer, but for many of its people beyond the Age of Anxieties. The airstrip is being lengthened to accommodate DC-3s, and the dusty gravel road winding over the great divide at Independence Pass is likely to be entirely paved, so one cannot vouch for space and serenity in the future. But there remains a certain peace in this kind of place and it dawns on one at last that a reason for it is that so many of the permanent residents are here by deliberate, often difficult choice.

Not all American professional and business people are caught up in the rat race of our time. Here one finds a group of exceptionally able young doctors who have deliberately turned their backs on far more lucrative big-city practices to build their little frame houses here, keep their Jeeps in gas and grease, their fishing gear cleaned and find time to sit on a verandah at evening and watch the gold turn to purple on the peaks. One meets the man who quit Wall Street and started the title abstract business on Main Street, the couple who sold their prosperous business in upper New York, headed West in a trailer with no specific destination and ended here in the real estate business. None is likely to get rich; all are likely to live longer, have a lot more fun watching their tanned and active children grow, and all seem to wear the air of people who know they have won the battle.

In time, of course, even the Aspens of this country can create their own rat race and there are signs of it now. Here one confronts the deep dilemma of this once-spacious country: the affluent population grows while the open spaces cannot grow. How are more and more Americans to make use of their national heritage without spoiling the heritage for everyone? The good places where one may breathe cannot be left eternally to the private rich, yet they cannot be permitted to be overrun in the ghastly manner of Coney Island. Who is to decide whether or how the few shall enjoy a major good or the many enjoy what then becomes a very minor good?

I would not pretend to know all the questions, let alone all the answers. But the more I have pondered this dilemma, the more it seems to me that the basic rule of thumb ought to involve a test of the individual visitor's or settler's *will* to enjoy the open places. The benefit must not be handed to him on a platter, by state or commercial facilities; he must prove himself willing to endure some hardship for the privilege. The governing principle ought to be *difficulty of access.*

This is a very different price of admission from the money price. It is not an un-democratic principle, since the means of access, whether the human foot, the pack horse, the Jeep or the car are as available to the millions of moderate means as they are to the limited number of rich. Only those willing to undergo dust and bumps and some fatigue to enter the Shangri-las of America are likely to treat the Shangri-las with the loving care they must have if they are to endure for posterity. The politician's banal bleat about "progress" has to be re-defined; it can no longer mean the best for everyone because the best then automatically and inevitably tends to become the worst. It has to mean the best for those who prove their love of the best, and the proof of that is willingness to pay not in money, but in effort.

I do not see what other principle can be applied. So I would join those who oppose paving the rocky, dusty and dangerous road that winds over Independence Pass and those who would leave the Aspen airstrip for the little planes that fly with some hazard and many sickening bumps. For entering the mountainous West, as for raising a child, the old rule of wisdom must prevail: what is easy to get is not worth the having.

Our own private New and Election Year's resolution is to bless and support any Presidential, Senatorial, Congressional or municipal candidate who proves he has read a few books. Not any books, but books like *The Quiet Crisis* by Secretary of the Interior Udall, who demonstrates the danger to the open spaces of what was once called God's Own Country, and the new book, *God's Own Junkyard,* by Peter Blake, who demonstrates what has already happened to America's cities, suburbs and roadways.

My hopes are faint. We shall all hear much in the campaigns

about saddling our posterity with a great public debt. We shall probably hear nothing about the real crime we are committing against our children and grandchildren. With breathtaking rapidity we are destroying all that was lovely to look at and are turning America into a prison house of the spirit. What was once the fairest of lands has become, by an increasing number of competent judgments, the ugliest community of man on earth. Little wonder that European tourists are reluctant to come here; what is there for them to look at in most of what a British publication calls "the mess that is man-made America?"

The affluent society, with relentless, singleminded energy, is turning our cities, most of suburbia and most of our roadways into the most affluent slum on earth.

There is not the slightest doubt any longer that we are losing our very special, God-given chance to create in this country a form, an order, a high civilization; this simply cannot be done in a physical setting of crashing vulgarity in the cities and dreary uniformity in the suburbs.

What is happening to New York, our richest city, a wonder of the world, once beautiful and thrilling as a Christmas tree, is pure vandalism in the name of economic necessities. As the Blake book reports, all eminent designers and city planners whose views are on record are appalled by the gigantic Pan American Building now astride Grand Central Station. In its own category this is surely the cultural crime of the century.

What makes a true and successful city is mixture, variety. As Peter Blake projects it, our cities are becoming totally "ghettofied" in terms of usage: "office ghettos, industrial ghettos, apartment ghettos, amusement ghettos . . . shopping ghettos, medical-center ghettos . . . so that most areas of the city will be alive for mere fractions of each day or week, and as deserted as Wall Street on a weekend the rest of the time."

From this "cancer of uniformity, of dreariness," the great cities are dying at the core of their spirit. Downtown Los Angeles seems dead already; downtown Detroit is dying; downtown New Orleans is in the throes, and even San Francisco now shows the blight.

The complex of forces doing this is intricate and powerful, but not unstoppable, as Blake has demonstrated. Nor do the endless, dreary rows of the real estate developer's suburbia *have* to be repeated. There are far better ways to design them, very specific ways; it can be done if people generally understand this, and will be done if people generally learn just where and how to express their demands and apply their pressure. None of the present horror was inevitable.

Endless vistas of townscape as well as landscape have been violated in the interests of what Blake calls "carscape." Much of our landscape can be restored to view by laws aimed at the billboard lobby. Who can disagree with Governor Brown of California: "When a man throws an empty cigaret package from an automobile . . . he is liable to a fine of $50. When a man throws a billboard across a view he is liable to be richly rewarded. I see little difference between the damage done by these two litterbugs."

There are laws to protect privacy, laws to protect us against overcrowding, against unsanitary conditions, against overt obscenity. There are virtually none to protect us against ugliness. Laws restrict or try to restrict what private individuals may do to the common air we breathe and the common waters we drink and bathe in. There are few laws to restrict what private individuals may do to our common land.

Surely there is a vested public interest in the American landscape and surely it is nonsense to say, as courts and other authorities have said, that economic interest is a necessity while esthetic interest is a luxury. It is nonsense to say that what is beautiful and what is ugly are not subject to definition, that there are no standards. If we do not attempt to erect such standards and enforce them, we are lost. To shrug and say that one man's Pan Am Building is another man's Seagram Building is moral surrender.

There is a fundamental moral and, therefore, ought to be a fundamental legal difference between ugly movies, ugly TV commercials, ugly music, ugly books and ugly buildings, highways and streets. The former can be avoided; we have a choice. The latter cannot be avoided; we have no choice at all.

2

The American
Cacophony

About 190 years ago the English writer, Horace
Walpole, opined that the next Augustean Age
in which the immortal arts would flourish would
open in the trans-Atlantic world, including what
is now the United States. Nobody would be
brash enough to say this is happening in America, but *something* is happening that confounds
the prophets of a few years ago.

Just a few years ago American sociologists
were about to give up on the United States in
terms of this country ever developing the life
of quality, as distinct from quantity. For a long
time the whole ideological thrust had been toward *more*—more for everybody of everything—
not toward better or higher. We were becoming,
they thought, a mobocracy; the world's first attempt at the education of *everybody* was producing a mass-minded society of conformists; the
higher qualities were being debased. We would
become a nation of many millions who held
meaningless high school and college degrees but
who read mass magazines, stared at TV for hours
every day, went to movies turned out in Gar-

38

gantuan dream factories, drove identical cars, wore identical clothing, lived in identical houses. Those with an instinct for taste and the higher reaches of art and thought would become an ever smaller and ever more pitiful group of huddling refugees in the great sea of lower middle-brow sameness. European intellectuals were sure of this and took a perverse pleasure in the spectacle; it made them feel better about the shift of world power away from Europe.

When this reporter went back abroad two and a half years ago I had the instant feeling that something was wrong with the argument. It seemed to me that it was now Europeans who were developing mass attitudes, mass production of both things and ideas; they seemed to me quite as materialistic as Americans in their new found prosperity. One young English writer, Peregrine Worsthorne, proclaimed in a London paper: "Americans are reaping a richer cultural harvest from their material prosperity" than are Englishmen.

Now, on this side, the columnist John Crosby is saying much the same. Conformity is already passé, he says, as witness the infinitely greater variety of cars and movies, the decline of the mass magazines and the rise of the small, quality magazines. Surely something is happening that is both healthy and exciting. In many states school kids are forced to work and think harder; in many colleges brain has become more popularly respected than athletic brawn. The rise in community groups that think and talk about world problems has been phenomenal; there is nothing quite like this organized hard thinking in the provincial cities of Europe. Theatrical groups have sprung up by the thousands; millions of Americans are learning to paint. More people enter the doors of the New York Metropolitan Museum every year than the doors of the Louvre in Paris; more visit the Detroit Museum than the famous British Museum.

Americans spent more than a billion dollars on books in 1960, twice the amount spent five years before; book sales have increased at twice the rate of the population growth. There is a popular interest in science to a degree never before experienced in this country. Our best universities have become centers of documentation and of distinguished teaching unsurpassed in quality by the greatest and oldest of the European schools. It is not a little surprising that for some time the number one non-fiction bestseller in this country has been a history of Hitler's Germany, the number one fictional bestseller a novel based on the life of Leonardo.

None of this equates with another Periclean or Augustean Age come to flower in these United States. But it does mean something worth observing. One thing this tremendous expansion of interest in scholarship and the arts *has* to mean is obvious enough—the simple *exposure* of far more minds to the world of art and ideas; but that in itself surely will mean that what potentially great artists, writers or scientists may exist among us are far more likely to be discovered and to discover themselves. Perhaps this is the final justification for mass education: the soil is turned over, which is the best way to make things grow.

A few years ago a story went the rounds concerning the American newsmagazine publisher who hired an editor for the religious page with firm instructions that he was to treat religion not only as part of the passing parade, but as "a damn good thing."

It is apparent that in the United States art has become a damn good thing. In the last fifteen years or so the number of symphony orchestras has grown to 1,100, operatic groups to 500, theatrical groups to 100,000; the cash value of good paintings has increased by more than 1,000 per cent, and approximately every fifth person dabbles, at least, in music, dance, acting, painting or sculpture. A cult of culture has risen from the general increase in wealth, leisure and education.

Only the hopeless misanthrope could be joyless about this phenomenon, although some question the relationship between numbers and genius—whether even such a tidal wave as this can be counted on to cast up a single Michelangelo or Shakespeare—but what is interesting for present purposes is the instinctive American move to organize even the spirit of the muses, to make the phenomenon a problem to be institutionalized, nationalized and "solved."

Officialdom, which avant-garde artists in all fields generally regard as the natural enemy of art in spite of the example of the Medicis, has moved in, and while there is no certainty that it will or can corrupt art as politicians and the military have corrupted the exalted reaches of science, still the argument foams more furiously in artists' circles, if not among artistic squares, than is realized by those who read as they run.

Some American artists of repute loathe the very concept of New York's massive Lincoln Center for the Performing Arts and the National Cultural Center envisaged as covering, if not adorning, 13 acres of the Foggy Bottom region in Washington, D.C. In the first instance the case for the negative ranges from those who regard Lincoln Center as a coldly impersonal real estate development where art-under-glass may be decorously enjoyed by those possessed of car with chauffeur for a sure getaway from the stranded crowd, to those fearful of a national pyramidal structure with Lincoln Center as the Yankee Stadium of the arts, to be fed with selected talent from the seventy-three smaller city cultural centers now rising or risen which would function as farm clubs.

In the arts, as in business, government or labor, bigness must certify considerable rigor mortis in the form of parasitical bureaucracy, controls, pork-barreling politics and an official corps of judges or academicians who will tend to entrench their own cult or school of thought, as the Museum of Modern Art became the Establishment for abstract expressionist painting. Art cannot be centralized, the argument runs, and in any case America is a decentralized community with more good art coming out of the Midwest than out of the East, and any further enthronement of New York is against the trend as well as the grain.

The concern about the National Center is that while funds will come from private sources, not from the government as in Britain, France, Italy or Austria, still its offerings must of necessity become officially approved art, safe, sure art, which in the minds of the young and rebellious—where indigenous American art must be born—is art already dead. Those so concerned may be counting their vipers before the egg is hatched—Establishments and "power elites" have a healthy impermanence in this country—but a more pertinent concern may be that the example of the state theaters and operas of Europe constitutes a false analogy. The truth is that while London and Paris are political capitals within a natural city, Washington is an unnatural city within a political capital. Its art will always have to cross the Potomac or the Anacostia, since Washington itself is almost barren of first-line artists in any field, as it is almost barren of first-line critics.

It required the Kennedy Administration to set the thing in motion. (Truman regarded abstract painting as "ham and egg" art, and Eisenhower's musical ideal seemed to be Fred Waring's band.) So art, even some advanced art, is now constitutional and non-subversive, although there are still a few unregenerate critics

41

who raise the question of which side is honored when great artists are invited to the White House.

The best way to get thrown out of the columnists' club is to be uncertain about anything whatsoever on this earth, but I confess I don't know whether this is a view-with-alarm or a point-with-pride column. I'm unsure about the whole business, certain only that "art as dinner party," to quote the *Washington Star's* critic, is somewhat remote from art as the transaction that reveals men's inner hearts to themselves, to quote someone now long forgotten.

Legislation is proposed in New York State to require labels on motion pictures categorizing those deemed by some public authority as unfit for children—as is done in England—and defenders of civil liberties have rushed to oppose in the name of constitutional and cultural freedoms.

My knowledge here is only that of consumer and parent, but if there is to be official separation of child from adult patrons I wish there were a workable way to separate the children themselves. It is not children "under eighteen," say, who can be adversely affected by scenes of sex and violence, but children under eighteen and over thirteen or fourteen. (A friend, the other day, was agitated to learn that his daughter of twelve had seen "Anatomy of a Murder" and when he cautiously inquired of her reaction, she said, "Oh, it was wonderful. There was a little dog that kept running into the courtroom!")

What is bothering many thoughtful people is a related but different question, the increasingly inescapable influence not of dramatized normality, but of dramatized abnormality. For violence is normal, while sadism is not; sex is normal, but perversion is not. We have all learned that the Platonic dichotomy of mind and body or matter and spirit was a false division from which our understanding of human nature has long suffered. Body and spirit are one and interacting. An abnormal or "sick" body is likely to be reflected in an abnormal spirit, in an outlook on life that has to be regarded as sick and therefore destructive if there are to be any standards at all and if standards are to have any meaning at all.

Like many others I have assumed that the current proliferation of themes of emotional sickness in stage, cinema and literature is a temporary vogue of "daring" experimentation, probably related to the spiritual wounds of the war or the emptiness of material affluence, bound to pass away as soon as their practitioners grew weary of their own themes as they now profess to be weary of society.

Now I am not so sure; I am inclined to think the nihilistic themes, based on the value of non-value, will continue to thrust upon us at every other turn and will cease only when the consuming public—not the laws—cries enough and refuses to buy any more.

I think this because many conversations in London, Paris, Rome and New York with responsible leaders in the theater, films, music, dress design and interior decoration have persuaded me that homosexuality in the popular arts is no longer the incidental presence it always was, but is now an *authority* and, in the sense that members of a minority tend to band together against the majority, an organized authority. A loose but effective combine of homosexuals exercises very considerable control of employment as well as of the product in the London theater, in the Paris fashion world, in the French and Italian worlds of film production.

The most obvious and omnipresent result lies in their picturization of women. The homosexual is capable of neither loving nor understanding a woman, so for his fashions the woman's body is merely a skeletal frame for his artistic experiments in design; for his films the woman is generally a prostitute or an overbearing clod. In the theater they portray neither high triumph nor high tragedy, for these involve acts of will and decision. In their world there is no decision and no will; there is only a degraded helplessness against "forces," because, being sick themselves, they must see society as the sickness.

When the sick band together and exercise wholesale judgment upon the healthy I know of no remedial action save boycott at the retail level. We can hardly apply the principle expressed by Macaulay in the last century in a famous speech on the civil rights of a religious minority: "... But if a man exhibits at a window in the Strand a hideous caricature of that which is an object of awe and adoration to nine hundred and ninety-nine out of every thousand of the people who pass ... such a man ought to be severely punished, not for differing from us in opinion, but for committing a nuisance which gives us pain and disgust."

In the present case no punishment is possible or proper, and

43

no remedial action unless the 999 simply refuse to look as they pass the caricatures in the freak show on their way to the main event.

No doubt the fact that the little quarterly slip marked "Bureau of Internal Revenue" lies on the desk has something to do with it, but we can't get the image of Joe Louis out of our mind: the greatest fighter of them all shoving into subways because he can't afford a taxi or a car. Joe Louis owes the government over a million dollars in taxes. He isn't sure exactly how much; neither is the government. And his is not the only such uncertain equation. This is one of the great shocks of adulthood, anyway—finding that even figures aren't exact, but have to be interpreted and guessed at, like a cubist painting. So don't feel guilty if you aren't quite sure what your tax bill should be. The august government isn't either.

Well, there is Joe, shoving into the subway, which we figure he can manage all right, and there is the government figuring they might let Joe have the first ten thousand he earns each year to live on and take everything over that for the rest of his working life. So hail Joe Louis, Federal tax ward No. 1, pensioned off by the government, not to quit work but to go on working. As it is, Joe's tax bill gets bigger each year because of the interest charges, and every year Joe's strength and abilities to meet the bill get smaller. An open-ended vicious circle that has to be closed, like the vacuum in the Middle East.

Maybe *all* boxers, writers, dancers, actors, singers and others whose sole capital is youth, energy or inspiration ought to have a new deal from the tax office. Something like the 27-per-cent depreciation allowance the oil men get on the premise that oil wells exhaust themselves in time. It's the same with all the above-mentioned individuals; a man has just so many fights, performances or books in him. The well of his spirit or his strength is depreciating all the time, every year that passes. But he doesn't get a 27-per-cent write-off enabling him to pass his twilight years in a cozy forty-eight-room bungalow with twelve-car garage attached, as they do in Texas.

It's all very mysterious. As close as we can figure it out the effect of the tax system is to encourage the investment of capital, not its expenditure, which is what life is all about, especially the expenditure of sweat, skills and talents. Under the tax system additional expenditure of these precious capital holdings brings, not additional return, but declining return. The government doesn't say, "Give and ye shall receive." It says, "Get and ye shall get still more." Somewhere along the line, government got mixed up and decided that human tissues last like iron while machinery wears out like human tissues. That's why a machine gets a depreciation allowance in its tax bill and your nerve ends don't.

Of course, people like boxers or writers or singers get into tax trouble for another reason. Figuring your taxes as you go along has become a complicated business and they just aren't businessmen. Their business is boxing and writing and singing and if they're worth their keep to society, their minds are on their business all the time. And that's where society ought to keep their minds. They can't balance a personal checkbook, anyway, and in the ideal society wouldn't be expected to. As things are, thousands of them end up in a tax mess. Like Joe Louis.

Or like William Saroyan; Saroyan is one of the most celebrated and—some think—most gifted of American writers. Saroyan isn't on the civil-service rolls, hasn't taken any government loyalty test, but he works for the government—full time. As fast as he can produce them in his shack on the California beach, his poems, his stories, his memories and dreams are collected by the government. For taxes.

But he has his moments. He hung a wacky, worthless smudge of oils called a painting in his shack one day. The gimlet-eyed revenue agent paid his regular call, pointed to the canvas and said, "What's that worth?" "Ten thousand," said Saroyan. "We'll have to take it," said the agent. "Monster!" said Saroyan with the best imitation of a sob he could produce at the moment.

When the small, egghead magazines said it, it wasn't news. It wasn't news when we said it here a few weeks ago. But when some industrial leaders come right out and agree that the economic law of supply and demand isn't working in this country— why, then it's news, almost as startling news as if the American Physical Society concluded gravity doesn't work anymore. The aforementioned industrial leaders came to this upsetting conclusion about the American economic system in replies to a questionnaire from the Senate Finance Committee.

The meaning of this revision of the ancient catechism is that the relationship of demand to supply no longer governs the price;

with goods piled up and demand low, many prices should have been steadily falling the last nine months—but they don't fall. Name your own cause—the rigidity of labor costs, conscious or unconscious collusion between industries to "administer" prices —the result is that the historic free market isn't free anymore; it got stuck somewhere.

Now, this alone is enough to force some fundamental re-thinking about our economic society, but there's deeper stuff to come. We are now being told that the centuries' old motivation of economic man in America, his very purpose, no longer pertains. The most eloquent heralder of this extraordinary news is Harvard's Professor Galbraith, who says, if we read him right, that *production* can no longer be the aim of our material society. The whole fabulous structure we have built was aimed at producing more, always more, for more people. This goal and god is toppling, he thinks. Necessity is no longer the mother of invention; the necessity is disappearing; most of us have as much or more than we can use already. He thinks we have to turn our attention to providing public goods, so to speak—roads, hospitals, schools, parks, etc., which is the province of government, not private enterprise, but we'll go into that some other time.

Before Galbraith is dismissed as a theoretician, let us point out that his cool, Harvard prose is matched, in part, by the hot Madison Avenue prose of a tough minded businessman, the head of the B.B.D. & O. advertising agency; Mr. Brower seems to agree that to keep the system going we have been manufacturing desires for products as well as the products and have been deliberately stimulating and encouraging debt.

Said Mr. Brower to other salesmen: "We have been the merchants of discontent, creators of obsolescence. This creation and stimulation of desire has put more people to work and, in turn, made their desires possible to fulfill. But what if this desire is gone? I will tell you. When a car becomes nothing more than transportation, when new clothes become nothing more than protection against weather and immodesty, when a house is only a shelter, when the thrill is gone out of buying and pride fades out of ownership, we are headed for something worse than a mere depression. We are headed for a whole new kind of economy that none of us are going to enjoy."

Maybe more than the desire for possessions is vanishing. Maybe even the desire to work is going. Says Brower: "This is the great era of the goof-off...the land...is populated with

laundrymen who won't iron shirts, with waiters who won't serve
... with executives whose minds are on the golf course."

Brower's remedy sounded a little unsatisfying, but he says
that what we have to do, or maybe he meant what salesmen have
to do, is to teach, day after day, that work can be fun, that the
thrill of achievement is the only real reward in life.

But suppose even the desire for a chance to work begins to
vanish? For Galbraith suggests that we just license the drones for
the health of the whole hive; he would pay the unemployed practically as much compensation as they would be getting at their
jobs, to keep the economy turning over.

Personally, we have only one gleam of hope to offer. If the
increase in traffic, and in congestion at theaters, beaches, night
clubs, etc., continues, then *fun* will be work, so much work that
real work might begin to look like fun.

In a week of mobile rediscovery of the American interior
this reporter has had talks with hundreds of students, teachers
and administrators in private and public colleges of a half-dozen
states, and the process has produced a dawning realization that
the United States is undergoing a profound sea change in its community life. It is not only that the financial and facilities problems of the universities are commanding incessant attention from
the President down to the rawest and newest of the state legislators; it is not only that the post-Sputnik struggle to raise intellectual standards is conscientiously continuing and in places already producing measurable results; it is not only that the passion
for higher education seems universal and is going to make the
generality of American citizens perhaps the most reasoned and
responsible mass society history has known.

It is all this but more. For one thing, it seems to me, the
local college or university in a great number of cities is becoming
the central, the dominant and characterizing aspect of the community life. It is still a struggle in many states to get sufficient
funds from hard-pressed, rural-dominated legislatures. But the
old divisions and antipathies are dying away—those between
"town and gown," those between the businessmen and the professors. No longer is the "city club," private haven of the financially powerful, the true repository of community authority and
respect. Not anymore does a professor invited within those pre-
cincts feel ill at ease, not anymore does the "hard-fisted business-

man" feel belligerently alien in the company of those he once thought of as "visionary theoreticians."

Never before has the "downtown press" paid such informed and imaginative attention to the local classroom and laboratory as a rich source of exciting "hard" news. The college is no longer simply a traditional, respectable adornment for occasions of official local pride and chamber of commerce brochures. The colleges have entered into the daily life of the cities and states and they into the daily life of the colleges in a degree remarkable to one whose memories of college life were fashioned in the thirties.

It is not only the flowering of the scientific revolution and the consequent need of corporations for the school, and vice versa, that has done this. Bad as so much of our secondary school preparation indubitably is, one senses a slowly gathering contagion of the excitements of the intellect in the middle and lower-middle levels of our economic strata, in spite of the honky-tonk vulgarities that affluence has smeared across our landscape and our surface.

It is all this and yet more. American intellectual isolationism and provincialism (long exaggerated by Europeans persuaded that Europe was the world's center) vanishes like April snow as thousands of faculty people go abroad each year on their various grants for foreign study, as more thousands of students make serious summer pilgrimages overseas and as hundreds of distinguished foreign intellectuals settle into American colleges as "scholars in residence."

Something else is happening. It seems to me highly probable that the flourishing of the universities is rectifying the sad geographical imbalance in the intellectual and artistic life of our country. There was a time, for example, when Chicago and San Francisco were distinct literary centers and "schools." In this sense they atrophied as New York more and more sucked in the bright new talents—in writing, in the theater, in the visual arts. This trend to centralize monopoly has been equally true in France and England, with Paris and London the centers for everything fresh and new. Only in Germany, with Berlin shattered and its writers and artists and actors and painters scattered to Munich and Hamburg and Dusseldorf, have we seen a large-scale movement toward regional redistribution in this generation. I have a feeling now that this can happen in America and is beginning to happen. It is the universities with their own new theaters and orchestras, their "writers in residence" and their vigorous local painters that will bring this about and restore creative adventure in the vast interior stretches of the land.

It may not be "regionalism" in the end products of the new creativity; that does not matter so very much. In all its forms the enduring art is universal art, and it is a universal America that we witness now, flourishing before our eyes.

Since we enjoy in this space what President Kennedy called the ultimate luxury of giving free advice, we may as well luxuriate to the limit and propose what is shockingly obvious—an Alliance for Progress for the mis-developed people of the United States.

We won't call it a five-year plan because that carries overtones of fur hats, communal kitchens and massed choirs singing official odes to the beloved bulldozer.

It will have to be an alliance of federal, state and local governments, universities, foundations and all other major sectors of that sprawling entity now called the American Establishment, the general repository of money, brains and power.

For twenty years the American people have been carried blithely and heedlessly forward, sideways and backward on the swelling tide of war spending and the happy, hectic seller's market of a world starved for the good—and bad—things of life.

The party is over. Now comes the hangover and we focus our bloodshot eyes to discover that: we have at least twice as many farms as we need, with chronic insecurity for most farmers and a malignant tumor in the federal budget; we have too many airlines, which are now facing bankruptcy after having helped bankrupt the railroads, the form of passenger transit of which we now have desperate need; we have developed, without plan or purpose, the monstrous social sprawl called the megalopolis, which is neither city nor country and is governed by up to a hundred overlapping units of government, which is to say that the communities are not governed at all but merely administered; we have allowed millions of our poorest, most unskilled people to drift from the South and concentrate, out of the need for human companionship, in the Harlems of the country, where relief and schooling facilities break down, tensions build up alarmingly and jobs for the young are not to be found.

With the swelling number of the unskilled at one end and the spread of automation at the other, we are now confronted with what looks very much like the certainty of permanent unemployment for several million Americans, this side of a vast public works program—but that, of course, would mean planning and planning is a dirty word for the eight months of the year Congress sits.

Those who enjoy the luxury of offering free advice also enjoy the luxury of asking unanswerable questions, and so some of us raise the plaintive query as to why America insists on a comprehensive national development plan in those countries recipient of our aid, while refusing even to consider a redevelopment plan for the headquarters country on whose order and well-being the recipient nations depend.

Various individuals and groups within the Establishment make a try from time to time. A Presidential group submitted an over-all, long-range plan to rationalize the morass of our transportation facilities. Rather, they threw it up for grabs and nobody grabbed. Senator Claiborne Pell has proposed a multi-state pooling of power and resources to make railroading work in the stifled and glutted northeastern states. The hard-headed Committee for Economic Development has come forward with a scheme for the "massive readjustment" of agriculture, which would mean, over a five-year period, the elimination of 2,500,000 separate farm units.

Every Congressman must know in his heart that all these things must be done if America in the immediate future is not to become a dizzying Disneyland of clamor, crowding, waste and, for millions, sheer wretchedness.

The President was wrong. The ultimate luxury is not to offer free advice. It is to possess the facts and the power and to do nothing with either.

Aspen, Colorado

From this continental watchtower where the tree line meets the gray rocks and the rocks meet the sky, a man can see, at least in the eye of the mind, the immense spread of the American Great Plains. One cannot put his eye or his mind to this scene without an overwhelming awareness that the great wheel of our history is making another turn, so consequential that it marks the end of one epoch and the start of another.

It is possible that the most important social phenomenon of

the past century was the tremendous migration from Europe and the Atlantic seaboard into the American West. The millions who came sought land, space to turn around in, and they built, here and in the true Midwest, a garden so wide and fruitful that it could virtually feed and clothe the human race.

Space, soil and human ingenuity were able to do in the American interior what the same factors were unable to do in the equally immense interiors of Latin America and Asia, including Soviet Asia.

But today contrary phenomena are occurring in these three open, interior land masses of the globe. By official pressures, many men are being pushed into the agricultural interiors of Asia. Many others flee the interior of Latin America to escape starvation. But here in the American Great Plains hundreds of thousands of their own free will are leaving the open spaces settled by their fathers and grandfathers and moving into the incessantly growing, increasingly congested cities. Psychologically, at least in my opinion, men need space even more than leisure, but it is clear that what they want, above space and leisure, is greater income and the greater stimulus of urban living.

Figures help one to grasp the scale of this reverse human tide. There are 433 counties in the ten states of the Great Plains region. Three hundred eighty-one of these counties have lost population in the last decade. The counties that have gained include the twenty designated as "metropolitan" counties, those dominated by a sizable city. Of the ten states, only Colorado, New Mexico and Texas have increased in population, which means that a great percentage of the human movement is right out of the Great Plains region to the big cities of the West Coast and the East.

So far, and happily, the majority of those moving from the western spaces into the cities have done well for themselves. But a hard core minority is doing badly because they do not have the training to get urban employment, which now goes more and more to the skilled. So this current of unemployables from the western prairies is added to the main stream of the unemployables pouring into the cities from the rural South and from places like Puerto Rico.

Competition for unskilled jobs in the ant hill cities is already severe and can become ugly. Technological changes may be the main difficulty, but racial hostilities, on the part of trade unions quite as much as industrial management, add intolerably to the painful pressures. Massive action on two fronts is clearly imperative.

On one, retraining programs, reaching down to include basic education in literacy, without which craft skills cannot be acquired, will have to be enlarged and intensified far beyond present efforts. But training in which specific skills? What kinds of jobs and precisely where will they be opening up? Industrial managements have repeatedly denied this information to unofficial investigators on the grounds they would be giving away business secrets and future planning to their competitors. Clearly, government authority must obtain and government repositories must hold this vital information, without which retraining programs will have neither chart nor compass.

On the second front, racial discrimination on jobs has to be broken down. And equal rights to vote and to go to school add little to a Negro's life if he has no equal right to work. Long overdue are changes in those many trade unions which vigorously exclude Negro Americans by the fiction that they are "voluntary associations" like country clubs or chowder-and-marching societies.

I am not sure that labor's right hand knows what its left hand is doing. In the same week that Negro groups put organized labor on notice that its racial barriers are to be attacked an official envoy of the AFL-CIO told a cheering throng of Jamaicans, now independent of Britain, that his organization would push for quota-free immigration to the United States.

More than a year ago, writing from Trinidad, I pointed out that the immigration and economic assistance buck would be passed to this country when the British West Indies became independent. This was, one must presume, what Premier Macmillan had in mind when he warned the West Indies that Britain would not be able to help them much, when he shut down West Indians' free immigration into the United Kingdom in spite of full employment there.

Illiberal as this may sound, we shall have to think carefully about opening our doors, in the names of all those already desperate in their search for jobs. And as we consider this problem our officials might take a hard look at the restrictive immigration policies of Jamaica's fellow Commonwealth nations, sparsely settled Canada and sparsely settled Australia. The United States has entered a new economic era and can no longer do anything and everything.

New York

Anger is a counterpart of joy and, since this is supposedly the "cool" and "beat" age of joylessness, it is logical to assume that the last angry man expired with the waning notes of the last hurrah.

Around Manhattan one encounters his ghost occasionally in the form of a brief, low-pitched whine, but that is the closest approximation of what used to be known as indignation, not to mention the "righteous wrath of the citizens." These terms now seem so archaic and arcane that one puts them down, even though fenced in by quotation marks, with some embarrassment.

We are by no means a nation of sheep in relation to other peoples, however big and formidable, as Khrushchev discovered in the case of his Cuban missiles, but we are truly sheep-like in our encounters with bigness within our own society. We sputter and that is all.

It is my fortune, or misfortune, to have been conditioned in the cohesive, unitary cell of the small town. An emergency meant that everybody turned out with extra efforts to make things work. If the men of the town did not open the school doors after a three-day blizzard, it was only because they couldn't find them. The other night I landed at Idlewild Airport in a gentle snowfall. The passengers' bags were dumped just anywhere; there was no order; there were no directions. Five hundred people milled about in exhausted confusion, eventually recovered their belongings, only to discover that most taxi drivers, those paragons of fictional ruggedness and bonhomie, had quit for the night. "Takes too long to make a buck," as one of them explained.

We are now in the throes of the typographers' strike which has, directly and indirectly, closed down every major newspaper in the country's biggest city. It is a strike which comes as close to utter senselessness as any that I can recall offhand. From the evidence available it is mostly a bid for greater power and prestige within the labor movement on the part of one local and its leaders—very little more. Literally hundreds of thousands of people have been hurt by this strike; many hundreds will lose their jobs for good if one or more papers fail to survive this blow.

The country's greatest community is without information save what it can get from the heroic extra efforts of radio and television, but there is no evidence that the strike leaders give a solitary damn. Nor is any bubbling of wrath among the citizenry even faintly discernible. The state of communal masochism is astounding. Either nobody dares say anything for fear of that dread label, "anti-labor," or everybody feels that no effort of his can possibly affect the situation.

And from the political leadership, municipal, state or federal—silence. No one, absolutely no one, is saying to the strike leaders what President Kennedy said to the leaders of Big Steel last spring: that they were showing contempt for the American people.

Big Labor has come full circle from the terrible days of the thirties when it won in sorrow and blood labor's overdue charter of liberties. Then, wealth did approximately equate with power, but now the managerial revolution and the diffusion of ownership have left wealth with responsibility half-shorn of power. It is an intellectual and emotional exertion, but one is obliged to revise Roosevelt's phrase, "malefactors of great wealth;" one is obliged to think about malefactors of great power and to apply it to Big Labor.

The laws are bound to follow suit, one day, and check this turning of the screw. Irresponsible power in a democracy is as dangerous when used by workers as by management.

In any case the day of the owner-manager, the "entrepreneur" of the economics textbook, is vanishing. Managers are increasingly "wage slaves" like the other ranks of employes within a big company. The labor movement, or what Jimmy Hoffa frankly calls the "labor business," was based on a class concept that steadily loses its validity. The division is increasingly a false one. The ultimate result surely ought to be a commonality of interest among all ranks within a firm or an industry, with stock ownership widely distributed among all ranks.

No doubt many union leaders would lose power and many union bureaucracies would be checked in their own kind of empire building. No doubt, also, this would be a happy improvement over conditions of the kind that now prevail in New York's publishing industry, where the greatest and best newspapers, which both mold and express the life of the community and provide its spirit and meaning, are now obliged to face the question of whether, after generations, they can carry on at all in the biggest and wealthiest city of the land.

This strike is a scandal to nearly everyone, apparently, save the men who called it. They possess what is known as the special strength of the shameless.

―――――――――――

There is a secret lesson from the long New York newspaper strike, a disturbing lesson that no journalist can easily accept, but which, I feel obliged to say, must be accepted and frankly taken as a starting point for the reformation of journalism in this country.

The secret truth is that great numbers of New York people felt a conscious or sub-conscious sense of *relief* at the absence of the daily papers and their saturating needle shower of unrelated facts―relief from the daily struggle to absorb and understand it all. In the first few weeks of the strike this was not the case; then, it was as painful as drug withdrawal. After that, most people felt no pain; indeed, they enjoyed a certain sense of freedom.

This is something publishers, editors and writers must think about very carefully as we struggle with the task of enlightening the American people, which is not the same as informing them. We might think about it in connection with a defiant, if not despairing, manifesto issued by the Center for the Study of Democratic Institutions, Dr. Robert Hutchins' "think factory" at Santa Barbara. John Cogley of that group asks the pertinent questions:

"Are our problems so vast, the technical aspects of modern life so tricky, access to the facts so slight and the necessary knowledge so elusive that American democracy will become simply a matter of living one's private life and turning over the management of the public sector completely to professionals? Are 'we the people' no more than a remote board of overseers, preoccupied with our private pursuits while experts carry on our affairs and make momentous moral decisions for us?"

My own nagging fear is that the answer is "yes," or is soon going to become "yes." Not because the generality of citizens are less intelligent than they were. Not because they are less interested―they are more interested. Not because they are less well educated―they are better educated. But because, with the growth of education and interest and the mammoth bulk of matters, both domestic and foreign, now lying within the realm of the "public sector," we have tried to take all such knowledge for our province.

In this we are failing. We are failing at the first level, the communicators' level, because in the media of communication

55

the swing to an emphasis on selectivity and constant explanation is too slow a swing. The daily needle shower of unrelated facts still tends to create a steamy vapor, obscuring vision. We are failing at the second level of the "consumer," it seems to me, for two reasons related to this.

In the first place, it is simply not true that there has been a general extension, in this country, of leisure time for reading, listening and study. It seems to me the extension of leisure has gone mostly to those Americans at the lower rungs of the economic and educational ladder, those whose desire for distraction competes powerfully with their desire for knowledge. Those Americans with a higher educational base, those in the middle and upper ranks of business and professional life—that is to say, those who *must* be well informed because of the importance of their decisions and their influence—these men and women are working harder and longer hours than their fathers and grandfathers. The daily cartoon of the exhausted commuter taking home his bulging briefcase is no sketch from fancy.

These people simply do not have anything like the residual time and energy to manage their families and concern themselves with community affairs, and still work their way to the truth of De Gaulle and NATO, disarmament, foreign aid, Latin America's bewildering predicament, Britain's lost position, the question of whether or not to cut taxes and whose taxes to cut, the meaning of the upheaval in Iraq, the best way to handle juvenile delinquency, overcrowded schools, immoral movies—you name it. They desperately need the aid of more skillfully edited, presented and explained news—not simply more news. There are only so many hours in the day; the more time spent scanning or hearing the cataract of "hard news," the fewer hours there must be for understanding it.

Mr. Cogley's manifesto goes on: "We are saying that the judgment of the people is still to be trusted." Of course, it is to be trusted—on the great, simple and immediate issues. On a hundred other important issues it cannot be trusted, because such judgments, under present conditions, are not expressed, and they are not expressed because they are not formed.

The town of Aberdeen, South Dakota, home of the quintuplets, is doing as well as could be expected. That is lonely country—or was. So flat you can see the railroad tracks come together on the horizon.

Kids grew up there, dreaming about the great, glamorous world far away. Now the world has descended on Aberdeen and the place will never be the same.

South Dakota's increase in average family income has been the lowest in the country—till now, anyway. Thirty or forty thousand dollars in gifts have already poured in. As you heard, big money offers from magazines, news syndicates, television are battering Andrew Fischer, the father. Money may solve some problems—it creates a lot of others. So Fischer went to his priest, who went to the local law firm of Agor, Seegal and Barnett; they're protecting Mr. Fischer's interests, for free. South Dakota's Senator McGovern, at the urging of townspeople, has a bill up to make the Fischer income tax exempt. The gifts aren't taxable; film and publication deals are.

Other places may call these efforts charity; in that country it's called being neighborly. In time, of course, local jealousies may develop, if the Fischer's do get rich. A *long* time from now men will say of Fischer, with his big house and big car, "I knew him when" or "easy money."

Well, rich society women endorse cold creams for money; successful actors now speak the commercials; ex-Presidents and generals sell their memoirs; Cabinet members and Senators have sold their stories, written from office records which presumably belong to the taxpayer's government. General Eisenhower got a capital gains deal from the Treasury on his war book, which made his personal fortune. Dave Fellin, the recently entombed coal miner, sold his story. So have the astronauts.

There have been exceptions. General Marshall wouldn't allow his memoirs to be printed till after his death, and he died poor. Secretary of State Acheson refused even to take any of the records home with him when he left office.

And Captain Carlsen, hero of the *Flying Enterprise*—remember him? He said no to it all, and just went back to sea.

If there's any moral, it's that Americans *like* to see a poor man get suddenly rich—because they dream of it happening to themselves, some day, some way. Although not necessarily the Fischer way.

Success hasn't spoiled Jimmy Hoffa; at least, it hasn't changed him or slowed him down. "What makes Jimmy run?" is a question the social historians may answer one day. Right now he's at the top of a very tough league; he's a carryover, an old-time street scrapper, surviving and flourishing in an era of labor leaders with manicured hands and uniformed chauffeurs.

He manages to run the biggest, roughest union in the country, while spending about as much time in court as Perry Mason, and about as successfully; and he doesn't do it all with his fists, which are still hard, or with his tongue, which is still sharp *and* ungrammatical.

Whatever he touches he changes, but not always the way he wants it. His attacks on Meany may only strengthen Meany; his approval of Rockefeller may only weaken Rockefeller, and where the governor needs support, in the Midwest and South.

For Jimmy Hoffa there is only one way to look at life—as a fight, and he's out to be champion. For him there is no resting place, and he intends to take over unions that have nothing to do with teamstering, for power purposes, as corporations take over businesses that have nothing to do with their own product, for tax purposes. He wants a consolidated, nationwide organization, which would give him enormous power because this nation lives on wheels. But he promises never to call a nationwide transport strike. The Congress would probably never permit one, anyway, as it has just demonstrated in the case of the railroad unions.

In a way, Hoffa is refreshing. In this age of indirection and the careful, lawyer-inspected statement, he can hate, and he's one of the few public figures not afraid to express his hatreds from the generous choice of words afforded by the richest language in the world. An un-polished diamond in the rough doesn't shine like the polished variety, but it's just as hard.

Nobody talks about the nobility of labor anymore, except the national labor leaders, and they've changed, too. In Washington their headquarters are in great glass and steel buildings; their offices are complete with a title on the door and a Bigelow on the floor. Some of them ride limousines, wear custom-made suits, smoke large cigars, and you can't tell the head of organized labor from the head of the chamber of commerce, without a program.

The unions themselves have changed. Years ago one authority said they had to function "as an army, a business and a town meeting." Most now function as a business. That, in fact, is what the eminent realist, James Hoffa, calls it—the labor business, not the labor movement.

It all happened in one generation. Once management held almost supreme power; then the unions exercised what at times

looked like greater power; now the real power in economic relationships is shifting to the state, to government. Recently the
Congress simply brushed aside collective bargaining, such as it
was, in the railroad controversy, and imposed compulsory ar-
bitration—a watershed, for good or ill. It's not the only watershed; the figures show the total membership in organized labor
diminishing, standing now at 18,000,000.

By the law, unions are private, voluntary associations. By the
facts, many of them are neither. And a lot of anti-union people
are trying to change the law to fit the facts. For all these reasons
labor leaders are worried this Labor Day. The thoughtful ones
among them are worried most of all about our 5- to 6-percent
unemployment, which, if it increases, does neither the unions
nor the American society any good at all.

Their next big push will be for the thirty-five-hour week,
as one move to put the whole people back to work. But we're
still a long way from what one writer, generations ago, called
"the insupportable labor of doing nothing."

March 26, 1964

This is a postscript to a television interview between this
reporter and Cassius Clay of Kentucky—or, Muhammed Ali of
Islam. It is a reaction to the reaction of the printed press, which
is obviously bewitched, bothered and bewildered, as the song has
it, by young Mr. Clay.

So we have columnist Robert Ruark of the grits-and-hominy
school of writing, who says Mr. Clay is a bum. We have columnist
Harriet Van Horne, who follows Freud to the higher truths, and
who finds despair and terror in the psyche of Cassius Clay, beneath his boasting.

For what it's worth, I would agree with neither finding.
There are two things amiss with the world champion. He is uneducated and he is humorless; he hasn't learned to laugh at himself. But he is very far from being a bum; his instincts, indeed,
and those of his younger brother too, are the instincts of a gentleman; they must have had good parents.

The army failed Clay on the intelligence test for reasons of
its own. He is not stupid, but quick of mind; he *is* ignorant, which
could be remedied and ought to be, for there is a rare life force
in this boy and he *could* be the example to youth that he yearns
to be.

Hidden despair and terror? On the contrary, he is happy as a bluebird in spring, on top of the world: He almost dances as he walks, bursting with life and exuberance.

Many people are upset that Clay fervently believes the faiths and dogmas of the Black Muslim cult. Some of these dogmas—their geological and astronomical notions—are, of course, fantasy. Their beliefs in the African origin of man and in ancient African cultures of a high order have much historical truth in them. But the pertinent claim made for this cult is that it helps restore the Negro's lost pride.

This, so I believe, it is doing for Cassius Clay. It is one source of his courage and his equanimity of spirit. This he needs. He is, after all, a boy of twenty-two, Negro, now the most famous member of his race, and in the turbulent time of the Negro revolution. Without an anchor, the ceaseless pressures on him could tear him apart. They may yet. But if they don't, the credit will probably have to go to this belief of his, and his own instinct for goodness.

3

The Purpose of America
Is to Be American

To institutionalize a sentiment, whether of joy or sadness, is not a natural thing; all of us feel a certain constraint on Memorial Day, because all of us sense that it is those with the most to say who are the most inclined to silence. So sometimes all of us must feel that the greatest tribute to those now gone and to whom we owe our freedom would be, simply, silence.

That is done, sometimes, in certain countries on such days of regret and memory as this; in Latin countries in particular, where all life is intermingled with a brooding sense of death and where the instinct to mourn goes always hand in hand with the instinct to rejoice. But we are not yet like that here in our country, where it is the future that always seems close at hand, not the past. Other national communities will accept a full day of silence; but we are the nation of the one-minute silence, and somehow this seems right and good for us.

Whatever our faults of national failure and our spurts of worry, fatalism is not yet a part of the American national spirit; it is good for our own health as a country and, we think, good for all of this uncertain world that this is so. And this is the deepest of all the reasons, perhaps, why we make this day of regretful memory and solemn ceremony also a day of picnic and party; this is why you see a few flags today at half staff, and the others flying as usual, bravely at the top. We behave on our Memorial Day as we do because, almost unconsciously, we are making certain assumptions. We are assuming, as we think of past wars, that wars really cannot happen to us again; we are assuming, as we think of a brother or a neighbor who died in battle, that our present neighbors and brothers will never share that fate.

Our friends in older and sadder countries are always a little disturbed about this characteristic of our nature, a little distrustful, feeling there is dangerous unwisdom somewhere in this; but they are feeling a kind of envy, too, as a man of heavy years feels as he watches youth. He knows it is heading for pitfalls and pain, but he also knows that without this irrespressible belief in life and safety there would be no life or safety, for him or anyone else, and that everything would come apart. From similar impulse, older and sadder nations have instinctively clung to us, not only from their belief in our power, but because of our power of belief. Inarticulate and unformulated though it may be this belief remains the ultimate wisdom.

And so, perhaps, we need not worry quite as much as we do about all the complaints that we do not really carry the message of America to foreign lands, do not really formulate and express what we call the "American way of life." One has a feeling that, should it be neatly formulated, that will be a warning sign that it is no longer in our bones, but only in our minds, a sign that its essence and strength are gone.

Even on Memorial Day, consecrated to tragedy, our flag flies at the top of the staff, and that, after all, is the truest expression and formulation of the American spirit. The tragic view of life is not yet ours, and if it should ever be, there would lie the only real tragedy.

So perhaps it would not be in bad taste to suggest to those among us with intense and private cause for grief on this day, to think a little of our curious holiday behavior in that light; to see the picnics and the parties, not as an affront to them, but as sign and symbol of reassurance for us all.

June 18, 1958

President Eisenhower said today that a gift is not a bribe; it is a tangible expression of friendship. Long ago another New England Adams named Henry wrote as follows: "One friend in a lifetime is much, two are many, three are hardly possible." But "friend" is a word that Mr. Bernard Goldfine uses to describe the men, numbering many times three, to whom he has made tangible expressions.

When the headline writers and investigators are through with the case of Goldfine and Adams no doubt the philosophers will take it up and they will seek for its deeper meaning, for this case, too, is not exceptional, but one of many that identify the mores and manners of twentieth-century American life. Just as the style of writing is part of its substance, just as a style of living is part of life's substance, so are symbols of substantive meaning. Those who wish may find the sign of political or moral decline in this current case; others will see in it one more sign that symbols themselves are declining. Attainability does this. The moon will never again be the symbol of mystery and romance once it is attained. The automobile was once the symbol of social stature; psychologists tell us it is now a symbol of nothing save transportation. The refrigerator and its cousinly gadgets were once the gleaming symbols of woman's rise above slavery, and they are now only things to be repaired.

Once the word "friend" had a precious meaning; it had to do with trust and love and refuge in distress. Now it is an item of mass manufacture and conspicuous consumption. The word is counterfeit coin, repeatedly used where the lead slugs known as "acquaintance" or "contact" are really meant, a malpractice associated chiefly with the worlds of business and politics. If the word "friend" has been debased, there is no escaping the debasement of the word "gift." A gift between human beings was once the most precious symbol: a sign of love, a sign of peace between tribes or kings, a sign of sacrifice by the giver, a reason for excitement on the part of the receiver, to be placed conspicuously in tent, or palace, or parlor as notice to all that a transaction in mutual affection and trust had taken place, not likely to be cancelled.

What, now, is the "gift" when politician or executive merely initials a list of recipients prepared by his secretary and places an order for wholesale lots? What has become of the gift of advice? This, too, was once a word with meaning. In politics and

63

business advisors are now hired, sometimes in groups at a per diem, or retained on a yearly basis and called "consultants." And what of the gift of hospitality? There are still tribes and regions where hospitality means shelter from nature's elements and rest for the sore in foot, where it is part of the accoutrement of character, part of a man's credentials for his day of judgment.

But Mr. Goldfine of this twentieth century, so his book-keeper tells us, would not possibly know about the separate hotel bills for Mr. Sherman Adams, charged to his account—indeed, not even to his own account, but to his companies' accounts. He is a busy man, she said; he cannot possibly know of such details.

Perhaps easy prosperity has done all this; perhaps the modern, corporate expense account and the modern tax system which has made much money, meaningless money. The philosophers can figure this out at their leisure, and perhaps they will tell us then to consider whether, when the symbols of human character and relationship decline in value, character and relationships themselves decline, and that when these decline in any human society, the society declines.

If there were a method of Presidents extending their news conference remarks in an appendix as Senators do their remarks from the floor, we would have hoped for a Presidential extension of his remark today that a gift is a tangible expression of friendship.

February 23, 1959

On an Army hospital bed in North Carolina an American gentleman is struggling with what may be his mortal illness. I use the word "gentleman" in its venerated sense, which relates to character, not in the spurious sense which relates to class or position. And I use the national adjective because the pith of America, the America we think of in our proudest vision, was expressed by this man's life.

I am speaking of the hulking, homely General of the Army, George Catlett Marshall. The man President Truman thought of as the greatest living American; the man the late Secretary of War, Henry Stimson, had in mind when he said, "Some day Americans will understand that a great man was living among them." It is a little painful to realize that already a generation of Americans have reached maturity, hardly recognizing his name, with no idea at all of what he meant to their country only a dozen years ago.

For the young who may be listening I can relate the obvious things—that he was the Army Chief of Staff during the war; that he was one of the true architects of victory, along with Roosevelt and Churchill; that later he tried to pull China together, failing because the assignment was impossible of success; that he was later Secretary of State when the Marshall Plan for Europe's salvation was born, and was back again in the Pentagon as Secretary of Defense.

I can only suggest the true nature of the man by recalling for you that he made Eisenhower the Supreme Commander in Europe, renouncing that glory and glamor for himself, to remain here where the real decisions were made; that during the war he was deliberately cold to his closest military friends in order that the human weakness of affection might not warp his judgments; that when he was returning from China and received the cable asking him to be Secretary of State, he wept—so weary he then was—but accepted because he was a soldier trained to obey; that when, after a lifetime's dedication, he was called a front man for traitors by Senator Jenner, he would not stoop to make reply; that he refused great wealth and refrained from publishing his memoirs on the ground that the published truth would hurt a few associates still alive and on the ground that history alone must be his judge.

More than any great person this reporter ever knew Marshall reminded me of Washington, whose commemorative holiday today happens to be. Like Washington, he knew how to remain silent and wait; like Washington, he had no dazzling intellectual brilliance, no particular wit or original humor, no gift for small talk or eloquence. But more brilliant and imaginative men leaned on Washington constantly, just as they leaned on George Catlett Marshall, in times of great anxiety. In both cases they did so because the General's shoulders were just a little broader than any others around, because the General's spine had a little more steel in it than theirs, because they knew, by experience and instinct, that his word, once given, was unbreachable and that his actions would have one, invariable purpose: the good of his country, the accomplishment of his duty.

I suppose when General Marshall dies that his headstone will be a modest one. But if there is room upon it these words, written four centuries ago, might properly be engraved:

"Who would dig and delve from morn till evening? Who would travail and toil with the sweat of his brows? Yea, who would, for his king's pleasure, adventure and hazard his life—

if wit had not so won men, that they thought nothing more need-
ful in this world nor anything whereunto they were more
bounden, than here to live in their duty, and to train their
whole life, according to their calling?"

America remains the Great Experiment in Living, without
equal in history, without its match upon this earth.

Many of us had come to doubt this giant fact in recent years,
and I among them. Many things had gone wrong in our affairs
at home and around the world, and we told ourselves: we are a
complacent people; we are a materialistic people; our young are
drawing inward, seeking private answers to life; our stride is
broken, our confidence crippled, and everywhere in a disillu-
sioned world men are putting derisory quotation marks around
the words "The American Way of Life."

We may lay aside our doubts. Of this I feel sure, having
lived abroad for nearly two years, come back again, widely traveled from east to west in this country, listened to a thousand
questions and comments and felt, like a strong but irregular
pulse, the conscience of a people demanding the best of themselves. After that experience I have this to say: if we are a materialistic people, no people on earth so relentlessly denounces
materialism or strives so hard to share its materials with other
people who do not have them; if we are a conformist society,
there is no other society that worries out loud so much about the
evils of conformity; if we are the richest country on the globe,
in no other country do riches alone attract less awe and public
merit than in the United States.

To those among us and to our foreign critics who say that
we are still isolationist in spirit, bumblingly ignorant of the rest
of the world, I would have a great many things to say, among
them these:

We do, indeed, have much to learn; but how can this be
wondered at? No nation in all time has been so suddenly thrust
into the affairs of so many other nations, including the most
alien and remote. Our major allies acquired their former responsibilities around the world slowly, deliberately, and possessed the power, including resort to force, to carry out their
policies and desires. Our present responsibilities were thrust
upon us; we did not seek this role, but have accepted it out of
common sense—and conscience—and we possess only materials,

good will and persuasion with which to see it through. This is why I cannot accept, nor should you accept, the occasional posture of our British friends, for example, as if they were citizens of a wise and mellow Athens who are proctoring a big and brassy Rome. Their premise is false.

There exists an American public conscience, pervasive and always growing. I know no other fundamental explanation for what I have seen and heard during these recent travels from state to state. Let anything go wrong, anywhere, whether it be an abandoned child in the local suburb or mass famine in far-off Asia, and there will be an immediate response, out of the instincts of compassion or indignation, from Americans, their number proportionate to public awareness of the wrong. In no other country I know, save England, does the public conscience function to anything like this degree.

Its important ingredients are at least two—a quality of innocence and a sense of guilt. I think, sometimes, that collective life in this exalting and terrible century would be without hope or meaning were it not for this element of innocence, because innocence implies belief in progress, and it is the world's good fortune that in America this belief is backed by power. It is part of the American spiritual tradition to believe that problems, however massive or distant, can be solved. Perhaps this comes from our successful experience in conquering and settling a most formidable continent. But it is there, it is instinctive and it never dies away. It *has* died away in certain older societies than ours, perhaps because they have suffered too much, and so their people have come to feel that time is life, that problems can never really be solved but can only be ameliorated and that the process of amelioration itself represents successful living.

I am not a philosopher, and I cannot assign philosophical values to these differing outlooks on life. I can only say, as a journeyman journalist, that life in many, many places on this earth would today be considerably worse than it is were Americans not possessed of this belief, this innocence, for then we could not act. If we are immature, as many Europeans say we are, the world has much cause to be grateful.

The sense of guilt involved in our collective reactions to the world's wrongs comes, I suppose, from the New England influence in our public life and, more remotely, from the Puritan strain in the inherited English spirit. It may well be a necessary element in our particular chemistry; but I have come to feel troubled about it, after these recent travels abroad. We feel guilty that China was delivered into the hands of Communists, yet I am certain we could not have prevented that. We feel guilty when a man named Lumumba dies a violent death in the Congo, when the peasants of northeast Brazil are revealed to be half-starved, when our Canadian neighbors resent our popular culture, which is drowning out theirs. We do not stop to remind ourselves that the original and fundamental responsibility for such conditions and such events lies with the peoples directly concerned, not with us.

Without this prodding sense of guilt we would not be quite the people we are; yet I feel sure, now, that we accept far too much responsibility for these things in our individual and collective breasts, that this is distorting our aim and purpose by putting matters out of focus. Our European friends always say, "You Americans seek to be loved, when you should seek to be respected." I think they are essentially right, and I have come to believe that our automatic reaction of feeling guilty for almost any mishap, anywhere, is no longer gaining respect for America but losing it. If we are eager to shoulder the load for every disaster, others become eager to help us do so. It relieves them of their own sense of guilt. (Three years ago certain Belgian officials in Brussels were not socially receiving American diplomats there, because they blamed America for Belgium's precipitous, unplanned grant of independence to the Congo. And Nigerians and others smashed our embassy buildings, because they accused us of murdering Lumumba in connivance with the Belgians!)

Respect is a two-way transaction, but it begins at home with self-respect. We shall be stronger and more effective—and more respected—if we can learn to live by a prayer my father used to quote: "Please, God, give me the courage to tackle those problems I have a chance of solving; give me the self-control to avoid those problems I have no chance of solving; and give me the wisdom to know the difference."

Innocence, conscience, goodness and implicit belief in progress both personal and public—these are qualities we associate with youth. In some derision Oscar Wilde once wrote, "The youth of America is their oldest tradition. It has been going on now for three hundred years." We are still at it, because, at heart, we *are* a young society. Only the young in heart are acutely self-examining; only the spiritually young endlessly tear up old ideas, customs, buildings and landscapes for something new and better. But even the young get tired at times, and the period of relative repose, inwardness and seeming complacency that followed the end of the Korean War can be regarded as a time of rest to gather strength and ideas for the new burst of political, economic and intellectual energy now beginning to dominate the public scene.

Still, our foreign critics will remind us, there are other qualities of youth—unsteadiness, recklessness—and since America's power is so vast these qualities are a menace to the world's peace. Sometimes our leaders have *spoken* recklessly; but how often, on the factual record, have they *acted* that way? What action of ours since the last great war has equaled in recklessness the act of wise old England in her invasion of Suez, or of ancient France in her bombing of the Tunisian town, which almost cost France all sympathy in her Algerian Calvary? Have we reacted hastily, unsteadily under the outrageous provocations of Cuba's Castro or under the massive insults of Khrushchev at the United Nations? I do not think so.

Peregrine Worsthorne, a British writer personally acquainted with the American scene and temperament—which so many of his critical countrymen, alas, are not—put it this way last year: "It seems to me the American people are always denied the benefit of the doubt. When they get excited and start calling for the Marines ... they are castigated for being hysterical children, too immature for world leadership. Yet when they remain calm and unruffled, they are castigated for being lethargically senile, too tired and flaccid for world leadership."

We are young, thank heaven, but we are by no means children.

I am certain we shall not lose the essential drives and hopes and beliefs of youth for a long, long time to come. The theory of the "discouragement of species" will not apply to us. This is an anthropologist's notion, applied to the social scene, that a nation does not fall, but slowly, almost imperceptibly slips behind militarily, economically and culturally until it awakes one day and realizes that the effort to catch up and regain its former place is too great for its strength, by now much softened, and it resigns itself to minor status for all time.

It is the very opposite process that one sees at work among the American people. If we do not see this clearly, it is because we have been confused by the recent *relative* decline in our power and world prestige—relative to the rise of Russian prestige and power—though we still out-match the Soviet in both respects.

In the *absolute* sense our power steadily grows; our economy grows in spite of temporary slowdowns; and—most exciting of all—there is a cultural, educational burgeoning that one can feel in the American air almost everywhere from coast to coast. There is a passion for higher education of an intensity I have felt in no other country I have known. The tremendous pressure on the universities is due not only to the rise in population, but to a general rise in family goals for the young. "The revolution of rising expectations" applies to the United States, highly developed as we already are, as well as to "underdeveloped" countries.

I have seen nothing like this anywhere. Say, if you will, that the television screens and the magazine racks are half-filled with trash; say that teaching standards are far too low in a thousand places; say that athleticism outranks intellectualism in a thousand places. I will agree, but I will say to you that all this is changing, slowly because the task is enormous, but most surely. A cultural explosion as well as a population explosion is gathering force among our people underneath the honky-tonk exteriors. There are over 2,000 theatrical groups in the United States. More than half the symphony orchestras in the world are to be found in the United States. Painting is a passion with millions.

To those who say, "Ah, but the general quality is not high," I can say that it is getting higher all the time, that only by cultural exposure can the true talents be found, and I would assert, as a prophecy, that from this vast and growing exposure there will rise the highest general level of education, understanding of the world and cultural awareness that history has ever witnessed. In the long run mass education is *not* the "enemy of excellence" and need never be if we use common sense.

If the system of educating the elite had withstood the test of time, Britain, where only a hundred thousand boys and girls are enjoying a university education, would not now be deeply troubled by its critical shortage of scientific brains; France, where nearly half the population never reads a book, would not now be re-examining her own educational system in some alarm; nor would Italy, home of the Renaissance, where one of every eight persons over the age of six cannot read or write.

America has not fundamentally changed, because its spirit has not really changed. Ours remains preeminently the land of the Great Experiment; for us life is always marked "unfinished business."

Other enemies in other times, before the Communists came along, believed us soft, tired, complacently wallowing in material riches, and found to their discomfiture that we were not. Whenever we have taken one step backward it was always to take two steps forward. We are stepping forward again; our historic cycle is not broken.

America, in its special meaning to the world, is by no means over. I have come to feel again what I have not always felt in these disturbing years since the great war—that the American Story in the Book of Life is really just beginning.

There is not the slightest danger that America is going to become a nation of Fascists or Communists, but a returned native has the impression we are becoming a nation of common scolds. True to our tradition of innovation we are original even in this. While the nationals of most countries scold other people, we scold ourselves.

It has become impossible to pass a newspaper and magazine stand without feeling the hot blasts of flagellation. "Are You A Good Mother?—Take This Ten-Point Test!" "How to Make Your Husband Smile Again." "Is *Your* City Dying?" "What *You* Can Do About Cancer"—or Juvenile Delinquency, Desegregation, River Pollution, the Melting Polar Cap, Atomic Fallout, Cholesterol, Bad Breath, Crab Grass, the Population Explosion, the Narcotics Racket, Itching Scalp, Middle-Age Spread, Psoriasis, Greek Orphans, Neighborhood Blight, Illiterate Polynesians, Smog, Apartheid, Body Odor, Protein Deficiency in Africa, the Creeping Girdle and Scrofula Among the Eskimos.

The biggest big business in America is not steel, automobiles or television. It is the manufacture, refinement and distribution of anxiety. It is the only business based on the maxims, "the customer is always wrong," "we aim to displease" and "send 'em away unhappy." Anyone from the age of ten is a potential buyer and, once hooked, may be a customer for life.

It is entirely possible that Khrushchev need not spend his money and energy on alternating threats and promises in his Pavlovian attempt to induce the ultimate state of *nevolya*—willessness—in the American people. We can do it to ourselves at our own expense. Our large, economy size do-it-yourself anxiety kit contains a book of instructions which begins with the reminder that Americans are personally and collectively responsible for each and every ill of mankind and can rectify all of them if the tools in the kit are properly used.

Logically extended, this process can only terminate in a mass nervous breakdown or in a collective condition of resentment that will cause street corner Santa Clauses to be thrown down manholes, the suffering to be left to pain and aid delegations from Ruanda-Urundi to be arrested on the White House steps. Either result would be marked on the credit side of the ledger for the next Congress of Communist Parties.

Anyone, for any cause, may now deal in the open market of the American conscience and make his profit. We stand in the world's dock, convicted of the double crime of success and stability and, having testified against ourselves, discover that we are sentenced to the guilt complex for the rest of our natural lives.

The American convicts suffering the most are, of course, many of our finest citizens—the sensitive, the imaginative, the liberal-minded, the men and women of conscience who wear not only heart, but liver and lights on their sleeves. It happens, or so certain psychological studies inform me, that the liberal has a deeper personal sense of insecurity than the conservative, the lunatic fringe aside. He suffers more for others partly because he suffers more with himself. He has an inborn, unjustified sense of guilt and vainly seeks to work it off. I do not belittle this; without this trait in our society life both here and in many places abroad would be considerably worse than it is. The American hairshirt has kept a lot of bodies warm from the Arctic to Bengal.

Yet a mass breakout from this suffocating prison into the clean air of common sense is long overdue. The great guilt complex, exploited for gain both commercial and psychic, is unnerving and distracting us, breaking our stride, wounding our natural pride and confidence. Our strength ought to be, but is not, as the strength of ten, because—we think—our heart is impure. In nature the weak are not permitted to weaken the strong, for then the weak are lost. But it seems to be news to many among us that sensitivity, generosity and compassion are possible without neurotic self-flagellation.

The latest noxious weed to grow from the compost of American neuroticism is the reaction in other, less-privileged countries. This is one respect in which we are most definitely winning "the battle for men's minds." We are convincing their more alert citizens that America *is* guilty, responsible for their troubles. This comes in very handy for their politicians, intellectuals and local Communists. It removes their own guilt. As things now stand our self-guilt and their self-pity fit perfectly, hand in glove. The fist is theirs, ours the chin.

October 1961

We are seeing the end of our adolescence. In its reincarnation as guardian, advisor and donor to half the world the United States is emerging from its teens. A certain glow begins to fade. The hard, gray thoughts of maturity take possession and there is some danger of the cynicism that is itself immature.

In our relations with allied, neutral and client countries we are like the half-boy, half-man who is chagrined to learn that his own best image of himself is not really shared by others, that many he has helped feel no particular gratitude or even obligation and that some he has trusted return the trust only when the occasion serves them.

We will persevere, no doubt, learning that we can re-make very little of the world in our own image, losing many illusions about others and ourselves. But one thing we dare not lose—our essential self-confidence, now shaken under strong assault from within and without. Every other consequential country save Russia and possibly China has already lost this. Not one of them really knows where it is going or how to get there.

In a profound sense the United States is alone in this world. Most Americans who grasp this heart fact have only recently grasped it, as it has dawned upon them that our major alliance *may* be pulled apart, beginning with loss of faith and will among the Germans; as they learn that the neutrals are not going to be "won over" to our side; as they learn that bringing internal stability to a long list of backward countries is a much, much more difficult, drawn-out and expensive task than ever faintly imagined by the advisors who inserted that paragraph called "Point Four" in Mr. Truman's inaugural speech of January 1949.

It is time we ceased clutching illusions to our breast. We have to let them go if our hands are to be free. Some were of a self-denigrating nature, in any case, and it ought to be a pleasure to let them go, a source of greater confidence. Such, at least, have been my own sensations as various items of impediments sloughed off during the two past years in Europe, Africa and Latin America. A few may be worth the mention:

Americans are materialistic. We are, in fact, as furiously moralistic and idealistic as any people left on earth. We are swamped by the materials, but their simple possession fills no hollow in our souls, as it seems to do with the French. For pure money and possession lust I think I would put the black Africans first.

We are status seekers. The most ironclad pecking orders of my observance exist among Africans and Arabs. The average well-off Latin American is so riven by class and status that he wants nothing to do with the poor, even in his thoughts. Some members of my English shooting syndicate, which hunted on Wednesdays, were young businessmen who felt obliged to demonstrate that they could afford a mid-week day off, which they could not. One stock broker carried the *Financial Times* in his cartridge case and consulted it between flights of partridge.

America is a conformist society. The reason for our fantastic profusion of laws and regulations is the fantastic variety of our manners, ambitions and desires. The true conformist societies, of course, are the primitive societies.

We have neglected Latin America. The neglecters of Latin America are Latin Americans. Somewhere between $5 and $10 billion owned by Latin businessmen is salted away in New York, London and Swiss banks, while their governments demand grants and soft-currency loans from us as a matter of ecclesiastical right.

Europeans understand the Communist threat more clearly than we. Less clearly, if anything, because we have to measure it in its worldwide framework. Not even the able British diplomatic establishment possess Russian experts of the eminence of Charles Bohlen or George Kennan. No European provincial city boasts a hard-working citizens group comparable to the Foreign Policy Study organization in Cleveland or in a dozen other American towns. No academic centers of Russian study in Europe are superior to those at Harvard or Columbia.

America is too impatient. We have been, in my reluctant judgment, far too patient with allies, neutrals and clients alike. This has won us no affection and now is losing us respect.

Goodness without power is impotent in this world. Power itself is impotent when there is no belief in the will to use it, if need be.

President Kennedy's "Peace Corps" so far is a bright stroke of domestic, not foreign policy. It is a prescription that helps to cure one of America's internal ailments, not ailing societies overseas. This is its effect if not its official intention.

It is a doctor's placebo, given to the organically healthy, educated youth of America to help cure it of its imagined illness: the feeling that their generation has no big and dramatic challenge as did their fathers in revamping America's economic society under Roosevelt and fighting the Fascists' threat to liberty. That is why the excitement here far exceeds the expectations in the distant destinations of this crusade.

The sense of frustration in the postwar college generation ran wide and deep. To them the days of great collective adventures seemed to be over. They were forced to look inward; they sought exclusively personal answers to the fulfillment of life in their times. So they married young, built private walls against the world, spawned a whole school of extremely funny, extremely cynical night-club scoffers at all that was political and public. They thought they saw a complacent, selfish, money-centered society all around them. They took it at face value, hedged against it, and their disappointed fathers called them security-conscious and conformists.

But America never really changes in its heart of hearts. It is constantly renewed in its better instincts because the best of its youth does not really change. It seeks to act, to find something above and beyond self with which to identify and give meaning to personal life. It finds something new in the youthful, gay courage of the President himself and in this "Peace Corps," token of his own spirit's kinship with them.

As an act of spiritual mobilization of American youth the "Peace Corps" is important. In terms of its potential, measureable, practical accomplishments its importance is far less.

Some months from now a few hundred picked youngsters with some degree of skill in languages, teaching, sanitation or crop rotation will arrive by car, Jeep or Land Rover in a tiny fraction of the towns and villages of Asia, Africa and Latin America. The full blaze of "human interest" publicity will focus upon them—for a while.

For a long time, in all these areas, hundreds of highly skilled, dedicated American adults have been working alongside their European counterparts at the same heart- and back-breaking tasks of development—men and women representing government agencies, universities, foundations, religious groups and private industries. One can visualize them now, sitting on their local club verandas or lying hot and weary under their mosquito netting, and reading the excited headlines about the "Peace Corps." Some of them will laugh and spawn local jokes about the coming of a children's crusade; some will feel bitter and unappreciated; some will frankly welcome any help that they can get.

Somehow, at some point in time, it will all shake down and work, if only for the reason that most Americans anywhere cannot abide failure and believe that any problem can be solved. But long before that time arrives the feature writers and cameramen will have turned their attention away, the young corpsmen and girls will no longer feel like heroes or martyrs, even to themselves. The rain and heat and drudgery and the local microbes will have occupied their bones.

But most of them will plod ahead—if they have been rigorously selected—feeling both sympathetic and superior about those who could not take it, and they will come home at the end of their terms, as their fathers who stayed the course of the war came home, older than their years, stronger than they were, privately aware that they are rightful owners of a little, special piece of their country's future.

"Pity the land that is ruled by a child," someone once said. The story of Lumumba and the Congo attests to this. But pity also the land whose rule allows no place for the childlike instincts of adventure, goodness and confident belief.

Shooting at sitting ducks is not regarded as either fair or fun in sporting and editorial circles, so I feel slightly embarrassed slipping this cartridge in the chamber. But since, by some optical illusion, so many important bird watchers still think the creatures are actually on the wing, it is necessary to fire and exhibit the carcass.

All orthodoxies eventually become squint-eyed and short-sighted. This has happened to orthodox liberalism in the United States. Since any definition of a true liberal must include willingness to accept plain facts, let us withdraw the old and honorable label from the myopic and call them "liberalists," as Mencken or somebody called routine preachers "religionists."

Among the influential liberalists excitedly exclaiming as they bird-watch through the wrong end of their rusty telescopes are some of the supper-club and phonograph-record political satirists and at least one of the gifted new cartoonists, the beguiling Mr. Jules Feiffer, who confuses the nature of individuals with the nature of governments as even trained psychiatrists so often do. It is Mr. Feiffer's perceptive observation that "People make up fairy stories about themselves and cast these as their real images and then try to relate this image to the fairy tale image of another person."

Substitute the concept of countries for individuals in the above passage and this is precisely what Mr. Feiffer does himself when he goes on to say, "Politically, we're a status quo country and our whole orientation is against change. One of the reasons we're hampered in the Cold War is that we feel change anywhere is a threat."

No wingless duckling lies flatter on the ground than this proposition. The most distinguished hallmark of the American society is and always has been—change. It is in this sense that the blare and thrust of America has been the greatest force for voluntary upheaval—economic, technical and cultural—the world has known in the last century and a half. The most powerful exterior engine driving today's "revolution of rising expectations" is the influence and example of America, not that of Russia. Allowed a free vote nine-tenths of the literate populace in nine-tenths of the "underdeveloped countries" would unquestionably opt to change as America, not Russia, has changed.

When all South America threw off Spain in the last century, the United States endorsed and protected the change. Lincoln's emancipation of the slaves sent electric currents of intellectual change through half the western world. It was the United States that brought the change to freedom in the Philippines and in Cuba, that inspired the drive for "self-determination of nations" in Wilson's time.

When Britain's Socialists were re-making that society we continued our absolute support of Britain with enormous loans. Dedicated Americans labored to change fundamentally the political institutions of both Germany and Japan. We made possible the immense change of the Middle East represented by the creation of Israel. We have not opposed the profound social changes Nasser has brought to Egypt. We encourage, not discourage, the great change that the European Common Market means, even though this may hurt us economically. We have refused to oppose the frequently violent and dangerous changeover from colonialism in the vast stretch from North Africa to the Congo, in spite of the frequent fury of our closest allies.

All over Latin America our political, technical and educational emissaries work day and night for change in the direction of democracy, enlightenment and economic progress. It is, indeed, the very premise of the "Alliance for Progress" that the local elites must give their own proofs of change to qualify for our aid.

Neither the American people nor its government "feel change anywhere is a threat." Because we have been obliged at times and places to work with and through dictatorial regimes, rather than abandon the field entirely, is no proof of love for those regimes. To assume, for example, that our military money has prevented Spain from throwing out Franco and installing a progressive democratic regime is to make an enormous assumption. It is also true, though liberalists won't face the fact, that there are places in this world—Viet-Nam seems to be one, like Greece, Korea and Malaya before it—where Communist attack has to be beaten off, and with the instruments at hand, before fundamental social reform can proceed.

America is a tremendous influence for change in the world. Even the African nationalists who berate us are quick enough to adopt our methods and send their future leaders here for study. For America to be a direct *agent* of forced change is another and far more hazardous proposition, though we have done it in our past and shall probably be forced to do it again. But in our last attempt, the bungled effort to restore freedom to the Cubans, the liberalists were the first to scream protest that we should even *try* to change that status quo.

Get ready, self-conscious America, to bleed from yet another self-inflicted wound. As one of the most perceptive of contemporary Frenchmen has said of the United States, "Any writer who bitterly denounces the vices of this country is listened to with special care and sorrowful appreciation, though he hurts ... and the writer who admires and praises this country has the nice qualities of a gratifying friend, to be sure, but is considered soft-headed."

So we sorrowfuly accepted the notion that affluence has fastened the spirit of materialism upon us, failing to notice that in no other country do riches alone produce so little respect, that no other people shows such a compulsion to give their riches away.

We accepted the notion of the "organization man" as if a new, stylized personality essence had come into being, a concept as false as that of "economic man" or "Socialist man." We accepted the notion of the brutishly ignorant "ugly American" abroad, unaware that no other foreign emissaries, in the round, show the same degree of humble deference to the views and values of "the natives" that most of our agents exhibit.

Now we are told in a new book, *The Image, or What Happened to the American Dream,* that we are becoming walking zombies, lost to reality, living a mirror life of pseudo-experience. We are indulging in "tourism," not travel, replacing fame with mere celebrity, treating pseudo-events as news, preferring reprints to originals, the corporate "image" to the corporate function— fabricating facsimiles of life, that is, even to the artifice of trying to project a "national image" in the world and appointing commissions to re-conjure the "national purpose," which supposedly faded away when we weren't looking.

This indictment, brilliantly stated within its limits by Daniel Boorstin, is likely to be accepted as another bright coin in the common currency of upper-middle-brow dinner-party talk. Some will agree with all of it; all will agree with some of it. (I suspect I contributed to the concept myself with a widely reprinted piece some years ago about pseudo-news and the "publicity saints.") The theme itself will become part of the "conventional wisdom" for a time. Then it will be put aside because, even were it true, it is, like pure pain, insupportable to the nervous system.

It approaches the terrible indictment of D. H. Lawrence, who "wondered whether America really was the great death-continent, the great No! to the European and Asiatic and even African Yes! . . . and all its people the agents of the mystic destruction! Plucking, plucking at the created soul in a man, till at last it plucked out the growing germ and left him a creature of mechaniam and automatic reaction, with only one inspiration, the desire to pluck the quick out of every living spontaneous creature." But the "image" theme is essentially untrue. There is something deeply superficial about it—that is not a total non sequitur—even though it is not as spiritually profound a profanation as the curse of Lawrence.

The "graphic revolution" to which Boorstin attributes many of his evils is wave action, not a sea change. The anxious, relentless search for spiritual certainties reflected in American literature belies the reality of the image life. So does the massive hunger revealed in the public turn toward painting, toward the theater, toward the museums of antiquities. So does the stumbling turn toward organized religion, the dead seriousness of much of the new college generation, the rise—so astounding to Europeans— in the quality of American science and general scholarship, in the immense increase in the reading of books. Boorstin's book itself and the furious argument it inspires belie its own theme of a widely pervasive fake life in America. So does the very attempt to restate the "American purpose," however embarrassing on one level this is.

It could, in fact, be argued that what happened to the intrinsic American purpose or ideal is simply that so many Americans have been so busy living it, realizing it, that it has not occurred to them that it needed fresh categorizing.

The author himself misses the central reality of America amidst the appearances that he believes have become our realities.

What is the central reality of contemporary America? It was stated by the aforementioned Frenchman, Jacques Maritain, a few years ago: "... The people who lived and toiled under this structure or ritual of civilization were keeping their own souls apart from it ... they were freedom-loving and mankind-loving people, people clinging to the importance of ethical standards, anxious to save the world, the most humane and the least materialist among modern peoples which had reached the industrial stage."

May 27, 1963

This, I'm afraid, is a short-range arrow aimed only in the general direction of a long-range target. It is part of the unsorted impedimenta left over from recent travels. No one can visit modern Greece without re-visiting ancient Greece through its written classics, and no one can do that without looking, of a sudden, at his own society with different, if not wiser, eyes.

It is an absurdly long jump from the golden age of Periclean Greece and the reasons for its failure in the end to the New Frontier of John F. Kennedy and the reasons for its failure in the beginning. If there is any connection, it is to be found only in general thoughts about the social biology of nations. The thought here is that the United States has reached middle age as a nation, knows this in its bones, but not explicitly in its mind, and therefore does not reflect it in its speech, including the programs of political leaders.

The familiar explanation for this government's failure to climb the steep passes of the New Frontier is not enough—the simple argument that Congress balks and that it balks because the mood of the country, which the Congress and election statistics accurately reflect, favors no great exertions. The argument adds that the American people have always behaved this way between wars and between depressions.

They have, but to be content with this explanation is to explain modern America only in terms of the short-range cycle of years and decades. Yet a case can be made for the proposition that a long-range cycle of generations and centuries is also at work, that the evidence for it is now abundant and can explain even such transient phenomena as the fate of the New Frontier.

All previous American generations have considered their country as synonymous not only with perpetual motion, but with perpetual youth. The youth of today, even more than their elders, know better, even if they can't express it. They know that quantities have little to do with qualities, that our traditional slogan of "bigger and better" is a non sequitur.

The essence of middle age for a person is that he knows he must begin to live within his means, physical, financial and spiritual. It is the same for a society. At middle age a person struggles to realize his final personality and a society struggles to give form, not merely dimensions, to its life. This has little, if anything to do with conservatism or liberalism. It has to do with reason, which the ancient Greeks revered, and a concept of the "good life" which they institutionalized.

Today, in America, reason is crying many halts, if only *sotto voce*. In the most obvious, measurable realm of natural resources it cries halt to the depletion of water levels in the name of more and more factories. It cries halt to the indiscriminate spreading of pesticides in the name of shinier red apples. It cries halt to the vast use of barbiturates and tension relievers in the name of momentary *nirvana*. It cries halt to engulfment of us all by more and more "news" when we can hardly grasp the meaning of the present news. Its gathering instinct is to cry halt to free immigration if this is to mean the compounding of tragedy, Harlem upon Harlems. It would like to cry halt to the piling of weapon upon weapon to kill enemies ten times over; to the fantastic spending for outer space when the problem lies in inner man and on terra firma. Reason says that we are overextended in foreign places, not in terms of our money, but in terms of our comprehension and our attention span; reason tells us our moral obligation to help others cannot extend beyond our practical capacity to do so. Reason would cry halt to further increases in our population. It tells us that more and more superhighways, bridges and parking garages in the already dense megalopolis is a self-defeating process; for the automobile, thus encouraged to proliferate, always saturates the temporary margin of space. Reason says the 50-mile hike is silly. The trouble with America is not hardening of the arteries. Its trouble is merely that it has grown up, reached maturity and, like the ex-athlete of middle age, is feeling bewildered and annoyed.

America knows, in its subconscious at least, that more bursts of "vigah" are likely to produce nothing more positive than a heart attack. It knows that what it really wants to do, what it really must do, is to slow down and sort itself out. For 300 years it has been told what it was going to become. Now it wants to know what it *is*.

January 1, 1964

The devoted students of Sherlock Holmes are as divisive as they are numerous, but they must surely agree that there was a certain respect as well as affection implicit in Holmes' exclamation, "Good old Watson, you are the one fixed point in a changing age!"

This must be the sentiment of many Americans, at least those of middle age or more, as they see the news films of Harry Truman striding out on his morning walk, each foot firmly planted, each crisp pronouncement—on Panama, Lyndon Johnson, Barry Goldwater—delivered with the finality of a man who has no regrets, who relishes his enemies as much as his friends and who enjoys the final freedom: contentment with life and no fear of death.

It is a good and inspiriting thing to witness, this evening of a life that was full to the brim and never seriously marred. A man's character is his fate, said the ancient Greeks. Chance, in good part, took Harry Truman to the Presidency, but it was his character that kept him there and determined his historical fate; he is, without any doubt, destined to live in the books as one of the strongest and most decisive of the American Presidents.

It was Dean Acheson, Truman's Secretary of State, who said once, in musing about the Presidency: "If a President will make decisions, you're in luck. That is the essential quality. And if he has a high batting average in the correctness of his decisions, then you're in clover."

About this quality of Truman's there was never any doubt from the beginning, in the minds of those of us who covered his Presidency all the way through. His simplicity, his honesty and his self-discipline were so obvious as to be non-arguable, however much we disagreed about some of his actions and appointments. We were aware of his sensitivity about the institution of the Presidency—"This is the most honorable office a man can hold," he used to say—and aware of his relative lack of sensitivity to criticism of himself. What we were not aware of, at least not I, was his sensitivity about the feelings of other people.

This has been a sadly belated discovery of recent days for this reporter. It was made during private and, therefore, privileged conversations, but I think he will not mind if I extract the small portion of the talk that illustrates my theme. The talk had wandered back a dozen years or so, and an aide remarked that Mr. Truman should have fired so-and-so. The man who had occupied the most powerful office in the world immediately said: "No, no. That would not have been right. There were other ways to do it. What you don't understand is the power of a President to hurt."

An American President has the power to build, to set fateful events in motion, to destroy an enemy civilization, to win or lose a vast personal following. But the power of a President to hurt the feelings of another human being—this, I think, had scarcely occurred to me, and still less had it occurred to me that a President in office would have the time and the need to be aware of this particular power among so many others.

Mr. Truman went on to observe that a word, a harsh glance, a peremptory motion by a President of the United States could so injure another man's pride that it would remain a scar in his emotional system all his life.

He recalled a painful episode during one of the lectures he loves to make to student audiences about the story and the art of governing America. A college boy stood up to ask the former President what he thought of the state's governor, whom he described as "our local yokel." Mr. Truman told the boy he should be ashamed of himself for his lack of respect toward the high office of governor. The boy turned pale and sat down. Later Mr. Truman made it a point to seek out the shaken, apologetic lad and to reassure him. He did much more. He had the boy's dean send him frequent reports on the lad's progress in school and followed his later career with the interest of a friend. What this interest by a former President must have done for the boy's pride and self-respect may be imagined.

The simple point here is that Mr. Truman had instantly realized how a public scolding by a former President could mark and mar the boy's inner life and his standing in his community.

I feel gratified to have heard this story. It has given me an insight to the responsibilities of a President that I did not have, and it has immeasurably added to my own residue of memories about the man from Missouri. He is nearly eighty now. He may live to be a hundred—his is strong stock—but this, I know, is the specific memory that will return to me when his time does come.

4

The Negro
Passion

February 10, 1959
This reporter has had his home the last thirteen
years in the Virginia city of Alexandria. It is an
old city, proud of its traditions and very Southern; Washington laid out some of its streets as
a young surveyor; its newspaper is the oldest
daily paper in America. It can be hard for a
community so imbued with and formed by the
old and the past to confront the new and the
present.

But Alexandria did so this morning, because when the final test comes the sharp wind
of the here and the now generally prevails over
the drifting mists of the past; three Alexandria
public schools admitted Negro children to their
classes. The adults kept their dignity; so did the
white children, as far as is known; and so did
the handful of Negro children who walked, without trembling, through the early morning gaunt-
let of officials, policemen and the staring knots
of the curious.

One of the three schools is the new city high
school a quarter mile up the lane from my house.

It *was* a lane. Just a few years ago this was open country, outside the city limits; there was a scrub pine wood where the school now stands; a place for secret caves, a place the quail would fly into for refuge when you surprised them on the lane. If you knew the hidden path, as my boys did, it was a place to idle your pony and cool him off on the homeward stretch.

Schools take a time to build, country lanes a time to widen and pave. The change came gradually, and we have all been accustomed, for some time now, to the groups of children walking up the road in the morning frost, swinging their books, kicking an idle stone. I can remember no tension, no act of violence along that little road. This morning there was the crowd, slightly tense; there were the policemen in their cars. There was trouble in the air and it was hard to bring back to mind the pine wood and the pony path. But the trouble did not erupt, and for selfish reasons, also, one can be thankful for that; an ugly scene at that corner, I'm afraid, would have wiped out and forever replaced the more tender memories all of us there would prefer to keep.

So Negro children can walk along there, too, from now on, kicking an idle stone if the spirit so moves. I can remember when they had to ride a bus some 30 miles if they wished a high-school education.

Perhaps it will be news to some in that old city if I say that this is not the first instance of racial integration in an Alexandria school. There is an elementary school there—a private, co-operative school—integrated now for several years, possibly the first integrated school of any kind in Virginia since Reconstruction days.

I know about this school because my wife and I were among the twelve families who founded it the year after the war had ended and the overcrowded public schools were in a bad way.

We decided at the start that if Negro kids wanted to come and their parents would pay and would work on the place like the rest of us—why, they could come. They have been coming for the last nine years; about twenty of them one year, as I recollect. When they started coming there was no fuss; only four or five families dropped out. The school is bigger and better and more prosperous now than ever. We integrated that little school, not as a challenge to anybody, not as a precedent, just because it seemed a good thing to do, on behalf of our own children, who must learn to live, after all, in a country that doesn't belong to any particular group.

We had no trouble; those three public schools had no trouble today. Letting *all* little children go to the school nearest their homes doesn't have to bring the world to an end.

September 10, 1962

By the time this appears in print the United States Senate may have done what a minority on the Judiciary Committee prevented for a full year and given formal approval to the nomination of Thurgood Marshall as judge of the Federal Court of Appeals. Thurgood Marshall, the history books will surely attest, was the sharp but tempered spearhead of the great movement which in this generation carried Negro Americans considerably closer to the citadel of full citizenship.

A man whose total public identification has been that of a Negro fighting for the Constitutional rights of Negroes can hardly escape becoming a symbolic figure. But symbols do not make judges; men make judges; and what is worth thinking about here is not the symbol, but the man.

The four Southern Senators of the Judiciary Committee who deliberately stalled committee action on the nomination and then voted against Judge Marshall can only have regarded him as symbol and his nomination as a symbolic case. They have bitterly opposed the Supreme Court decision on school segregation as a wound in both the flesh and the spirit of the Constitution, and they considered their opposition to the chief instigator of that decision, therefore, as a perfectly logical expression of doctrinal consistency.

In addition to this they acted out of what they regard as political necessities, just as many of the Northern, big-city Senators acted when they voted in favor of Marshall. For them, too, the hulking Baltimorean, who has become one of the most famous lawyers of this legalistic age, is a symbol and perhaps nothing more.

All this was inevitable, but it is a pity, and not only because it is wrong in spirit. It is a pity in this particular case because it is wrong in fact; that is, it is a misinterpretation of the man. If there are Southern Senators who are against Marshall because they believe he will pass his judgments as a Negro, if there are Northern Senators who believe the same but do not, for political reasons, care if he does—then both sides are in error. I say this on the basis of an acquaintance with the judge which has not

87

been intimate, but which happened to take place in circumstances sharply revealing of the man's cast of mind.

My first chance meeting with Marshall occurred in London, where he had arrived in the company of Tom Mboya, the young Kenya politician, after Marshall's trip across black Africa inspecting the condition of constitutional liberties in the new African states. The second encounter was at a small round-table conference this summer with highly charged anti-American students from various foreign regions, including Africa.

Thurgood Marshall would not have been engaged in these enterprises, as, of course, he would not have engaged his whole career in our domestic wars over civil rights, were he not intensely aware of the color of his own skin and faithful to his racial heritage. But what stayed with me, what was to me impressive and humbling, was that in everything the man said on both occasions, in his every expression and gesture, one was made conscious of the presence not of an American Negro, but of an American, period.

I don't know how else to express it. An eavesdropper unable to see the man's skin color could not have known that a Negro was talking. His attitude toward Mboya was not that of one colored man to another, but that of a lawyer passionately concerned about individual liberties wherever they were suppressed and whoever was suppressing them. I have no doubt that if the new Kenya government is oppressive of human rights it will find the spirit of Thurgood Marshall hotly opposed to it. I have no doubt at all that the oppressions practiced by the Nkrumah regime in Ghana are favored by no justification, no rationalization whatever in the thoughts of Thurgood Marshall. And in all this he is very different from any number of highly sensitized American Negro intellectuals.

When we argued matters this summer with the young, darkskinned student leaders from around the world there wasn't any doubt as to where Marshall sat. He sat with the Americans present. The attitudes and notions of the foreigners that made the rest of us impatient made Marshall impatient and for precisely the same reasons. He tried to make them understand what this domestic battle of ours over civil rights is all about, how far we have come already and how far we hope to go. And when he said "we" he was not talking about American Negroes, he was talking about America.

Perhaps others do not find this either impressive or humbling. If I do it is because, when I try in imagination to "walk in their shoes," I wonder that any sensitive, intelligent American Negro can avoid becoming a neurotic enemy of this society of ours. Whether the secret lies in his genes or in his upbringing, or in both, I would not know, but the essential fact about Thurgood Marshall is that he bears no trace of this virus in the emotions. A Negro, he remains a whole man in a society half-sick from racial prejudice. Whatever his qualifications as a legal thinker— and they must be considerable—Marshall qualifies as a human being of the first rank.

May–June 1963

By its dominant voices, its most unforgettable faces and its chief acts of bravery does a generation recognize itself and history mark it.

For America, this postwar period is surely the era of the Negro passion. The most moving voices are now those of Negroes; the most searing, lasting words are put on paper by Negro writers; their music is the American music most penetrating and persuasive to other parts of the world. No cause is now so fundamental to the health and integrity of this society as the Negro cause; of no other leaders are so much stamina and courage demanded as are now required of Negro leaders.

They are bound to win, somehow, not only because their present aims are so limited and unarguable, but because they have succeeded in involving us all, whoever we are, wherever we live within the nation frontiers. They have caught the attention of the whole American people and, more than that, they have caught up the conscience of the whole people, however many of us may try to deny this to ourselves. A newspaper or television picture of a snarling police dog set upon a human being is recorded in the permanent photoelectric file of every human brain.

This generation is not likely to find surcease from the Negro passion; its source springs and the resistance to it are too deeply grounded for easy resolution, and its present outburst too long delayed. Its more violent manifestations are not going to be confined to the Deep South. The head of black steam building up in places like New York, Washington and Chicago are finding outlets too few and too small, at the present rate, for the permanent avoidance of combustion.

Because this unfolding drama involves the automatic reflexes of the instinctive sense of justice, because it involves namable, hearable, countable individual persons of flesh and blood, it is going to dwarf the general and social pageants of this domestic era, whether they be the struggles to rationalize the inchoate megalopolis, to preserve the open spaces, to eradicate a disease, to "conquer" space, or whatever.

The time is coming, soon, when the Negro passion will truly dominate American politics. It is going to change the prism through which we consider the problems of far-off nations; romanticism will have to give way to realism. Liberalism of the academic or cafe-society brand—the motivations of those who rhapsodize over the Peace Corpsmen in Ethiopia or journey 6,000 miles to sit at the feet of Dr. Schweitzer, but who would never dream of visiting the night police court in their own city and observing the tragedy of the American Negro—such impulses are going to lose their present status in the hierarchy of the virtues. There will be a noticeable dearth of hiding places for those professing belief either in their religion or the American Constitution.

An education in the facts of life and history is in store for those pained by the messy contradictions built in to the Negro passion. Those bewildered at the Negro uprising ("after all, they had made a lot of progress") may learn that this is one of the eternal lessons from past rebellions against oppression. It is not when the oppression is most complete that these revolutions begin to revolve, but when concessions are given, hopes are born, light is glimpsed at the end of the dark tunnel. It is when an oppressed people feels close to its goal, not far off from it, that their action becomes frenetic.

Those who are cynical or upset by the moral duality in the Negro phenomenon, by the spectacle of lofty courage and self-sacrifice among the Negro leaders, side by side with the spectacle of spreading crime and moral squalor in the slum-bound masses of the Negro poor, may learn that the first is a direct reflection of the second—its natural, not its unnatural, partner. Desperation, like war, ennobles some among its victims and debases others. No true people's revolution was ever neat, clean or devoid of sad anomalies.

If the Negro passion of today is not a true people's revolution, it is as close to one as we have ever known in our land.

The struggle of the American Negro for full citizenship—a true, seminal, people's revolution—is a dual struggle. Contained within the obvious black-versus-white showdown in the South is the black-versus-black showdown within Negro ranks.

After fifty years the Negro intramural contest is no longer one between the "accommodationist" strategy school, of which Booker T. Washington was the mentor, and the "militancy" school, led by the NAACP. The contest is now between the militancy school and the extremist school, now most loudly represented by the Black Muslims.

The militancy of the NAACP, whose work in Birmingham before the mass rioting began was in the direct line of the position taken at its founding meeting in 1909—"absolute refusal to differentiate the rights of human beings"—has never been intended to mean violence, while recognizing that violence might occur. It was intended to mean force, interpreted as the force of massed numbers, incessant protest and the force of law employed to the hilt. The aims have always been limited to those simple human rights common to the rest of us and shared within our common society.

The Black Muslims preach hatred of the whites as a race, which is a negation of the principle of the individuality of guilt, and total, geographical separatism, which is a practical impossibility.

For some years now the old-line accommodationists among Negroes, those humbly willing to work their way through self-improvement, have been in sharp decline, and the strategy concept and staff of the NAACP have been in control of forward Negro ranks. Until Birmingham they appeared as extremists in the eyes of many whites, particularly in the South; now they will appear to everyone as the moderates.

What they have been trying to do, in a phrase, is simply to undo the undoing of the Emancipation Proclamation and the Thirteenth, Fourteenth and Fifteenth Amendments, the undoing that was accomplished by an intricate series of laws and regulations in the South during the last twenty-five years of the nineteenth century, culminating in the 1896 Supreme Court decision which sealed the whole package with the stamp of "separate but equal." It was the 1954 school-integration decision which tore the package open again in what Negro leaders regard with some right as the first official re-affirmation of the Emancipation Proclamation in almost a century. If, as I believe, we are in the presence of a true people's revolution, the history books will most probably date its combustion, if not its origin, from the 1954 decision. When the President's Commission on National Goals in 1960 came to the matter of the "sordid or timid techniques of unequal treatment that still leave millions outside the circle of first-class citizenship," it added these words: "If this means that some men must renounce old privileges in order that other men may enjoy new liberties, then that is the way the knife of democratic aspiration will have to cut."

That is the way the knife began to cut in Birmingham. All that whites there stood to lose were some old privileges, not rights; all that the Negro leadership there sought to gain were common rights and liberties. They did not seek privileges of any kind. Until the undirected rioting began the distant observer, at least, could not believe that the privileges whites stood to lose could be half so important to them as the prosaic and limited rights the Negroes sought were to them.

The present national Negro leadership rejects the term "gradualism." Gradualism as a concept may be rejected, but gradualism as a fact will surely remain. It took thirty years of organized agitation in this century to put an effective end to lynchings. We still have poll taxes and extralegal voting barriers. After nine years of the school-desegregation decision only about 8 per cent of Negro pupils in Southern and Border states have been integrated. A total and sudden overturn of racial restrictions and abuses in this country is not conceivable to any informed person.

The American Negro will go on, conquering one formidable height of legalism after another. But new and massive social obstacles rise before him. He has been excluded from the spreading suburbs, and now the scythe of "urban renewal" cuts away shelters left to him. He has won some painful victories for legal equality in hiring, and now the impersonal force of automation sweeps away unskilled and semi-skilled jobs by the thousands each week, the kind of jobs left to his people.

He is frightened and he ought to be. So ought all Americans confronted by the prospect of a permanent body of unemployed of massive proportions. What the denial of ordinary rights brought to Birmingham will be nothing to what the denial of livelihood can bring to many cities.

However painful this is for most of us, the plain truth of the Negro revolt is that the American Negro has, at long, long last, lost faith in the white man and his society. He no longer believes in the words of promise. He no longer believes that the laws will be enforced unless he, himself, forces their enforcement. This is what the most patient and enduring of American races has come to, and we who are white have no one to blame but ourselves. There is no place to hide anymore.

But there is a second barrel to this weapon pointed at the dominant white culture in our country. With the end of Negro faith in the white American has come the beginnings of the Negro's faith in himself. Respect from others denied, he had nowhere to go to find it save in a self-generated self-respect. He could not find it from the passive moral and intellectual assurances of religion, or science and logic; he could find it only in action—an old precept of psychiatry, but an extraordinarily difficult bootstrap operation for an individual or a group.

It should go without saying that when such a transformation occurs in the individual breasts and the collective ranks of the most cohesive voting and acting bloc in America almost anything can happen. There are likely to be both events and remarks of a brutish as well as of a noble nature, and one is tempted to think that political alignments will never be quite the same again. The Negro vote has been an indispensable political sword in the hands of the Democratic Party for thirty years. But no "white power structure" owns this sword anymore, and it could be very quickly turned against the vitals of that party and this President, who merely inherited this upheaval, as President Hoover inherited the depression of the late twenties.

If the generality of American Negroes have now lost faith in the good intentions of white Americans, educated Negroes long since lost faith in the practical common sense of white Americans. They are aware, by the hard statistics, that for a supposed materialist society we are stupefyingly wasteful of our materials. Here we are—exhorting, planning, wracking our brains for ways and means of getting the country moving economically —while right to hand lies the most certain, if not the fastest, remedy of all.

That is to allow 19,000,000 Negroes to fully join the American common market. It would be like adding a whole nation of producers and consumers to increase our common wealth. As Harry Golden has recently put it, this would not only mean the lifting of a great burden from the white man, but it would mean "a boom so charismatic that the white Southerner will one day wonder what his resistance was all about."

If Negroes were employed to the same degree as whites and paid as much (right now both gaps are widening, not narrowing) the economic turnover in this country would increase by a mammoth $12 to $14 billion a year. And that figure represents only about half the price we now pay for maintaining a Negro subculture within the general culture. For we must also pay, in billions, for swollen forces, for ever-increasing charity medicine, children's homes, penal institutions, unemployment compensation and straight relief checks, an immense portion of which is directly due to the stupidity of trying to keep the Negro "in his place"—that is, semi-illiterate and unskilled. The full and equal education of American Negroes is not only a moral, but a practical necessity; not an act of charity toward others, but of enlightened self-interest. I believe it to be far more certain of results than the spending of billions for the advancement of people in various foreign countries.

Education is the key. As the President said in San Diego, less than half the non-white population of this country has finished high school. In actual numbers this proportion of the unskilled increases every year, while the actual numbers of unskilled jobs decreases every year as automation spreads and we become more and more a white-collar nation.

It takes no brains to see that unless we quickly get about the business of educating every child capable of it and training or re-training every adult now devoid of usable skills, the problem will get beyond us. We shall then have to carry a permanent albatross of many millions of unemployable human beings. Tax loads will only get heavier, bureaucracies thicker; police forces will multiply because crime will become a normal, not an abnormal way of life.

In this twentieth century the uneducated man is not a man. He does not quite exist. In its deep-seated, visceral motivations the Negro revolt is, in part, a desperate spasm of reaction against non-existence.

(A speech delivered on November 26, 1963—four days after the assassination of President John F. Kennedy—at a Freedom House award dinner in honor of Martin Luther King and Roy Wilkins.)

The events of the last five days have acted as a catalyst upon Americans everywhere. By instinct people have drawn closer to one another.

The assassination in Dallas revealed in a flash the depth and extent of the things that divide us. The reaction since then has revealed something else—an essential goodness in most of the American people, what H. G. Wells called the "conspiracy of good will."

Everyone in this room is part of this conspiracy. We will all remain a part of it. This is a good company under this roof. We feel in our hearts that President Kennedy would have wanted such a meeting as this to go on. We are all of us, in a certain sense, his spiritual kin. We think he would have approved what we say tonight, what we do and the rare personalities we have asked to grace this table.

Freedom House had little difficulty this year in deciding whom it wished to honor or, rather, whom it wished to be honored by. These men had walked in honor—a long road, a long night's journey into day—before they reached this room. We seek only to add our own certification to what history has already made so manifest.

There is a kind of law of collective life that pre-determines such choices as these that we have made. For society nearly always, by some self-preserving instinct, tends to endow with honors those individuals of whom it has the most *need*.

For a long time America has needed these men. Every person in this room tonight has needed them. We have desperately needed leaders to call up our sleeping conscience, to help us open our hearts, to rid our American civilization, not of a thorn in its flesh, as the Negro travail has often been called, but of the one deep stain in its soul.

They are our moral monitors, who have taken away the hiding places from all those of us who want to believe in our religions or in the original charters of the American purpose. They are our physicians, who have obliged us to face the painful operation upon which our health depends and who will take away our moral crutches, one by one, and prove to us that we can walk upright, however rough the ground.

Let there be no mistaken notion that these men are the leaders of American Negroes only; they stand in the front rank of the leaders of America. It is their hands that hold and wield the cutting edge of history for our time and our country. It is these men who stand at the growing points of our society more closely than any others we can call to mind. It is they, more than any others, however high in office, who are changing the structure and the processes by which we live and before our eyes are altering the relationships of citizen to citizen.

The conventional wisdom has told us that we live in a bland and cautious time and are bereft of heroes. We have been told that our generation is as embarrassed in the presence of the noble as our Victorian ancestors were embarrassed in the presence of the base.

Freedom House, for one, has decided that it shall not be so base as to be embarrassed in the presence of the noble; we are sure in our own minds that a hundred years from now the books will agree that there were giants in these days.

This house is saluting courage, first of all. It is courage, as Winston Churchill said, that makes the other virtues possible. We stand in awe before the kind of raw courage that enables a man to set in motion a people's revolution; and if this is not a true people's revolution it is as close to one as anything this land has known.

We stand in respect before the kind of wisdom that seeks to hold such an upheaval within the bounds of law and to limit its natural and inevitable excesses. And we are surprised and comforted to find these two qualities combined in the same human breasts.

Many revolutions have devoured their own children. We persist in believing this will not happen in this limited revolution which seeks, not power, but common rights—not supremacy, but equality.

The Reverend Martin Luther King, Mr. Roy Wilkins would be made ill at ease by any suggestion that they alone have brought about this long overdue showdown in the old conflict between our mores and our laws, this climacteric in the continuing drama of this country. Some of the help they have had has been white in color, and Freedom House would have been honored to have had upon this platform tonight such men as Ralph McGill of Atlanta, journalism's sword and buckler in this battle, and Joseph Cardinal Ritter, Archbishop of Saint Louis, who desegregated the Church schools in his region a year before the Supreme Court spoke its unanimous mind, who did not regard segregating children as impractical or as a social lag or immoral. Who regarded it as a *sin*.

The revolution led by such men as these and the two men we honor tonight has by no means ceased revolving. The statistics —on schools, churches, housing, public facilities desegregated, on Negroes successfully registered to vote—are impressive already, though they have just begun. But there is a spiritual by-product of this practical process, one long overdue, which seems to us of enormous portent.

For a long time we have been told, occasionally by men of highest office, that you cannot legislate changes in the human heart. You can; we have. Because laws, enforced, compel changes in human conduct. New conduct develops new habits, and new habits develop new attitudes, since man, to live within himself, must justify his conduct to himself. Action *does* change feelings, an old lesson of history, an old principle, I believe, of psychology.

In this lies the seed of the ultimate triumph for human justice and for the true equality, mutual recognition and respect. The black American is no longer invisible to the white American, because he has seized the white American by the shoulders, spun him around and forced him to look, long and hard, upon his fellow man. There was no other way left to the American Negro. He has done it, and the American landscape suddenly seems much richer than it was.

For this, for all that has happened in these climactic months, this organization is grateful. It feels confirmed in its own beliefs and purposes. We feel more certain now than ever that the house of America will *not* be divided, and that, therefore, it will stand.

5

Man Is Still
a Political Animal

March 28, 1956

Every four years around this time we consider it our humble duty to serve as medium between the political tongue and the voters' inner ear, to translate what the candidates call "plain speaking" into the plainer truth. We offer this service free of charge.

For example: when a candidate says "I'm glad you asked that question," what he means is "Oh, oh, give me a moment to think."

When one of his supporters says "My candidate is a man of the people," he means that his candidate was also born in a hospital.

The phrase, "I am not a candidate for Vice-President," means "I gotta keep my Presidential bandwagon rolling until after the first ballot."

"I'm in this fight to the finish" means "The law sets the election day and I can't do a thing about it."

"I intend to be the President of *all* the people." Translation: the Constitution has fixed it so nobody escapes.

When he says "We must return to the principles of our forefathers," he means "Things must have been simpler in those days."

When he says "I intend to hew to the line, let the chips fall where they may," he really means that he intends to put his shoulder to the wheel and let his voice be heard.

When he says "I can't tell you what a pleasure it is to get back home with you folks and away from that Tower of Babel on the Potomac," he is really saying "If I get licked, I can always open a law office in Washington."

A party "leader" is a politician just like himself, whereas a party "boss" is a politician just like himself, but in another state.

And, of course, when a candidate tells you "A vote for me is a vote for the American way of life," what he means is "I ain't running in Southern Rhodesia."

We trust this brief glossary will serve as a handy guide to help you get through the season; we might even expand it from time to time if things get more confusing than they are at present, a contingency that scarcely bears contemplation.

Of course, a political glossary is useful to most of us only every two or four years; an even more pressing problem is the terminology of everyday working life which is also becoming a special language. We have long thought that somebody should issue a handy guide for us millions of office workers, and somebody has. We don't know the name of its compiler, but it seems to serve equally well in governmental and private office work, and here it is, in part:

A program: any assignment that can't be completed in one phone call.

To expedite: to confound confusion with commotion.

Channels: the trail left by inter-office memos.

Co-ordinator: the guy who has a desk between two expediters.

Consultant: any ordinary guy more than 50 miles from home.

To activate: to make carbons and add more names to memo.

To implement a program: to hire more people and expand the office.

Under consideration: this means, never heard of it.

Under *active* consideration: we're looking in the files for it.

To negotiate: to seek a meeting of minds without a knocking together of heads.

A conference: the substitution of conversation for the dreariness of labor and loneliness of thought.

Re-orientation: getting used to work again.

Reliable source: the guy you just met.

Informed source: the guy who told the guy you just met.

Unimpeachable source: the guy who started the rumor originally.

We are making a survey: we need more time to think of an answer.

Note and initial: let's spread this responsibility around.

Let's discuss: come down to my office; I'm lonesome.

Let's get together on this: I'm assuming you're as confused as I am.

Give us the benefit of your thinking: we'll listen to what you have to say as long as it doesn't interfere with what we've already decided to do.

Will advise in due course: if we figure it out, we'll let you know.

And "a clarification" means to fill in the background with so many details that the foreground goes underground.

That's the list. Brief enough to fit neatly on one sheet of paper—the large memo size—and it can be slipped under the glass top of your office desk for quick reference. It can make office work a lot more simple, but, we should warn you, a lot less fun.

October 15, 1956

Devices change with the times; politics changes with the devices; men don't change much with either, but they get temporarily warped out of shape by both. Wilson could command the printed page any day in the week because he had the English language at his command; Roosevelt was the political star in the radio medium because there was a kind of happy music in his voice; Eisenhower has television working for him and Stevenson hasn't—anyway, not yet. Print was neutral, radio almost neutral, but television is either for you or against you; you lick it or it licks you. Eisenhower has it licked, because the whole Eisenhower physical apparatus—voice, face, gestures—are so natural and instinctive that the battery of studio gadgets simply fails in what one often suspects is their true purpose—to stiffen, distort, intimidate and generally make unreal the real personality of any man who faces them.

Mr. Stevenson is getting better in this contest of man versus machine, but in this campaign so far the gadgets have taken most of the rounds, hamstringing, nerve-wracking and generally subduing what is in reality a buoyant, charming, bold and impressive intellect and personality.

TV allows few compromises; if you can't lick it, you have to join it, or pretend to. Mr. Eisenhower licked it by joining it—long ago, sometime after his miserable political debut in the rain at Abilene, Kansas. Long ago he did what Mr. Stevenson is just now getting around to doing—he hired the most expert counterintelligence professionals he could find to infiltrate and subdue the phalanx of gadgets. This is easily done once you learn the trick, because the gadgets, like German soldiers, are over-disciplined, lack imagination and do only what they're told to do.

Take the teleprompter. After that one fiasco in 1952, when he audibly cussed out the thing, Mr. Eisenhower has learned that if you just stick to your own pace, the teleprompter will keep up with you; Mr. Stevenson apparently could never get over the feeling that he had to keep up with it, so he's just abandoned the thing and gone back to a script.

Mr. Eisenhower has had the benefit of the real experts, who are those who know there are no experts in this field. Pseudo-experts told Mr. Stevenson to get up from a chair and walk across to a desk. But the President's real expert, Mr. Montgomery, knows that to walk naturally across a room is one of the hardest things that even a professional actor can master. Mr. Stevenson's pseudo-experts thought it was very professional to use two or more cameras. This is the reason for that sudden, startled look on the Stevenson countenance—he'd just caught sight of a frantically waving arm, the signal to turn to camera two. From now on he'll confront only one camera, as Mr. Eisenhower usually does. The camera will do the moving—with a Zoomar lens—not the candidate.

Ignore all the tricks of the trade, as Mr. Stevenson and his people were doing, and the speaker can be so uncomfortable his audience suffers with him. Use too many tricks of the trade, like planted questions, pretty actresses and tiny tots, and you run the risk of turning a serious political process into a soap-opera jag for unemployed minds. The central problem is how to be natural without being nauseating, how to be smooth without being slick. If he weren't so obviously sincere, Mr. Stevenson, we'd say, has been running a grave risk of appearing pedantic; and if he weren't so naturally natural, Mr. Eisenhower, we'd say, has been running the risk of appearing corny.

The TV contest is expected to even up a bit from here on in. Small voices have spoken in the night to the Stevenson advisors, persuading them that he will have to do some rehearsing ahead of time, as Mr. Eisenhower does; that his director will have to case the studio joint, not just before, but long before the broadcast, as Mr. Montgomery does. And no more rushing in by the candidate, three minutes in advance, still revising the speech.

As we said, you have to sneak up on, infiltrate and outwit the TV battery; try to rush it in a surprise attack and you're bound to go down before the volley from its automatic weapons.

April 26, 1957

A beleaguered, browbeaten committee of five U.S. Senators will announce next week who they think are the five greatest Senators in our history. Historical hades is expected to break out, since more human beings are willing to fight for their notions of the past than for their visions of the future. If sheer courage is the criterion of choice, we would nominate Ohio's Senator Corwin, who in 1847 stood up and denounced our war with Mexico. The speech was considered traitorous by many, but, strangely, it did not ruin Corwin's career; in fact, Lincoln later made him Minister to Mexico.

If the House ever gets around to naming the five greatest Representatives of all time, we would nominate J. Proctor Knott of Kentucky. For he did something that required even more courage—he was funny. Furthermore, he was funny at the expense of a *place*. This was worse than treason, it was heresy, for as all politicians know, all states, cities and towns, theirs and their colleagues, are always at least "great," if not the new Eden on earth, and filled with the "good people of."

On January 27, 1871, J. Proctor Knott got up to oppose a big grant of land to a railroad proposing to lay tracks along the Saint Croix River to Duluth, Minnesota. J. Proctor gave Duluth the business, in part as follows: "Duluth! The word fell upon my ear with peculiar and indescribable charm, like the gentle murmur of a low fountain stealing forth in the midst of roses... 'twas the name for which my soul had panted for years, as the hart panteth for the water brooks. But where was Duluth?... Sir, had it not been for this map, kindly furnished me by the legislature of Minnesota, I might have gone down to my obscure and humble grave in an agony of despair.... I see it represented

102

on this map that Duluth is situated exactly halfway between the latitudes of Paris and Venice, so that gentlemen who have inhaled the exhilarating airs of the one, or basked in the golden sunlight of the other, may see at a glance that Duluth must be a place of untold delights, a terrestrial paradise, fanned by the balmy zephyrs of an eternal spring, clothed in the gorgeous sheen of ever blooming flowers and vocal with the silvery melody of nature's choicest songsters."

The map indicated "vast wheat fields" adjoining vast herds of buffalo and the Piegan Indian tribe. So J. Proctor Knott explained the immense commercial possibilities of Duluth. "Now, sir," he said, "when the buffaloes are sufficiently fat from grazing on these immense wheat fields, you see it will be the easiest thing in the world for the Piegans to drive them on down, stay all night with their friends, the Creeks, and go into Duluth in the morning . . ."

Well, the House roared, the bill was killed and, in fact, Congress began to quit the whole business of lavish land grants to the railroads. But J. Proctor Knott was ruined. Humor was a deadlier thing than treason. His reputation as a humorist ruined his reputation as a statesman—a chapter in history probably never read by Mr. Adlai Stevenson.

May 22, 1958

American diplomats around the world must be feeling a bit confused these days, unsure, from what they read in the press, whether they are the country's great white hope or the country's Achilles' heel in white tie and tails, if you can imagine a heel dressed like that, and we've seen a few.

The older hands among them will not be unduly surprised by the news they're reading; Washington experiences an annual freshet of this argument. It never runs deep, but it always runs true. So here is Senator Johnson of Texas saying in Secretary Dulles' presence that personal diplomacy by commuting is no substitute for the well-trained and dedicated diplomatic corps posted abroad. Listeners had no doubt that Johnson was suggesting that if the Secretary stayed home a bit more, the Ambassadors we keep in the capitals Dulles is always visiting might make out pretty well on their own.

Score one for the professional diplomats. But then, in another part of the forest of newsprint, they learn that they are *not* making out well on their own, because they are frittering away too much of the twentieth century in cocktail parties and are, therefore, out of touch with the common people, including Latin American students, Reds, pro-Reds and potential stone-throwers in general. Also, they tend to drink wine in countries like France. This last accusation has truth in it, though it may seem strange to our diplomats abroad since it comes from Congressmen; strange, because these diplomats have often had to entertain traveling Congressmen and know that the word "stoned" has more than one definition.

Folklore dies hard, and in the annual fuss over the State Department budget there is always one Congressman who remembers that he represents the plain-spoken, church-goin', baby-havin' salt of the earth back home, folks who don't want no truck with those sinful foreign capitals full of mixed drinks and French perfumes and who see no reason why their hard-earned tax dollars should be squandered for any such goins' on.

Well, that's normal—and perennial. But now a new factor has entered this familiar picture. The Vice-President himself has discovered that a lot of our diplomats in Latin America spend a lot of time seeing their diplomatic colleagues, at parties and elsewhere, and little time down in the streets, pubs, slums and schools talking to the plain-spoken, baby-havin' folks in *those* countries. The implication is that if the diplomats bent their ankles more and their elbows less, Washington would have known in advance that a lot of Latin Americans are sore at us for supporting local dictators. The *Herald Tribune* even had an editorial with the title, "End Cocktail Diplomacy," exclamation point, which is not quite as funny a recommendation as the mythical *Readers Digest* title, "Let's End Puberty Now," but about as futile.

Well, a good many ex-foreign correspondents here take all this with a grain of salt of the earth. Including this one. The very nature of most diplomats' jobs keeps them chained to their desks and to their confreres' offices and homes. They are accredited to governments, not to whole peoples. Some, of course, *are* stuffy and un-alert; American newspapermen knew more about what was happening in both Budapest and Cuba than did our diplomats there. The theme of anti-Americanism because of anti-dictatorship, running all through Latin America, had been written and broadcast about very often before Mr. Nixon ever went there. The blockage is right here in Washington, where the information was freely available to the highest officials if they were paying attention.

Returning journalists used to be able to see the American President privately and tell him what they knew; they can't do that, anymore. They can't even talk to State Department intelligence officials, as of this week, without a press officer listening in. The recommendation now that our foreign envoys mingle with potential rebels, Reds or even left-wingers will indeed be salt in the wine of those envoys who remember how many of their colleagues, especially those in China, were denounced, investigated and ruined for doing just that only a few years ago.

July-November 1960

One of the inalienable rights, unanticipated by Jefferson, to which every modern American is born is the right to practice popular psychiatry. Since any number—preachers, GPs, over-divorced actresses or Radcliffe sophomores—can play, there is nothing to disbar a political columnist from the game.

And since it has been proposed under scholarly auspices that all Presidential candidates be subjected to psychiatric as well as physical examinations, we shall inaugurate this era of scientific politics with John F. Kennedy on the couch:

DR. VON SEVAREID: Mr. Kennedy, you have satisfied me that your childhood was happy and that your sibling rivalries were healthy, but are you not still afraid of your father?

PATIENT: No, but I get the feeling at times that he is a little scared of me.

DOCTOR: I'm interested in your own image of yourself. What do you think it is about you that makes people say you are too young?

PATIENT: I can't figure it out. Dewey was my age when he ran in '44 and nobody said he was too young. Nixon is the fellow with the baby face, not me. It must be my hairdo.

DOCTOR: Now, about the time you saved the men on your PT boat—did you experience a conscious desire for martyrdom? Did you wish to be loved?

PATIENT: Look, Doctor, I guess you've never read the oath and rules a Navy officer has to swear to. I got them into that mess. It was my job to get them out. Besides, I knew I was the best swimmer.

DOCTOR: I see. You like to be the best, don't you? How do you feel when somebody beats you at something?

PATIENT: I don't know yet.

DOCTOR: Now, about your repressions. Why is it you cannot impulsively throw your arms around people the way Senator Johnson, for example, does?

PATIENT: He's from Texas. I'm from Harvard.

DOCTOR: Why is it you can't let go with a belly laugh, the way Mr. Stevenson or Mr. Humphrey can?

PATIENT: I'm also from Boston.

DOCTOR: Let us turn to your ego-expression mechanisms. The previous Democratic subjects I have mentioned all have their own trademarks. Mr. Humphrey identifies himself to others by his poverty, Mr. Stevenson by his phraseology, Mr. Johnson by his initials, which he puts on his cuff links, his guest towels and the flag at his ranch.

PATIENT: Oh, Hubert just tries to be different from everybody else, hoarding his debts that way. It's reverse log-cabin snobbery. Words help Adlai to feel alive. I know I'm alive, already. As for Lyndon, I get the feeling he needs to be reminded all the time who he is. I know who I am.

DOCTOR: Most interesting. Who, exactly, are you?

PATIENT: The next President of the United States.

DOCTOR: I see. How about guilt feelings? When you beat somebody, do you have an impulse to apologize to him? Do you lose sleep worrying about him?

PATIENT: Well, I don't rub it in, but I don't feel guilty, either. Doctor, the way I see life, the strong have to take care of the weak in the end, and the weak have to give way so the strong can do it. Maybe the meek will inherit the earth some day, but the bold first have to earn it for them.

DOCTOR: I haven't had a patient like you in some time. Now, about any possible passive-aggressive dualism in your nature—do you regard your wife as your "partner"? Does she, for example, manage the family finances?

PATIENT: No!—to both questions, for heaven's sake. I'm the man around the house and I know it. She's the woman and she knows it. In fact, she takes pride in being a woman. That's why I married her.

Following this interview the doctor submitted his sealed report to the statutory Commission on the Mental and Physical Fitness of Presidential Candidates. A strong, but perhaps misguided, sense of patriotism, however, induced him to leak the contents to a columnist and they read, in part, as follows:

"In keeping with the Commission's terms of reference, which oblige the examiners to determine age by the measurement of psychological maturity, I conclude that this subject is the oldest of the group under recent scrutiny. He appears free of the self-doubts shown by the subject Stevenson; free of the ego-exhibitionism and resentment of criticism shown by the subject Johnson; free of the occasional melancholia shown by the subject Nixon. His emotional pattern is strikingly similar to that of the subject Rockefeller.

"If I may be permitted a note of sociological jocularity, I would say that he is un-American in his lack of guilt feelings and self-pity and in his strong instinct of male dominance. Should he achieve the national leadership and American males generally seek to emulate his example, the deplorable economic consequences to my profession may easily be imagined."

Distance does lend enchantment, and I don't think I have ever enjoyed political conventions so much as the one by the gilt shores of California and the one by the Chicago slaughterhouse. Of course, distance lends ignorance, too, so I could be wrong, but my impression is that in the first transaction the earnest followers of Stevenson, Johnson and Symington suffered from the same failing that caused the miseries of Picky Paffenhofen.

I didn't grasp Picky's trouble at the time, but after more experience in life I concluded that he couldn't understand the forces of nature. He was the best counter, plan-layer and odds-guesser in the sixth grade in my home town. He would bet you how many cows would move down the path under the classroom window during the history hour, or how many jawbreakers would be left in the glass jar in old man Oleson's Racket Store by Saturday night, and he would win every time. But things like rain clouds bringing rain always caught him out. I think his mind was just too complicated. I think natural forces were too simple to interest Picky, so he would forget about them until too late.

There was the time, after the town saw its first airplane, that Picky decided to build a plane of his own. He made it out of apple crates and boards in the hayloft at the farm. It had wings, it had a propeller, it had a tail and, as he explained, it was a whole lot lighter than the one that came down in the ballpark on the Fourth of July. So he sat in his apple-crate airplane and told his little cousin Otto to push him out the hay door. Otto didn't want to, but Picky insisted. So Otto gave a push, and Picky suffered only a broken arm that time. I shouldn't say "only." It happened right at the start of the summer vacation.

The next thing after that was the time Picky and I were riding bareback one evening, bringing in the cows. Picky had this new whip which had just come from Montgomery Ward. It was a beauty with a varnished leather handle, 8-foot thongs and a little strap that you fastened around your wrist so you couldn't drop the whip while riding. Well, we started racing across an open pasture for the barn, and Picky caught sight of a lone fence post ahead. He began to yip like a cowboy and galloped toward the post, whirling that whip around his head. As he came up with the post he curled those thongs smartly around it, and, as I recall, he suffered a wrenched back because there was a badger hole right where he fell.

Some years later when I passed through the town, Picky was gone. I couldn't swear that his peculiar failing had anything to do with it, but the neighbors did tell me that he had married a fourteen-year-old girl and they had moved out west immediately after the wedding.

I don't mean to make an exact comparison between Picky and those delegates who were for Stevenson or Johnson or Symington, because Picky wasn't old enough even to vote, let alone get sent to a political convention. But those delegates and managers were figurers and plan-layers, too; they were rational thinkers who naturally expected rational results. The apple-crate airplane looked just like a real airplane to Picky, and their candidates looked just like Presidents to them. Stevenson had the best statesman's mind, Johnson the most political ability, Symington the most statesmanlike appearance, and so on. They didn't seem to understand that the force of nature was with Kennedy, not their men. Call it "crowd appeal" or the "magic touch" or whatever you wish, you can't figure it or second guess it because it is elemental.

Like gravity in the case of Picky's plane or the principle of the continuity of direction of moving objects in the case of the fence post, it's just there and always has been there. Roosevelt proved that, even in the fourth-term campaign, when all logic was on Dewey's side. Eisenhower proved it. I don't say that more simple minds always understand natural forces, but they go along with them, while reasoning minds resist them and often have their summers ruined.

I can't help wondering about all those reasoning Republican minds who did the logical, rational thing and nominated Nixon this week instead of Rockefeller. For eight years he's been almost President, separated only by a prefix; he already knows his way into the White House and has tried the chair for size. But, somehow, Rockefeller seems to fit the elemental forces of nature better. I'm sure those Republican delegates will have a nice summer, but I'm doubtful about their Thanksgiving holiday.

So far, all that Nixon and Kennedy have received from the American electorate is what Damon Runyon used to call the "medium hello." Members of both parties have clapped on command, but in his heart every other Republican I know is a little uneasy about Nixon, every other Democrat I know is a little uneasy about Kennedy.

Why? Not, I think, for the reasons usually assigned. Not because of their "youth." Not really because of Nixon's "white-collar McCarthyism" of long ago; not really because of Kennedy's church or his toughness or his father's quick money. Most of us are uneasy about these men because they represent a clean break with the past and we have not yet adjusted. We cannot relate them to our life-long images of power and statesmanship and the shrine of the White House. These tidy, buttoned-down men are clothed in no myth or mystique, and where shall our mind's eye place them as it ranges back over the majestic skyline of American history and calls up the rugged and wind-blown captains who once led us?

The "managerial revolution" has come to politics, and Nixon and Kennedy are its first completely packaged products. The processed politician has finally arrived. The well-trained civil servant is to be handed the ultimate power. We shall have government of the people, for the people, but *by* the certified manager. And while professors of political science may rejoice, most of us are uneasy, for we know that the Presidency is neither a business nor a science, but an art, and that a very great artist is now required.

Nixon and Kennedy are not princes of the blood or sons of the soil. They are not captains of industry, like a Willkie, or of armies, like an Eisenhower. They are not luminaries of the intellectual world, like Wilson or Stevenson. They are not powerful proconsuls who grew bigger than their provinces, like Governors Roosevelt or Dewey. They are junior executives trained in the home office with an unerring eye to the main chance. The managerial revolution came to industry when rugged tycoons like Henry Ford were replaced by skilled committeemen. It came to labor when the John L. Lewises and the Phil Murrays were replaced by the Reuthers, when, indeed, the labor movement became the labor business. Now, with Nixon and Kennedy the great, eccentric and indefinable art of leading a nation has become the leadership business. The organization man has found room at the very top.

I have no right to say it won't work. Their souls may yet prove superior to their skills. They must, or it will not work at all. Skills will do for a quiet country in quiet times, but only lofty character and iron purpose can lead a turbulent America through this tumultuous time. (Alas, even the clichés of convention oratory are true.)

Many of us remain uneasy about them because neither one has acquired a true identity; their faces and voices are familiar, but their meaning as men escapes us. In the past, more often than not, we identified our nominees because of what they had already done or said, by their association with great deeds or great ideas. They came to us already clothed in their own mystique. Sometimes, to be sure, the cloth was made of shoddy, but we thought it was wool and at least a yard wide. And their raiment was hand- and home-made, not synthetically processed of water and air, whether their name was Lincoln or Grant or Wilson or Eisenhower.

But the washable, wrinkleproof Brooks Brothers garb of these new and skilled practitioners of the leadership business— what is it made of? How much is real, how much synthetic? Where are the deeds, where the inspiring ideas or rebellious words? They would lead us over the passes to the "new frontiers," they say, but we see no dust on their boots or dirt in their nails, and the graphs and charts they trace with their store-bought pointers leave us still untrusting.

If I am unjust, forgive me. It is hardly the fault of either nominee that we have run out of available rugged characters with ready made records. Perhaps what chiefly bothers me is the fact that this should happen precisely with my own age group. In my college generation—the Nixon-Kennedy generation—there were brilliant, strong, idealistic, unorthodox individuals in great supply. They sweated to grasp the new ideologies of Fascism and Communism sweeping the world; they marched in "peace parades;" they sickened at the Republic Steel massacre of strikers; they got drunk and wept when the Spanish Republic went down; they dreamed beautiful and foolish dreams about the perfectibility of man, cheered Roosevelt and adored the poor.

I can't find in the record that Kennedy or Nixon ever did, thought or felt these things. They must have been across the campus on Fraternity Row with the law- and business-school boys, wearing the proper clothes, thinking the proper thoughts, cultivating the proper people. Men of measured merriment, as Thomas Wolfe put it, and of measured tears. I suppose those boys were smarter than my crowd of bleeders. I always sensed that they would end up running the big companies in town, but I'm damned if I ever thought one of them would end up running the country.

Vice-President Nixon is one of the shrewdest politicians I have known. But there is a difference between shrewdness and wisdom, and my horseback impression—subject to change—is that Nixon is most unwise in the "personality appeal" he was sketching out for himself as the campaign began and prior to the first poll results.

Reporters in his entourage agree that he deliberately chose the underdog role. In other words, he initially took the defensive position. He has gone further. Senator Kennedy has used harsh words about Nixon's principles, so Nixon intends to campaign in a more lofty manner, avoiding "personalities." Kennedy is tough, so Nixon intends to give the impression of a "nice guy." Kennedy was born rich, so Nixon will emphasize his own grocery store childhood, when he made hamburgers that were cheap but honest. In other words, Mr. Nixon is cutting his cloth to Mr. Kennedy's measure.

This is extraordinary strategy for a man who for eight years has held with distinction the second highest position in the land, who has been intimately identified with the very source spring of power, involved in the most consequential national decisions, a man who has done hand-to-hand combat with the world's most formidable leaders.

To adopt this strategy is to conform to Kennedy's strategy. It is to allow oneself to be upstaged. It is to betray uncertainty about one's own meaning and public identity. If persisted in, it will surely play straight into Kennedy's hands by reversing what should be the natural roles of the two men—just as Kennedy intends to reverse them. For it is Kennedy who is creating the image of supreme personal and political confidence, that is to say, of *strength*—whether he truly has it or not.

Strength is the key to this election. Millions of Americans vaguely felt that Adlai Stevenson was not strong enough; millions now feel that Eisenhower is not strong enough. What the country yearns to see in the White House is power; "likeability" is not enough in this American mood. Beyond impressions of strength or weakness, sad as the thought may be, people will not discriminate very much. They will not vote for an underdog out of sympathy; the "soft sell" will not deliver the goods. Nor will Mr. Nixon accomplish much by humbly asking his audiences to "study the issues, then vote for principles, not for a man or a party." There is not that much difference, in policy and principles, between the two parties or the two men.

In any case, it is an astonishing and revealing phenomenon that a man in the spotlight of eminence for eight long years should even be thinking about manufacturing an "image" of himself. To a man who knows what he is, what he wants and what he can do such thoughts do not occur. He is carried past them by the passion of his ambitions and convictions. Harry Truman was not at all shrewd in 1948; he was merely convinced, simple and, in his stumbling way, passionate. So he won.

Many of us detest what one reader calls the "fraudulent farrago of the calculated effect," though I suppose we must live with it. Kennedy's self portrait may be quite as mechanically assembled as Nixon's, but surely it better suits the seasonal taste of those millions in the gallery who don't know anything about art but know what they like. They are tired of watercolors in genteel pastels; "nice guys" among the political painters are apt to finish last. Bold strokes in bright oils are what is wanted to make the immense canvas of American existence come to life again.

Nixon, who was not intimidated by Khrushchev, gives the curious impression of being intimidated by the junior Senator.

Perhaps there exist deep-laid psychological reasons for this. He has just begun, after all, his first real slugging match; politically, he was spoiled early in life. As he once said himself, "Political positions came to me because I happened to be in the right place at the right time." Perhaps eight years of self-discipline too deeply ingrained the emotional reflexes of the understudy, the second man.

I don't know. I do recall a private session around a lunch table some years ago in the rooms of the Secretary of the Senate. At one end sat Governor Dewey; at the other end sat Richard Nixon. Dewey was advising Nixon about his forthcoming trip to the Orient, from whence Dewey had just returned. He described how Asiatic reporters and photographers had besieged him everywhere, as an illustration of the world's intense concern with America.

"And," said Dewey, "I was only a state governor and titular head of a party. But you," he said, dramatically stabbing his finger toward Nixon, "you are *Vice-President of the United States!*"

His tone was that of one man desperately trying to make another man understand himself—to *know* in his bones, viscera and nerve ends who and what he is. On the basis of the Vice-President's current behavior I cannot help wondering if Dewey made his point.

The final or manic phase of the political campaign has now seized the candidates and ancillary orators, the phase in which frenetic politicians regret only those statements that lose them votes, whatever the loss of their own dignity or of the country's flexibility of strategy in a warring world.

This brief period is always dangerous and often damaging for men and for national policy. This goes double for the present campaign in which, as we suggested weeks ago, a single remark could decide the outcome. Only mass euphoria obscures the sheer ghastliness of a condition in which the Presidency of the United States may be decided by statements about the presence of Nationalist soldiers on those two off-shore islands—soldiers kept there by Chiang Kai-shek in a primary hope of ambushing America into war with Red China, weird as this may sound to those ignorant of what Chiang has been living for these past ten years.

In this phase of a Presidential contest, as in a war, truth is hounded down, disfigured and tattered by half-truths, exaggerations, innuendoes, cut-rate debating points, impossible promises and a blatant re-writing of history that the editors of *Pravda* must admire.

In terms of the search for truth it is as preposterous to compare the oral tennis matches on television with the Lincoln-Douglas debates as it is to compare Quemoy with Berlin in terms of the search for world safety. A spectacle of volley and countervolley in which neither man concedes a single point or admits a single error, past or present, by himself or his party, is merely an exercise in point scoring, a travesty on the debating institution in its academic or parliamentary sense. Truth is neither turgid nor neatly packageable; it is elusive, many-sided, a harvest gathered only with patience, humility and largesse.

On and off television the hailstorm of selected facts and claims, exaggerations, lies both little white and big black, is lashing the crop, filling eyes, ears and nose with dust and chaff.

No doubt a desperate plaintiff or defendant (to complete this mixed grill of metaphors) testifying from a witness chair perched on a soap box in a shouting courtroom cannot be regarded as in full possession of his faculties, so a mistrial is not apt to be called after November 8th on grounds of perjury. But, in the absence of the recording angel, let us perform the functions of the court reporter and jot down a few of the non-truths so far loosed upon the jury.

Considering first those of an apocalyptic nature, reason whimpers in pain at Mr. Kennedy's accusation that Mr. Nixon is trigger-happy, as it does at Nixon's solemn assertion that loss of the rocky ridges of Quemoy and Matsu would lead us into World War III. It was Ike, not Dick, who cut his palm showing Mamie how to fan a six-gun; and Khrushchev's game is blackjack, not dominoes, falling or otherwise.

And if Nixon's observation that three Democratic Presidents led us into war means that they acted arbitrarily, we find ourself troubled by his claim—while defending Ike in the first TV argument—that Presidents only do what the people demand. He might also now rewrite his St. Louis speech of years ago in which he praised Truman's courage for the Korean intervention.

We note down, but with invisible ink for sheer embarrassment, Truman's claim that Nixon "never" tells the truth, Nixon's sanctimonious concern that Truman's racy language will corrupt our young and Kennedy's claim that 17,000,000 Americans go to bed hungry every night. Our trust in American technology is quite firm enough to discount the probability of jammed locks on that many gleaming white refrigerators.

No amount of butter on burned political fingers can account for a grasp so insecure as to "lose" an object as big as China or even one as small as Cuba, and we cannot accept Nixon's claim that Washington mislaid the first or Kennedy's claim that Washington mislaid the second.

Nixon's statement that American prestige has never been so high, while Russian prestige is slipping, approaches Hitler's big prevarication in dimension, if not in intention, by its sheer audacity, so we are obliged to record it with lamentations. In awareness that politics is the art of the impossible, we record Kennedy's balancing act in boldly attacking the Eisenhower performance while timidly refusing to attack Eisenhower.

With a sigh of the weariness born of familiarity we note Lodge's "pledge" to put a Negro in the Cabinet; Nixon's idea of using a weary, aging, powerless ex-President as world peacemaker, globe-trotting style; both candidates' belief that they can solve the totally unsolvable farm problem; both men's genuflexions before that hoary children's crusade—preventing the rapacious federal government from "telling teachers what to teach." (Fifty major federal acts on education since George Washington have not yet produced that horrendous result and one simple clause in forthcoming legislation could prevent it, in any case.)

The final entry in our little notebook of judgment is a large black question mark, a block to arrest for further examination the candidates' most basic pretensions, their implied claims to a mystique which, far more than any stated "policies," ought to make up the national mind. One is Nixon's theme that he is pre-eminently and wisely mellowed in the ways of this revolutionary, unprecedented world. The other is Kennedy's implication that he is another FDR ready to loose a repressed floodtide of brilliant ideas and bold actions that will remake America's life and re-grasp America's world leadership.

We do believe that *he* believes this and that he would try. Sadly but deeply do we doubt that the early sixties will even faintly resemble the early thirties. The great simplicities of Roosevelt's problems are gone; the old elbow room is gone. The age of complexity is upon us.

Mr. Henry Cabot Lodge, who eagerly seeks the job of putting his shoulder to our Constitutional fifth wheel, the Vice-Presidency, is not celebrated in the land of the knowledgeable for profundity. Yet it is he who has blurted out the lumpy, unpalatable truth—that "we are in for twenty-five years of international tension."

He might have stretched the timetable even further. But, while the Back Bay pecking order may ordain that the Lodges and Cabots speak only to God, there is no evidence that God has ever answered, so twenty-five years is a bold enough guess, even for a Brahmin devoid of doubts, without the double-check of a countdown from on high.

Lodge is Dennis the Menace in this campaign. In his barging insouciance he fails to detect the raiment on naked emperors, and with this blunt prophecy he has cheerfully denied the implication of nearly everything Nixon and Kennedy have been saying. They have been suggesting in their sales pitches that they keep remedies just under the counter for all our ills, from Latin gunmen and African tribalism to the Communist obsession with world revolution. Now Lodge has gaily announced that all that stuff under the counter is just palliatives, plasters and concoctions not yet approved by the AMA.

Like most present-day politicians, with the noble exception of Stevenson, the two Presidential candidates have been pandering, in effect, to that deep glandular urge we all feel but all know to be false—the desire that history come to a stop, at least for a breathing spell. The Communists not only know it will not stop, but jam down the accelerator at every opportunity. Kennedy and Nixon know it too, but only Lodge proclaims it in the tones of the instrument that both announces and penetrates fog.

There are no "solutions," no magic formulae, American traditional belief to the contrary. There are only palliatives, stop-gap preventatives and new experiments to be tried, for ours is the age of limited opportunities. That is why this campaign does not really represent a choice of "policies." The totally honest voter has to admit to himself that he just doesn't know whether getting rough with Castro will "solve" that problem any better than adopting what the British call "masterly inactivity;" he doesn't know whether giving up or defending those off-shore islands is the better way of avoiding war with China; he has not the faintest notion whether delivering atomic arms to Germany or withholding them gives the better prospect of quieting Russia in Europe, whether we should encourage De Gaulle to be tougher or more lenient with the Algerian nationalists, whether tight or easy credit offers the better long-term prospects for our economy.

So only a relative few will cast their vote on policy. More will vote on party and the vast majority will vote on personality. Woodrow Wilson once said that the national instinct is "for unified action and it craves a single leader. . . . A President whom it trusts cannot only lead it, but form it to his own views." This is still true fifty years later. Even in our age of pulse-taking, endless committees and commissions of experts dedicated to "finding the way," we fall back on the simple, tribal instinct of choosing a Man.

In any case, the problems of America and the world are now so fluid and unpredictable that present "policy positions"are almost meaningless. What counts are the intelligence, understanding, emotional balance and, above all, the strength and will of the human mortal we assign to the frightful task of trying the new experiments. Little wonder that in the television debates the country has been weighing two men, not two arguments. I have been trying to do the same, reassembling my own impressions of Nixon and Kennedy over the years. They are these, in part:

Both men have been deeply, single-mindedly dedicated to self-education in public affairs. Both are workhorses; either would accomplish in a day three times what Eisenhower accomplishes.

Kennedy has the wider liberal education, though he is by no means the literary scholar his handy quotations from the classics would suggest. Kennedy is liberal by conviction; Nixon is liberal through political pragmatism and has no systematic, philosophical base to his thinking.

Nixon assumes middle-class mores and values to be the normal life—he has never known any other; Kennedy is fundamentally indifferent to them. Neither is a religious man (as Eisenhower is not), all the public posturing to the contrary.

Nixon's self-confidence is somewhat febrile; Kennedy's goes to the roots of his being. I would say that he is the "whole man," save that in his absolute lack of fear, self-doubts or awe of the Presidency there is something disturbing, as with those medal-winning infantrymen in the war whom psychiatrists concluded lacked some chord or nerve cell normal to men. By the same token Kennedy is devoid of self-pity, while Nixon can indulge in it.

In the sense that their ambitions rule their lives and the lives of their intimates, both men are intensely self-centered. Nixon is sensitive to the hurts suffered by himself; Kennedy is sensitive neither to his own hurts nor to those suffered by others. As President, Nixon would act a great deal of the time with an eye to the votes for his re-election. Kennedy's supreme confidence would make him less cautious and calculating in this respect.

I am not at all sure that Kennedy is a more intelligent or conscientious man than Nixon. What I feel quite sure of is that he is a stronger man, the kind of human creature who can make a fateful decision and, like Harry Truman, sleep soundly in his bed.

If it were not for the risk of being tarred and feathered by 65,000,000 fellow citizens, we would like to ask the two Presidential candidates if they would mind repeating it all once more, just for our sake. We didn't quite catch it the first 300 times around.

A lot of you feel you did, so you will cheerfully line up at the polling booth and crisply mark your ballot, confident that you voted for the better man and exactly why. We would envy you, save for a still, small voice. The voice speaks to us in dim, though not blank, verse with a re-written version of Kipling's "If," saying: "If you can keep your head while all about you are losing theirs—maybe you don't understand the situation!"

As a supporter of The Situation, without which we would have had to go to work or into real estate long ago, our personal view is that neither Kennedy nor Nixon has answered the real questions about America or the world or themselves. Not, at any rate, the questions that bother us.

We have been totally unable to find out if either man truly understands and accepts that:

In spite of all their promises about parity payments, wage levels, defense appropriations and pensions, it is the quality, not the quantity of American life that is the great domestic concern. A system that has found opulence is blindly searching for its own cultural form and tone among the civilized societies. America knows what it can do and get; now it must know what it can *be*.

Americans in their heart of hearts wish not only to like their

President, but to respect—indeed, revere—him and his office, and they yearn for loftiness, so utterly lacking in this shrewd and sharp campaign.

Americans will forgive error and understand inconsistency if only there is honest candor.

Humor remains one mark of the large-minded man, and the people will respond to the leader who laughs at himself, knowing it is only the unsure man who will not.

Americans want to be led, not to be given "what they want," for in numberless contexts they cannot know what they want until experiments are tried.

"States' rights" has become the wooden, totem-pole language of far too many who cite one letter of the Constitution in order to deny another letter, as well as the spirit.

Equality for Negro citizens cannot wait upon "changes in the hearts of men," as Eisenhower seems to believe, for it is the illumination of action that produces changes in the heart more often than the other way around.

The farmer is not necessarily nature's nobleman nor the salt of the earth, and the family farm is no more sacred in a rapidly changing economic pattern than the family flat—it is only more difficult to move out of.

In an era of total wars that make every fifth or sixth adult male a "veteran" by the mere act of donning a uniform, only those veterans and their families who suffered directly from the fighting have special claims upon the national treasury, and the rest of it is organized greed.

"Non-interference in the internal affairs of other nations" is a standard to aim for under normal conditions, but cannot be a policy straitjacket in a revolutionary world struggle in which the United States affects the scene in other nations when it *fails* to act about as often as when it acts.

Israel is a sovereign nation among other sovereign nations, to be treated as such; it is not our orphan ward with special claims upon our moral sense.

"Matching Russia's rate of economic growth" is an unnecessary as well as an undignified purpose. Russia is late in the race, and in any sprint the acceleration during the first few yards is faster than that during the final few yards.

Russia's advance in wealth, though not in weapons, is a happy and not an ominous thing, for by this process are revolutionary societies altered to conservative societies.

NATO's fabric is shredding away, partly under the strain of viewing strategic nuclear weapons not merely as the war preventative, but as weapons for actually waging war. For any crowded European nation this proposition wipes out the ancient choice of victory or defeat and replaces it with the choice of survival or extinction, which is no choice at all.

Great Britain, in spite of her Commonwealth, can no longer go it alone and must attach herself to a larger context, preferably an economic "Atlantic union," which will require an American action of immense size and consequence.

By no means are all backward peoples ready for political independence, whatever the anguished backlash against the American leader with courage enough to say so.

"Masterly inactivity" is sometimes the hallmark of diplomatic wisdom, in spite of the American tradition to the contrary. To admit that the United States cannot directly deal with every threat in the world is not to be an appeaser. A danger postponed often *is* a danger averted. We will know no absolute peace but will live in the twilight between peace and war. This is not insupportable. Time is life.

Surely these are among the real truths involved in America's choice of a new leader, truths which neither Nixon nor Kennedy has spoken or clearly indicated they are aware of.

Election-night's drama wrung out the spectators as well as the principals. In the gray early hours of the next morning, when these words are being written, the spirit can hardly match the size of the event. So these words may be poor companions in the general parade. But all professional observers imagine themselves addressing a new leader in person, and my own communication, to President-elect Kennedy, goes about like this:

You have done an astounding thing, considering that your face and name were obscure until one night in the Chicago stockyards four years ago. But perhaps this is astounding only in traditional terms. Communication is instant, now; instant reputations can meet the times.

Anyway, the country has not responded to what you were, did or did not do in the past. In your case the country considered the past "a bucket of ashes." Your past record was no more than the record of a hundred others. You were neither hero nor sage. The people have taken you at face value, voice value, first value; that is, present value. We are the most contemporary of peoples. Our youth is our oldest tradition, as Oscar Wilde said, and in that perfectly valid sense you are traditional and well rooted in the American soil and story.

Like most political writers, I am a romantic at heart; belief in heroes is my secret vice. It has been bad form in recent years to reveal this particular vice. I hope you turn out to be a great man in the book sense, in the history professor's sense. But you have to arrange about that yourself. Tuesday's vote didn't prove it. I hope you discourage press agents and quick-book biographers who try to prove it *a priori*. They will make things harder for you in the long run.

On its face the vote seems to say that half the country is against you. I don't think it is. You have too much thrust to be intimidated by the statistical result anyway. A house divided statistically can stand. But it can't move unless you move it.

On its face the divided vote gives you no mandate. Forget about that. Lincoln was a minority president; so was Truman. What the statistical stalemate gives you is the wonderful chance to write your own mandate, and a whole Congress of your party persuasion is there to witness and endorse your signature.

On the face of the divided vote half the country wants to "move forward," as you have put it in a manner that makes even the emptiest clichés seem bursting with meaning, and the other half wants to sit where it is. This isn't quite true, either.

Actually, the country wants to go somewhere; it just doesn't know the address it has in mind. It knows it wants something different but doesn't know how to label it. You are in the position of the advertising man—you can "create wants." A trial offer is all a President can give us, anyway—returnable after four years if not fully satisfactory.

I am persuaded that you are one of the men in politics, one of those who want position, in order to do something with power —not one of the boys who want position in order to be something with title.

So the place ought to be jumping for months to come. Covering Washington in recent years has been a bit like covering an endless convention of certified public accountants. Most of us have been turning out noiseless copy from our noiseless typewriters. The exclamation-mark key is rusty. Most of us will love to bang on it, praying the finger for that key hasn't totally atro-phied. This isn't just our problem; unless you stir our glands, you aren't likely to stir the glands of the nation.

Still, while you seem very young yourself, many of us are getting along, and with age comes inconsistency as well as cau-tion. So we want you to be impatient with many of the hideous, haggard problems still cluttering up the place; but we are also afraid of your impatience when it comes to the explosive prob-lems like Berlin or China or Cuba.

When we were a kid country we could blunder around. Now America has large feet and the yard is full of land mines. Hire at least a few scared worriers to help guard your mind, if not your body.

It's strange how the world's image of America always be-comes the image of the single individual who sits in the White House. So you can't create a new image of America until your own image is completed. All we've got so far is the outline sketch. Believe me, a lot of us want to fill it in and we're reaching for our strongest, brightest colors.

October 9, 1961

Sam Rayburn stood on feet cemented in the original Amer-ican rock. He did not merely believe, by the evidence, in the strength, goodness—the rightness—of America, he assumed it. This is a quality that has been thinning out since the rock was fissured, beginning with World War I. The new enlightenment of self-analysis and self-doubt is not necessarily a good trade for the old implicit belief, since we remain under assault by forces that deny self-doubt.

I can see Mister Sam now, hunched behind his big desk in his inner sanctum on a quiet Saturday afternoon when the House was empty. The square little man with the sad, squinty round face would pour a little bourbon and branch water and talk about his patron saint, Robert E. Lee, whose pictures dominated the wall above the black horsehair furniture. It was a good place to bring one's small sons just to let them hear a little talk of their country and the past from someone who had no doubts. The young ones walked out of there very solemnly and self-con-sciously, the way children file out of church.

I know only the story of Lee fascinated Mister Sam, only Lee was his real hero—not Wilson, with whom he began his career in Washington, nor Roosevelt, with whom Sam rose to his great power. It was not just that Lee meant the South, it was that Lee meant duty, love of country, self-abnegation. I don't think Rayburn ever confused himself with Lee in the attainment of these qualities—he kept Lee there as a goad and goal. When he looked at Lee's photographs you had the feeling that Mister Sam was silently offering a toast to a man perceived in the iron embrace of his sense of duty.

At the opening of the '52 Democratic Convention in Chicago the Speaker read a long speech which few in that restless, not yet orderly hall, really heard. The next day *The New York Times* expressed astonishment that the country had never understood the passionate feelings of the crotchety old Texan about his country, or sensed his human tenderness and concern.

Not many did know this; just a few old friends, including the man who wrote the speech for him. This was the man who is always associated with Mister Sam in my memories—David Cohn, another sage from Greenville, Mississippi, one of the wisest, most truly talented lovers of all things, however preposterous, about this country ever to go unheralded in our disregarding life.

David Cohn, who died a year ago in Denmark, once wrote of Rayburn: "He was born on the farm in the pre-packaging era when folks got their cheese off the big round and their crackers out of the barrel and so . . . he clings to the outmoded concept that the contents are more important than the package. His voice doesn't quaver when he speaks about 'the people.' He doesn't bait labor or capital, quote the Bible or call the farmer 'nature's nobleman.' "

Mister Sam was one Texan who did not wear a ten-gallon hat, never slapped a back and called his cattle ranch a "farm."

Northern liberals called him a Southern conservative—the man who rammed so much of FDR's New Deal through the House! Conservatives called him a liberal. The labels merely made him impatient. If you asked him to define his philosophy, he was apt to say, "Well, a little applied Christianity wouldn't hurt."

He thought only in human, not doctrinal terms. Once, years ago, when somebody was complaining about the farmers spending their money on frivolous things like automobiles, Sam bristled and said, "When I was a boy, I used to hang on the fence all day on Sundays, just hoping somebody would come by in a buggy. God help the lonely. I'm glad farmers can get out and see people now."

I think the gruff old bachelor was lonely himself. Perhaps something happened far back in his youth so that he never married. I would not wish to pry or to know. In his rough way he expended his parental love on the House of Representatives. It was his home.

He was a just parent and ruler, patient, scrupulous. But he was not a permissive parent. Rules were rules and "no" meant no.

Mister Sam was a little bigger than life; a little bigger than Texas.

He was of the salt, soil and substance of our political system and inheritance. We shall not see his like again in the Speaker's chair, for the old ways, the old image of America, are going, as the old men go.

As I write this he still clings to life. He will die hard, but well. Courage is poise under pressure. In the loneliest moment of all he will not admit to his loneliness. I am sure he will die as my old father died, of whom he so much reminds me—reassuring those about him, patting the nearest hand and saying, "Everything is all right."

March–November 1961

The jet plane has made travel sudden transition, a blow to the brain. One week I was in the cramped, gray towns of England, where thousands of the educated refuse to understand that the external Communist threat is deadly real; the next week I was in the wide, bright towns of the American Middle West, where thousands of the uneducated refuse to understand that the internal Communist threat is really dead.

On a street in Kansas my host stopped his car to point to a new office building. "He owns that, and a lot else beside," the host explained. "He's got money and influence. He couldn't tell a Communist from Robert A. Taft, but he's trying to get his crackpots onto the school board and a lot of us are worried."

"He" is the local boss of the John Birch Society, one manifestation of the rank, posthumous aftergrowth of McCarthyism now spreading its weeds among the grass roots in Main-Street country.

"They organize in task forces," my host went on. "They call

schoolteachers and local college professors in the middle of the night and denounce them as Communists. They recruit kids as spies to take down classroom remarks of their teachers. They plant people in public lectures to ask loaded questions. They try to get their idiotic films and maps used in the high schools. Maybe it's hard these day to get a man smeared in Washington or even in Hollywood, but in a small city like this, where people live awfully close together, it can still be done."

The maps show every country in the world in the color red, except a few such as Spain, Portugal and the Dominican Republic. All the neutralist nations, all those like Britain or Sweden with any degree of public ownership, are Red.

These are the people who think of Chief Justice Earl Warren as a Communist, of social security, income taxes and minimum-wage laws as planned stages to Communism.

This phenomenon is not that most frightening of all things, ignorance empowered, as was McCarthyism; it can hardly make a dent in the collective sanity of any large and sophisticated community. But it is beginning to strain the nerves of intellectual leaders in the middle cities that possess the social evils of the great cities and none of the simple virtues of the small town. The soil was always prepared for Main-Street McCarthyism, for these are the centers where "they" means the government in Washington—alien, far away, always threatening the nest eggs long "scrimped and saved" for.

The phenomenon is not new; indeed, it pre-dates Joseph McCarthy by many years in its essential spirit. My own initiation into this weird world came in the mid-thirties when, for the purpose of a newspaper exposé in a Midwestern city, I spent weeks in prim parlor meetings of the "Silver Shirts," listening to pinch-faced retired clerks, accountants, corner merchants explaining how the Communists were about to seize the country. The memory is vivid of one elderly host leading me, with mysterious looks, down to his cellar to show me the food hoard he had accumulated against the coming siege. He even knew the precise date—the next October 15th—for the nationwide Bolshevist uprising.

Education has failed such people, or they have failed education. America is pre-eminently the land of change and any kind of change bewilders and upsets them, and they must seek simple answers. They cannot tell the difference between a spy for the Soviets—the only real internal danger, which police specialists must deal with—and an old-fashioned Socialist or a garden-variety pragmatic liberal. They cannot understand that their own leaders are not conservatives but anti-Constitutional radicals.

There is, it seems to me, a certain inverted kinship between these uneducated Americans and the often highly educated neutralists and unilateral disarmers of Europe. Neither group comprehends the damaging confusion it sows. The first does not know that the Soviets are delighted with any movement that creates distrust and disunity among Americans and transfers our attention from the real world menace to a fictitious domestic menace. The second does not know that the Soviets are delighted with any movement that propagates the misleading notion that the Russian quarrel is with the United States alone, the wish-belief that the world is at peace, a peace that would be universally serene if only the Soviets and the Yanks—equally dangerous —would cease irritating it and reach compromise on specific issues.

The European neutralists who see a potential settlement under every Cold War issue are doing far more damage than the American Know-Nothings who see a Communist under every bed. The American Union is not going to drift apart, but the Western alliance *can* drift apart. The Cold War can be lost on the world scene; it can hardly be lost on the Main Streets of Kansas.

The President's western speeches represent a bolder effort to isolate and weaken modern McCarthyism than any effort made by President Eisenhower against the vintage ism—or, for that matter, any effort made by Congressman John F. Kennedy—but while the Presidential whistle will warn off many of the wavering, it will only solidify the hard-core extremists themselves.

They are that kind of people. Unconsciously they welcome isolation, and martyrdom if attainable. They are lonely in their sullen resentment, anyway. They are people who have never made, or have abandoned in bafflement, the intellectual effort to understand the real nature of the Communist world threat, and hug to their breasts the domestic-devil explanation of freedom's reversals as the magic talisman vouchsafed to them alone, the chosen few, in the midst of the ignorant multitudes.

Ten years ago they had both a national leader and the American press to inflate their influence. Today they have only the press which, because the bizarre is always news, tends to nourish them, just as the London press has nourished their complete opposites, the neutralists and pacifists in Britain, whose great prominence has little relation to their small numbers.

Our indigenous extremists are doing surprisingly well without a leader in terms of the attention they get. But they cannot concentrate and bring their influence to bear without a political leader, and unless General Walker should somehow land in Washington, it is hard at the moment to see where they will get one. Senator Goldwater, as he indicated on television last Sunday, is playing it cool. He opposed those "Minutemen" flatly, but refused to be pinned down on the Birchites. Few politicians, standing on the first steps of ambition's lofty staircase, willingly invite additional enemies. But the odds would seem against the Arizona Senator identifying himself with the outer fringe of political respectability. He may be of the extreme right intellectually, but his is not the emotional order (or disorder) of a McCarthy.

In any case he must know that as champion of those obsessed with the devil theory he would throw away all chance of the Presidential nomination, to say nothing of election. Neither his party nor this country is or will be disposed to do orgiastic battle against shadows.

The President would not have spoken out as he did unless he were worried about the indirect effect of the extremists on his conduct of foreign policy. He knows they do not require a leader in Washington to hamper in some degree his painful effort to avoid a world stance either of belligerence or appeasement. They can do this merely by silencing some men on Capitol Hill who would otherwise publicly support him, just as the pressures in his own Massachusetts district silenced him when, as a young Congressman, he privately yearned to speak out against McCarthyism.

Any leader the new extremists may place in Washington would have a glorious booster-stage ascension on the magic carpet known as Page One, quickly followed by a sputtering descent. For he would be obliged both by his supporters and his opponents to specify, to name names, to prove the existence of traitors in high places; and he would end up, as McCarthy ended up, proving the opposite.

The real battlefield in the war with Communism, of course, is outside, not inside, this country. And the real issue inside this country is not between those who believe and those who do not believe that we have Communists in high office. The issue is between those who believe that the Russians have limited aims, that Communism is chiefly a concept of life that must be opposed by a more attractive concept, that conciliation can end the Cold War—and those who believe that the Russians have unlimited aims, that Communism is chiefly a weapon for political aggression, that we must vigorously prosecute the Cold War by every possible means from local negotiations to local force if we are to stop both the Cold War and its cause, which is Communist aggression.

The President warns against belief in "total victory." Even among those who follow the second line of argument few believe in that, in the sense of eradicating Communism in its heartlands. They do believe in victory in the sense of preventing or eradicating Communism in areas critical to us.

True enough, as the President begs the people to understand, the problem is complex. But the art of leading and organizing the will of a vast and diverse nation has more to do with simplifying than with complicating. There is something to be said for Goldwater's plea that the President make the plain declaration that we intend to win this world struggle. When the leader does not simplify in responsible manner, frustrated citizens will simplify in their own manner, which can be a foolish and divisive manner as the aforementioned extremists are demonstrating.

October–December 1962

California is not a state of mind, as alleged; it is at least three states of mind. It is a personality split three ways, like a rapidly rising investment, which it also is.

There is the California of the pleasure-seeker, the sun-worshipper, the love goddesses of Muscle Beach, the hot rodders and the strolling blonde with sunglasses and manicured poodle, pretending that Hollywood still exists.

There is the California of the pure intellect, working at the highest growing points of modern thought, trying to master the age of overkill and represented by the best laboratories in the world, the world's greatest concentration of Nobel Prize winners and by some of the most effective continuing seminars in the humanitarian studies this country knows.

And there is the California of the retired Iowa farmer and small-town banker with his half-rim eyeglasses and string tie, of the white Baptist church, the mission society, of front parlor anti-Communism, anti-vivisectionism, anti-alcoholism and anti-godlessness. This third California frowns with extreme distaste upon the California of the first part, and looks with wonder and fear at the California of the second part so busy taking apart the complicated universe which God put together in exactly six days of twenty-four hours each.

This third California also regards standard California politics, with its Nixons and its Browns, as hopelessly impure, and so it has put forward a third candidate for governor, a tall young man the rest of the country has *not* heard about, but a young man who just might decide this election and subsequent national events by pulling in enough extreme-right Republican votes to guarantee the defeat of Richard M. Nixon.

Thirty-five-year-old Robert L. Wyckoff, who practices medicine, law—and now oratory—could win a quarter million votes, and, in a condition where Democratic registration is far higher than Republican registration, that just might put period to the career of Mr. Nixon, now in his seventh crisis.

Trailing a ton of electronic clutter for the purposes of a CBS report, we descended on the candidate of the Prohibition Party (now undergoing a name change to the American Party, because it will settle for state liquor stores and charging the beverage industry with the cost of treating alcoholics, which sounds like a fair idea) in one of those curving canyon streets of endless, modest ranch-style houses with their built-in garages, built-in kitchens and total, built-in uniformity.

It was no surprise to find that Mr. Wyckoff is not a very smart man; but there is a difference between smartness and intelligence and it *was* a surprise to find him a very intelligent man. He is currently pursuing a doctorate in medical law at Yale between dosing patients and trotting around to neighborhood schools and church meetings with his "campaign manager." He must have been born grave of mien and mind; he looks at one with the steady, but slightly shy and soulful gaze of the reformer who has seen the light, and the old-fashioned courtliness of his manner was a positive refreshment in this era and region of sloppy, cocky youth. You can't help but like him and you can't help but admire his total integrity, slightly suffocating as it is.

It is pretty hard to make fun of an earnest, unworldly man who believes that only morality and applied Christianity will save his state, nation and world—who's to say him nay? The night before my visit one of the scornful wiseacres who command large audiences as "commentators" in the Disneyland of Los Angeles television had made merciless public fun of Dr. Wyckoff in an interview. "Oh dear, but it was humiliating," said the candidate. "I just crept out of there like a whipped dog." But Californians, like other Americans, quickly sense the presence of a decent man, and it was the wiseacre who was tongue-whipped by hundreds of indignant phone calls. The rating of the commentator must have gone down, that of the candidate up.

Dr. Wyckoff wrung his hands over the clutter of papers on the table in his dining nook. "I have to do all my own research," he said, "and it's so terribly time-consuming." He has an idea that taxes could be controlled or reduced by a $50-per-semester increase in university and junior-college tuition, now ridiculously low by most standards. He has an idea much of the state bureaucracy dealing with welfare could be eliminated by a private unemployment insurance plan whereby one day's pay is withheld each of the first twenty weeks of a person's employment, to be handed over when and if he loses his job, and state aid to be given him only when that fund is exhausted. Offhand, I couldn't see what was so terribly wrong with either idea.

I asked if he thought he would win the election. He hesitated, blushed and said, "I don't want to mislead you, but they tell me a candidate must appear confident at all times. So yes, I will win."

This is an intramural exercise. I hoist the warning flag at once because I have no clear idea of the public interest in, or the intrinsic importance of, quarrels among pundits of the press and the airwaves. Put it down to what psychiatrists on the witness stand call the "irresistible impulse."

Perhaps my resistance was lowered in London, where there is no such thing as "cold print." In London every morning's newsprint steams, smokes and sometimes belches flame. Their worst papers are worse than our worst; their best are better than our best in style and intellectuality, if not in news content; but nearly all meet on one level in the art and practice of slamming each other's columnists and editorialists. To the outsider it may seem an endless tempest in the breakfast teapot, but it stimulates the gastric juices no end.

If Fleet Street resembles a cockpit full of flashing spurs and flying feathers—and occasional tumbles of high hilarity—there are reasons for it besides the English tradition that no gentleman insults another, save on purpose. In Britain the life of a journalist is a grubby life unless he can draw attention to himself, and if he can't do it by verbal skill he can try it by verbal violence. The London papers are nearly all national papers, intensely competitive, with no safe circulation districts in which to relax. And British writers, I suspect, take one another as their targets partly because what they write about the world no longer matters so much to the world.

American pundits did not behave so very differently when America was a small and isolated power. But today we are a sober-sided lot, instinctively respectful of one another's toes and thin-skinned to the point of hurt feelings when a confrere takes us on in our very cold print.

Fortunately, the young Mr. Emmet Hughes, clearly destined for a major role in American journalism, possesses a quality of toughness matching the quality of his talents. He will not feel that I am doing a terrible thing to him when I say that he has done a terrible thing to former President Eisenhower and several others with his revelations in a magazine and a forthcoming book of Eisenhower's impulsive comments about other American leaders made in his unguarded moments with his intimates, of whom Hughes was one.

It is not news to many of us who worked in Washington during the Eisenhower years that the President was often bored by John Foster Dulles, regarded Adlai Stevenson as a self-conscious "faker," and distrusted Richard Nixon's essential capacity for the Presidency. Indeed, some of these attitudes and outbursts found their way into print in one informal manner or another. But to print them now in the form of semi-official biographical material, privileged material of the most intimate kind, carrying the cachet of one who accepted the President's trust and not as a future biographer, but as a present confidant—to print them now with Mr. Eisenhower so recently out of office, still alive and active and in public contact with men he then excoriated—surely this is wrong.

Presidents are human beings, harried human beings, and they cannot possibly maintain their public face with their private friends and assistants. If they cannot let down in private, whether to curse, denounce or even to weep, they would soon crack up. How are they to work, to endure, if they are daily haunted by the thought, not "Ah, that mine adversary had written a book," but the thought, "Ah, God, my closest colleague may write a book tomorrow?"

No private journalist is entirely a private citizen. To some degree he carries a public responsibility and therefore abjures some materials. His own sense of history and his own taste determines that degree; no hard rule of limitation is ever possible. But when a certain, however indefinable, line is overstepped it becomes apparent; it is glaringly apparent in the case of Mr. Hughes, however brilliant and fascinating his revelations are.

Of course, truth will out; it must, even the little, personal truths about such a one as a President of the United States. But life is long. The country will endure. Journalism may be "the first draft of history," but there is such a thing as a draft that is too soon, with too much. We need not be in such a fever to uproot, masticate, devour and relish every intimate morsel concerning the private thoughts and impulses of our public men, as if there were no tomorrow. We seem, in this country, to be losing the healthy element of space in our life together. Let us not destroy time, which heals many things, and along with space is a precious protector.

In a democracy that works, the highest attainable goal for the master ego is just short of absolutism. The titan is permitted the status of a benevolent tyrant—no more—and always provided we can count on fresh benevolences.

Since Robert Moses of New York had, at any given point, done something for us lately, and has still to cap his career with the forthcoming World's Fair, his reign as the Last Angry Man was permitted to continue to his seventy-fourth year. There never was any evidence that his head lay uneasy, though he wore eight crowns at once, all of them of the thorny variety, as Governor Rockefeller discovered when he reached to pull one of them off.

For the benefit of outlanders innocently assuming that the most powerful man in the nation's biggest metropolis is its mayor, it should be said that save for the chronically bedridden there are no New Yorkers now alive who have not sat in Moses's parks, swum from Moses's beaches, driven over or through Moses's bridges and tunnels and sped along Moses's superhighways, while viewing Moses's golf courses to the right and Moses's dams and reservoirs to the left. Unlike his scriptural namesake, Moses did not perform as mere intermediary in the provision of this manna in the former wilderness of brick shacks, where this Moses also labored a fully forty years.

A man who has this much handiwork to survey and has invariably pronounced it good, a man who has immortalized himself in his own lifetime and has the temples and monuments to prove it, is not a man to genuflect before the passing politician, and so when Rockefeller asked for one crown, Moses handed him five, thorns and all, keeping his three municipal chairmanships, including the World's Fair job. (One is not technically a chairmanship, but where sits Moses there is the head of the table.)

Master egos like Robert Moses and Admiral Rickover never fail to fascinate this observer. Their biographers will be tempted to say that their supreme arrogance, their furious intolerance of all opposition develop only after years of proving and re-proving that they can do the job and others can't—so will the fools and foot-draggers please stay the hell out of the way? But the ego was there to begin with and if something like paranoia develops instead of the mellowness of success, that, too, was incipient and shouldn't bother us too much provided the tyrant remains a titan and his handiwork good.

No, their working environment didn't make Moses or Rickover what they are; it was they who worked upon their environment since they were always what they are.

The question, of course, is whether they could have done what they have done, however brilliant, dedicated and honest they were, without these attributes of anger, impatience and callousness. I think both have to be given the benefit of the doubt, because neither man held a position of final political power with the weapons that go with such positions. Both worked in essentially bureaucratic surroundings. Either they conquered their surroundings or the surroundings would conquer them.

I incline to think that under such conditions brilliance, honesty and dedication are not enough—not nearly enough—for a man who is a little larger than life to reach his full growth. I have known of many occasions where the finest men were totally trapped in the Kafkaesque jungle of bureaucracy, in private business as well as in government, and had to resort to the meat axe to cut a way through. Those who couldn't lay hands on an axe simply got out.

The careers of men like Moses and Rickover suggest that we

may be coming full circle in the organizational life. We are going from the era of the masterful individual back to the masterful individual after passing through a delusory period of infatuation with the "science of management," with its tables of organization, channels of command and all the other Rube-Goldberg contrivances which keep an organization alive by feeding on its own flesh but which cannot recognize or push to fruition a big idea.

You can beat City Hall, but you had better be a Moses if you are going to try. Since most men are not, they follow the precept of joining what they can't lick. That would never do for a Robert Moses, certainly not at the apex of his career. If he can't lick 'em, he leaves 'em, and it's a neat question which one is out in the cold, he or the governor.

All other explanations having failed, my own theory is that the polar cap slipped, tilting the globe and shifting the weather. The July–August dog days have moved into the November–December period, and the Mediterranean mistral now blows across North America with its usual effects on the nervous system.

How else explain the recent behavior of otherwise shrewd and sure-footed men in public life?—Richard Nixon's self-destructive speech blaming his defeat on everybody but himself; Howard K. Smith's notion that Alger Hiss's analysis of his prosecutor's motives carried validity; the article by Alsop and Bartlett in the *Saturday Evening Post,* impugning the courage of Adlai Stevenson while excluding any Stevenson statement in his own defense; the speech by Dean Acheson, life-long Anglophile, which made his British friends instant Achesonphobes.

(Let's leave out the statement made in Rhodesia by Senator Ellender, because he sees everything in black and white, anyway, recognizing nothing gray save some uniforms of a hundred years ago.)

The great pageant of American public life has a built-in continuity in spite of the aberrations of the players on the stage and the scribbling critics seated on the aisle. The show will go on and the Kennedy cast, after its magnificent performance in the Cuban drama, may even move from triumph to triumph, as they say in theatrical biographies, although some of his players might have to turn in their horn-rimmed glasses for contact lenses to avoid splinters in the eyeball in case the villain doesn't blink in the next stare-down.

A roving critic poking about the wings of the Washington stage quickly becomes aware that the sweet song of success from the Cuban performance has been all but drowned out by the penny-whistle notes of the postlude as provided by the *Saturday Evening Post*.

Everyone involved has been injured, but there is no point in repeating at this late date the inventory of specific damages. It is perfectly clear that a President cannot maintain an intimacy with any particular Washington reporter because of the ever-present danger of embarrassment to himself and because it destroys the reporter's critical independence. What needs pointing out, because it is less well understood, is that there are inherent dangers as well as solid advantages when the palace guard is thick with self-conscious, history-minded professional intellectuals blessed and cursed as they always are with "the double vision."

They tend to act, not just for the sake of the action, but for the newsprint of the present and the history books of the future. They are, therefore, not only highly attentive to their own witticisms at Georgetown dinner parties, but jealous in advance of their own roles as the books to come will cast them. With one eye they are constantly watching themselves as actors on the great stage. Washington has not yet reached the point of pre-war French politics, when government was virtually conducted on each morning's front pages, but such men do have a special relationship with journalists and this carries built-in hazards.

Given their intellectual hypertension, their intramural hates as well as their loves are bound to be intense, and they are quite unable to carry either in silence. I believe the late Joyce Cary said something to the effect that no vendetta among African tribal chiefs can equal in savagery one among Western college professors.

But against the extramural world outside the palace (Congress, for example) they are generally united by a bond of self-satisfaction, nicely if unintentionally revealed in the *Post* article. The palace atmosphere reflected in those references to the "Trollope ploy" during the terrible Cuban crisis, and to the "doves and the hawks" merging into the "hoves and the dawks" was the atmosphere of "we happy few." I have not known quite this climate in Washington before. It may suit British affairs of state as conducted in Whitehall and Belgravia salons, but it fits badly and embarrassingly on the American body politic.

Perhaps that is the worst one can say about the Cuban postlude. The play itself was marvelously done. Yet I did hear one elderly, wise American, a greater scholar than any in the palace guard, remark: "This has made me wonder if these are really serious, responsible men around the President."

I think that they are. But since they are quotation-lovers, one can hope they will always remember that the play's the thing, not the ploy.

May 1963–March 1964

Two years ago, in May 1961, President Kennedy sent his special message to the Congress in which he said that he himself believed we "should go to the moon." It has taken two years to develop the beginnings of a national debate on the question among Congressmen, scientists and editorialists.

I say the "beginnings" of a debate because, on its public plane at least, the argument has not yet come into its true focus. The true question is not whether we should try to land men on the moon—the nature of this political world as well as the nature of man's curiosity and the unquenchable spirit of science make it inevitable that we try—but how we go about it. The real argument is going on in semi-private between the Cold Warriors, including the military, who want a "crash" program, and certain scientists, deeply aware of the difficulties and dangers, who fear the atmosphere of a "race" in this delicate operation. They discount the lasting value of the prestige attendant upon being first.

They would like to see the whole psychology of strain and rush, of looking over our shoulder, rooted out of this endeavor. They believe that with this step toward the moon we have reached the point where haste will not only make enormous financial waste, but very probably produce failure and human tragedy.

Congressmen now expressing doubts about the moon program are being contemptuously assailed as pinch-penny mossbacks living in the last century. This comes a bit gratuitously from partisans of the President, since he himself, in his message of two years ago, urged every citizen and Congressman to "consider the matter carefully in making their judgment," because, he said, "it is a heavy burden and there is no sense in agreeing or desiring that the United States take an affirmative position in outer space unless we are prepared to do the work and bear the burdens to make it successful."

Only now are many of us, including the worried members

of Congress, beginning faintly to comprehend the order of magnitude of the efforts and the burdens to come. A new and fathomless world of human endeavor is swimming into our ken. It is natural and not necessarily a sign of stodgy un-imaginativeness that practical men instinctively and immediately try to estimate the practical costs involved; indeed, they must. And the more they try the more dismayed they feel.

They have a few present facts to go on: they know that the budgets for NASA have been doubling every year for the past five years. They know that a successful moon landing in this decade would cost at least $30 billion and maybe more. They see that of the 400,000 qualified specialists now working in "R and D"—research and development—60,000 work on NASA projects, and that this percentage must sharply rise, raising the gravest questions about scientific priorities in the American society of the future.

They see what our present budgets for normal military preparedness are and they see no way to reduce them substantially. Now they see, dimly on the horizon, a second realm of uncontrollable expenditure which can match and even surpass normal defense expenditures as the years go by. Space is limitless and there are only staging points in its "conquest"—there is no stopping place.

Being practical men of the present, with present and practical responsibilities, of course they feel dismay. What is a vision to some men is a specter to others. The immediate specter these men see is a permanently growing federal debt, a permanently unbalanced budget, a permanent level of extremely high taxes.

This is only the beginning. Anyone has only to let out his imagination a short notch to see the ultimate possibilities—to see humanity's push into space transforming this society, dominating its intellectual pursuits, absorbing its resources, altering the training of its youth and its moral and religious concepts, upsetting the priorities for its social and humanitarian efforts on terra firma.

Those who scold the worriers say that to cancel the moon voyage would be as if Ferdinand and Isabella had canceled Columbus' voyage, which opened the New World. They are more right than they know. What is at stake are not only the new marvels to be found, but also the profound transfiguration of the source of the search.

After the voyage of Columbus the Old World was never the same in political, economic, military, social, religious or intellectual terms. After the first men walk upon the moon Old Earth will never be the same and the change will begin in the two societies, Russia and America, now competing for the cataclysmic honor of commencing the alteration.

The Goldwater phenomenon has already reached proportions far beyond anything that most serious observers, especially those in the eastern centers of thought, imagined it could attain a year ago, and the phenomenon is just hitting its real stride.

If it is to be described as a conservative movement, clearly it has little connection with the ideas and the climate that surrounded Senator Robert A. Taft, the true, traditionalist conservative of the postwar period. Taft largely created his own following the hard way; a great deal of Goldwater's following has rushed to him, including groups he is bound to find an embarrassment sooner or later. Taft knew exactly what he thought and the philosophical and historical reasons behind his thoughts, and he built a systematic program from this foundation; Goldwater's domestic ideas spring essentially from negative reaction to what he sees about him, and the emotional battery that gives them energy is all but pure nostalgia for a society that is gone.

For these and other reasons, including his simple, homespun sincerity and charm, he is much more another Eisenhower than another Taft. Like Eisenhower in both his campaigns, and unlike Stevenson and Kennedy in theirs, he is making no demands upon the people for greater and greater intellectual and physical exertions. In his domestic proposals he issues no rallying cry for the people to charge the barricades or cross unknown frontiers. He seems, instead, to be issuing a rallying cry for passive resistance to the baffling problems of a nightmarish age.

When he advocates turning civil rights over to the states (that is, turning desegregation in the South over to the segregationists), when he asks that the progressive income tax be abolished, when he suggests that family relief in the vast, sprawling Harlems of America be turned over to lodges, unions, private charities and relatives of the indigent—when he says these things he is not solving the problems, he is wishing them away.

Yet he is perfectly correct when he retorts that the problems of our time and our society are not being solved as matters are going. And in this profound frustration must lie the key to Goldwater's large following. It is not half so much a movement with a program as one with a protest. It is desperate, confused protest against a desperately confused new world of human living rising around us at home and abroad. Millions have simply given up trying to understand it, let alone cope with it.

Most of the human race abroad is convulsed with the paroxysms of a revolution that is essentially socialist and non-white. These parts of the world refuse to "turn out" as men like Goldwater had wanted to believe they would. At home labor-union power has grown enormously; giant corporations become supergiants, beyond detailed comprehension; the people migrate needlessly, draining the farm states, inundating the cities, where the slums and the maddening traffic increase. Crime spreads, technology baffles and disorganizes our daily lives, throws millions out of work, and before these monsters of the scientific Frankenstein even educated men seem powerless.

Problems we have always had with us, even massive problems, because we are not and never have been one of the inert societies of earth. But what is different this time, what many of us have sensed increasingly and what maddens people who make up the Goldwater following because they believe there *must* be a simple answer, is this, as Mr. Robert Heilbroner has put it: "They (the problems) do not respond to our existing means of correction and control."

It is in a profound sense that, as Heilbroner states it, "Our society seems no longer under our control. Running its masterless course, it disposes of us as 'it' sees fit and not as we might desire."

The traditional agencies of correction and control—local governments, limited federal government, the Congress, the marketplace, the most exhaustive reporting and analysis of facts by the press—these agencies are no longer truly effective. Nor is the agency to which Goldwater appeals, traditional horse or common sense. It is not to be wondered at that Negroes have taken to the streets or that a crime organization which should have been dealt with in the quiet of grand jury rooms becomes the subject of a Senatorial, TV and press circus.

We have entered the age of what Heilbroner calls the "Great Paralysis." I do not know how the paralysis is to be broken, but broken it must be. The last thing we can do is escape it, as so many of Goldwater's followers seem to wish, by thinking ourselves back to a simpler time.

However he fares in New Hampshire the Senator from Arizona and the political writers will not be finished with one another for some time. In a certain sense he is much the most interesting of the candidates, yet he has not really been explained. His views have been explained, and the vision of America that he would like to recall to reality seems clear enough. But the special psychology of the man, the *method* of his thought, as distinct from its substance, has not been revealed.

Nor have we who presume to unravel the daily mysteries accomplished this in respect to others who claim competence to act as first trustee of the fate of millions. Mr. Harold Stassen is a good example. Who has really detected what it is, deep in his viscera, that makes him stir and paw in his harness every four years like the proverbial firehorse at the sound of the gong? It is something more complicated than simple ambition.

I have often thought that political writers make very poor use of the tools of modern psychology. Sports writers and Hollywood gossips do better laying bare the inner souls of their heroes and villains than we who write of the characters who perform upon this far more important stage. One of our troubles is that we are habitually judging political men in their relation to the "themes and issues," as if the warp and woof of their minds consisted of "positions" on this objective problem or that.

This is what we have been doing with the fascinating Goldwater psyche; yet, surely, the interesting and special thing about him is not the conclusions his thought has led him to, but the process of his thinking. Admittedly, getting into this is, for the amateur in psychology, to tread a minefield in poor light. One can booby-trap himself very easily and that may be what I am about to do.

Right or embarrassingly wrong, I have come to the conclusion that in the world of political thought he is the mechanic as contrasted with the engineer. Woodrow Wilson once said that government is not a machine, but a living thing. He explained that it falls, not under the Newtonian theory of the universe, but under the theory of organic life, that it is accountable to Darwin, not to Newton.

Perhaps, after all, the simplest way to explain Goldwater is to recall his passion for mechanical gadgets—the household panels that slide, the flagpole that lifts at the push of a button, the radio and automobile knobs and panels that respond to his touches. This is an entirely reputable avocation; the point is that it is the hobby of a human psyche that is very different from the one that paints or writes or gardens, or even the one that creates furniture in the basement workshop. It is emphatically not the psychology of the ponderer, the shaper and leader.

The Senator appears to view American society and the stream of world history in static terms. Touch this button, he seems to be saying, and the Cuban problem will be transformed; pull this lever and China will be taken care of; put your finger on this clause of the Constitution and policy X becomes literally and unquestionably un-Constitutional.

I have the impression that he sees American society as General Eisenhower seemed to see it in 1952, as if through the lens of an elementary civics book: a fixed mosaic with labor in its place; management in its; industry, agriculture, city and small town all in their proper and appointed spheres; with political philosophies, whether "liberal" or "conservative," neat, self-contained and separate, never flowing in and out of each other's main currents.

One gets this impression much more from his extemporaneous speeches and much less from his writings. But the speeches are the pertinent evidence for the reason that his writings are essentially done for him by others.

The mechanistic approach to government and world affairs is not synonymous with the conservative philosophy of life; there are nominal liberals who are governed quite as much by this state of mind, who are also intellectual button-pushers. If there is a difference between them, it is that when the liberal wants to push a button he thinks it will automatically open something; the conservative, that it will automatically close something.

Perhaps there is a better and more accurate imagery to help explain what I am so awkwardly trying to explain. It might be found in the words of Sir Harold Nicolson, most reflective of British diplomats, who suggested that the statesman is not an architect creating on a blank page, but a gardener cultivating "forces of nature" toward a desired end.

6

Dallas to Washington:
The Trajectory of a Bullet

With the end of a young and remarkable life, with the end of an unusual Presidency, we may possibly have also seen the end of a family political dynasty—a dynasty that gave evidence it might stand in history with the great Adams family of the nineteenth century.

The Kennedy family was a family blessed by strength, wealth, popularity and power, and a love of life—but a family star-crossed as well. The admired older brother killed in the war; a sister killed in a European air crash; a baby boy, dead soon after birth. Now John F. Kennedy, who had carried on, and carried to the very pinnacle, the hopes and dreams of this remarkable Boston Irish family.

What *was* John F. Kennedy? How will he stand in history? It is hard even to assemble thoughts at this hour of national paralysis; easy to misjudge such a complicated human being. The first thing about him was his driving intelligence. His mind was always on fire, his reading was prodigious, his memory almost total recall of facts and quotations and ideas.

A friend of mine once crossed the Atlantic on a liner with the Kennedy family many years ago. She remembered the day twelve-year-old Jack was ill in his stateroom; there lay the thin, freckled little boy reading Churchill's early life, other large books scattered about his bed.

His was a directed intelligence; he did not waste his energies; he always seemed to know where he was going and he put first things first.

John Kennedy's intellectuality was perhaps the hallmark of his nature as President, even more than his youth, the thing that made him different from so many Presidents. But few thought of him as an intellectual in the sense of one seeking truth for its own sake; he sought it in order to act upon it. He was that rare and precious combination, the man of contemplation as well as the man of action, not un-like Wilson. He had a sharp sense of history from his immense reading, and was acutely conscious of what his own place in history might be. In a sense, he lived for that; much of his personal correspondence as President suggested his awareness that those letters would be part of the American archives and story for all time.

He brought a new style into government; he surrounded himself with intellectuals, as did Franklin Roosevelt in his first years; but in his own style he was more like President Theodore Roosevelt. Like the first Roosevelt, President Kennedy believed in action; he had no patience with those who were tired or skeptical or cynical, no patience with those who could not keep up, mentally or physically.

He became, with his young and beautiful wife, the symbol of America as he and most of us like to think of America: itself young, itself always hopeful, believing, and believing that government could change the face of our land and our lives, and that America could do more than any country in the world to change the face and the nature of the world itself.

He showed no signs, even after three years in office, of growing tired, either in body or spirit—but the built-in obstacles to practical achievement were, and remain, big and complex. He began some entirely new practical courses of government action —as with the Peace Corps and the Alliance for Progress. These, perhaps, were more imaginative than his domestic conceptions; in any case, it is in the domestic field that his difficulties were the greatest and progress the slowest. Early on he showed that his way would be to try to conciliate and persuade the Congress, and to compromise with it where he had to, rather than to try bulldozer tactics. Of his bold actions his nuclear confrontation with the Soviet Union over Cuba was the boldest, one of the boldest, most dangerous and most successful acts of statesmanship the history books will ever tell the future about.

But at bottom President Kennedy was a cautious, prudent man. He liked to have all his ducks in a row before he moved. However vibrant in his political behavior, he was, in his deepest emotional nature, a conservative human being. Rarely did the people become aware of his deep feelings about anything. When he spoke to the country by radio and television his head usually ruled his heart. Only in very special circumstances, as on the day of the brutal events in Mississippi, did passion rise in his voice as he spoke. This is why some professional observers said that President Kennedy had opened his mind to us, but not his heart —that therefore, he had captured the admiration of the people, but not its heart.

If that was so, it is so no longer; the heart of the people is with the young President in death, with all of his family. Its hopes are now with the new President.

We are all of us dazed and spent at the end of such a week, a climacteric in the American drama—all of us, those who must act, those who write and speak about it, those who read and listen and wonder.

We wonder if our people will stand together now in shocked sobriety behind their new leader, leagued in common sense, their heads ruling their unruly spirits. We wonder if they will divide even further as the shock wears off, spreading the cancer spots of venom that exist in a thousand places.

This is a fair land. For most it is a prosperous land. We have always been a people to whom the future beckoned more than the past. We have been an idealistic, a moralistic, a passionate people. Were we a jaded and cynical people perhaps these things would not have happened. No one would have cared that much.

But in these years, it is clear now to all, our passions have taken many crooked courses. Suspicion and hatred have surmounted trust and love among too many large minorities. Hard, unmelted lumps are revealed at the bottom of the American melting pot. Almost daily legal force must be called upon to restrain illegal force.

144

We are deeply infiltrated by the Negro-haters, the white-haters, the foreigner-haters, the city-haters, government-haters, the haters of the rich and the haters of the poor, those of the political right who hate and those of the left.

Americans are struggling for the soul of their country. A century ago the struggle by means of free discussion broke down. The government broke down, the nation broke apart, Lincoln died and vengeance took possession of men otherwise good.

John Kennedy has died in the midst of this present struggle for the national soul, a kind of civil war, in which the cohorts are many and the battle lines not very clear. It is not a complete answer to say that one individual lunatic was responsible and that all cities, all countries have their lunatics. His lunacy was fortified by its alignment with one of many irrational political mystiques. The additional furies that his act released destroyed him in turn, as the furies released by John Wilkes Booth destroyed Booth a hundred years ago.

The events of this past week have pulled aside the curtain of our rationalizations, our old habits of mind, and have revealed the naked state of the American soul. The history of this generation has never allowed this people to rest and to calm its spirit. We have been sobered and frightened by a great Depression, radically re-aligned in the social revolution that followed, caught up in two long wars, one—in Korea—that we could not understand, maddened by years of the devil-theory of politics; we have felt somehow betrayed by the advance of world Communism, frustrated by the seeming lack of results from our own great efforts overseas; we have packed ourselves, more and more, in great urban centers with all their tensions, which have reached an explosive stage with the rise of the Negro's long-delayed revolt.

It is more than the American nervous system that is frayed; it is our whole organic system of traditional beliefs and hopes and assumptions. Men, as individuals or as communal, racial or class groups, or as nations, must possess a firm image of themselves if they are to live and work in calmness and sanity. When the mirror becomes cracked and streaked they begin to lose their sense of identity, and with it their self-control.

It is hard enough to stand steady during one revolution, and we are trying to endure several at once—political, scientific, racial, cultural and demographic. Order is not going to surmount disorder, the shattered pieces of our fragmented society will not find their proper places again, unless we can somehow re-discover our common trust.

If the death of our vibrant young leader, our happy prince, our symbol of America's youthful hope and belief, can bring us to our senses, then John Kennedy will have done far, far more for his people than he will ever know.

All the Presidential assassins were men tortured and consumed by hatreds. They hated life and society as they existed; perhaps, at bottom, they hated themselves. They struck at the head and chief symbol of society to fulfill their own sick selves, to give their meaningless lives some kind of meaning. It is fruitless to blame society itself; such men have existed, and acted, in all types of society.

Lee Harvey Oswald of Dallas, Texas, was like John Wilkes Booth and unlike the others in certain respects—he tried to escape the consequences of his alleged act and, like Booth, he never came to trial. The violent act of each one set off further violence. After Lincoln's death violence and violent feelings spread deep in this country. Retribution and counter-retribution took many forms.

This is what must *not* happen now after President Kennedy's death, as Chief Justice Warren warned us when he spoke beside the President's coffin. Violence can beget violence, but calm also begets calm. The days immediately ahead, therefore, will place us all on trial. The country will be on trial before a doubting world which wonders if the United States is qualified to act as the leader in the effort to bring law, stability and peace to other nations.

There is no certainty that we will surmount this trial. Deep strains of violence in our society and in the American nature have come to the surface in recent months. To anyone now listening who may have murder in his heart, a brief scanning of history has something to say.

Political murder is one crime that does not pay in America. Assassins and would-be assassins are always caught. The result expected by the murderers never comes. The effects are always the opposite of what the murderer has in mind. John Wilkes Booth damaged the Southern cause by his act. If Lee Oswald, the probable killer of Mr. Kennedy, had any thought of aiding Communism or Cuba or Russia, he has pretty surely accomplished the reverse.

146

White men who shoot or bomb Negroes hasten the end of white supremacy. Negroes who kill white men delay the time of Negro equality in their community. In countries where personal rule is the tradition, murder can and does change governments, policies, whole social structures. It cannot do so in a country that lives under the rule of law. The overwhelming instinct of most citizens is to band closer together and to seek their protection behind the law, not behind a gun. That is the reason we have a government of law, not of men. No bullet can strike down the law.

It was hatred concentrated to the point of paranoia that killed President Kennedy. About such a state of mind very little can be done. But it was sheer disrespect for the legal rights and processes which make civilized life possible that killed the President's killer, and about this condition much can be done.

The events in Dallas revealed in a blinding flash the degree of venom that has been poisoning the American society. They also revealed for all to comprehend the alarming degree of carelessness and callousness with which police, prosecutors and all the information media have for a long time and in many cities handled everything that is implied in that precious phrase "due process of law."

It is hard to disagree with the Civil Liberties Union, which asserts that Oswald could never have received a fair trial. He was convicted by the police and, thereupon and therefore, by the news media, neither of whom have any business convicting or acquitting anyone. It is hard to disagree with those who oppose turning the Ruby trial into a public spectacle, even though his guilt will be admitted at the outset.

For a long time now, in this age of publicity, we have been debasing the very things by which we must live. We have debased the word "fame" by substituting "celebrity." We have elevated the athlete over the scholar, the police and prosecutor over the judge, the public arena over the courtroom. Justice by publicity is not justice. We have reached the point where most of the ablest lawyers in the country refuse to take criminal cases for fear of taint by publicity, as we were once in the condition where most of the best lawyers were afraid to take loyalty cases. The late Senator McCarthy did not invent guilt by accusation—we were getting there on our own—but he helped condition this society to the strange and frightening process.

What the Dallas police did in the case of Oswald any number of other police in other cities have done in the cases of hundreds of other suspects. Even the FBI, which by the uncanny inversions of publicity has become more sacrosanct than our highest court, has declared men guilty before any trial was held. It has been common practice for police at all levels to announce confessions which ought not be revealed outside a courtroom.

What ought to be our most august law-making body, the United States Senate, has felt unembarrassedly free to provide a national platform so that the cheapest of cheap crooks could broadcast accusations against men not yet tried and found guilty. The news media have simply gone along in most cases. Indeed, we have endured the spectacle of microphones and cameras thrust at a suspect freshly caught and handcuffed with the demanding question, "Why did you do it?"

A certain number of lunatics at large is something any society has to endure. But a spreading disrespect for the legal procedures without which the substance of law, and therefore of order, cannot be protected is not endurable and need not continue. This wretched condition is not a helpless matter of human nature. It is a matter of offices, organizations and formal codes of conduct. The organizations of policemen, prosecutors, lawyers and journalists have their own codes, written or understood. They have only to live by them.

Since Biblical times and before, wise men have seen and acknowledged that power and money are corrupters. The twentieth century has added a third factor to the list—publicity.

Our period of mourning for the death of a good but mortal spirit is ending as the period of joy for the birth of the immortal spirit of goodness itself is beginning. It is as if we had need for the happening of a month ago to make us remember what we ought to be in this country, as well as for that of 2,000 years ago to make us remember what we ought to be in this life.

. This is the second time in one generation that such a concatenation of events has scraped the bones of our being. The first time was the December season of 1941, when we had to try to believe that all men are brothers and that love shall conquer hatred hard upon the stunning act of organized lunacy known as Pearl Harbor. Twice this American generation has been struck from behind and twice it has tried, in the name of Christ, if not to forget and immediately forgive, at least to save itself from the poison of hatred.

We are an immature people in many minor ways; there are cancer spots of venom and panic in our system. Yet, when the major tests have come upon us the world has observed that we stand steady in our shoes. It is this steadiness that leaves room for goodness. In the American hierarchy of values it is not brilliance or strength or even success that crowns the structure, but goodness. This is the true secret of America, and if so many foreign observers miss it, it is not only because goodness does not make news, but because we do not know how to talk about it except now and then in mawkish embarrassment.

Foreigners are not alone in their misapprehension. There are more than enough native Americans, including the remaining Communists, the white supremacists and the Birchites, who do not understand that the real force which is driving them to defeat is this simple one of good will. It is why "isms" do not take hold in this country, why our economic system is so flexible, why social stratifications, even those of race, break up. It is why, one might observe in passing, the attempt of the Birch Society one week ago to re-stir the hatred by means of full-page advertisements—even before the official mourning period was over—produced more shame than anger.

Where lies the root of this constant groping for goodness? To Jacques Maritain, the French philosopher, it was revealed in the remark of an American friend—"We are bruised souls." He meant the effect of the whole cargo of ancestral sorrows and wounds, and the present cargoes of moral distress and physical poverty that arrive with each arriving ship.

Our bruise, said Maritain, is of an evangelical nature; it has produced compassion. It is, "The deepest reason for the sense of mercy and pity, and the sense of responsibility toward all those in distress, which are rooted in the collective American psyche, deep beneath the hardness and harshness of the hunt for material interests.... This spark of the Gospel lying deep in people who more often than not do not think at all of the Gospel, is not a thing that one speaks of.... It exists, however, and is active in the great mass of the nation. And what is more valuable in this poor world than to find a trace of Gospel fraternal love active among men?"

The sense of civic pride, like the sense of nationality, becomes part of a man's personality in this life. When news came of the absurd county jailbreak, a friend in Dallas said to me with a groan, "They hated us last November, now they will laugh at us."

People are just people. In no fundamental sense whatsoever are the people of Dallas, Texas, different from other Americans, though their professional boosters at times like to think they are. What happened to Dallas is that the principle of randomness in nature—including human nature—caught up with them. It is the principle that makes events come in clusters, from the grouping of the galaxies to the "run of luck" at poker.

The murder of President Kennedy led to the murder of Oswald, which led to the trial of Ruby, which led to the jailbreak. "People will think," said my stricken friend, "that we just can't do anything right."

But Dallas has done many things right, and some things much better than some other American cities, including, it may be argued, its handling of the most difficult civic problem extant —the process of racial integration. Racial hostility is certainly there, but it hardly compares with the massive, sullen hatred developing in New York or Chicago. Dallas has more than enough of crime, but nothing like New York, where the nightly non-fatal shootings and stabbings are so numerous they do not even make the papers. It has acquired more than its share of those bitter little political hate groups, and one reason they stand out so sharply is that they exist in the middle of a human climate that is breezy and openhanded in the best tradition of Western friendliness.

And this brings one to the specific practicalities of why Dallas, or Dallas officialdom at least, *has* done some things wrong, unfortunately at critical moments of her civic history. These mistakes were not due to corruption; they were not due to laziness or ignorance. They were a direct result of this same Western, casual, small-town easiness of nature. The "Big D" is a metropolis in body, but not yet in spirit. It got big too quickly for that. It doesn't want to part with the chummy, back-slapping, first-naming spirit of its youthful Main Street days, and I can't say that I blame it. With sophistication goes formalities; Dallas wants the former but instinctively resists the latter.

By the book, a city hall or a county courthouse ought to be centers of formality, rules and—if possible—dignity. In a medium-sized Western city they become centers of informality. The nickname camaraderie around the Ruby courtroom both beguiles and astounds the European journalists covering the trial.

To go back to the beginning, when the law of randomness caught up with Dallas: when the first policeman to rush into the

Book Depository building saw Oswald sitting in the refectory, of course the man in charge said, "He's okay, he works here." And for the policeman, of course, that was enough. When the press and cameramen wanted a look at Oswald during his transfer from the city jail, of course the chief of police wanted to be accommodating. When Jack Ruby joined the throng, of course the officers let him stay; what was familiar was okay. The courthouse jailer who failed to lock the door behind him I can't fully explain; I suspect those desperadoes had become familiars, too; he probably called them "the boys."

Dallas wants the rewards of big city-ness, but it doesn't want to pay the penalties. One of the certain penalties is the sacrifice of cozy good-fellowship in high places. The police chief who was in office last November 24th is still in office. Everybody likes him as a decent man. Everybody likes Sheriff Bill Decker, too. On the evening of the county jail break, while two or three of the criminals were still at large, Sheriff Bill took his wife out to dinner as he had promised.

The newspaper accounts next morning seemed to take this as a reassuring sign of steady calm.

Dallas has reached the awkward age. It's part boy, part adult; and at the awkward age, very awkward things happen.

The United States right now is like a man who has had a bad fall; he has picked himself up and is feeling himself all over to see if anything vital has broken. The whole purpose of what we have all been seeing in Washington since the assassination is to show us—and everybody else in the world—that *nothing* vital has been broken, that we can just start up where we left off last Friday.

The thing that makes the difference between a mature country and an immature country is the orderly transfer of power. That is the trick; countries that don't master it are in *real* trouble.

Truman to Eisenhower to Kennedy to Johnson: in eleven short years we have seen the trick performed three times. The individuals never outlast the office as they do in some countries. And none of the three men we've just heard confused *himself* with the office; each clearly thought of himself merely as the temporary tenant who would move on when his lease ran out. Each had that curious detachment, as if one part of him was

151

acting while the other part was standing off and watching him act. Each had a sense of humor about the exalted and wretched job.

All three did the job in a different style and created different atmospheres around the White House; they picked different kinds of helpers; they worked at different speeds. None was a brooder. All quickly realized in office that the task was much, much harder than they had anticipated and all of them seemed to grow in office.

Truman and Kennedy seemed to enjoy the exercise of power most of the time; Eisenhower some of the time. All knew that *words,* at certain moments, are *deeds.* Truman and Eisenhower seemed to struggle with their words, as if the words got in their way; Kennedy, whose formal education was extensive, enjoyed the use of words for their own sake as well as for their effect.

Now Lyndon Baines Johnson will learn of the office as we learn of him. He comes to the office possessing, very probably, fewer illusions about it than any of his three predecessors. Harry Truman was a product of Main Street, Midwest; Dwight Eisenhower of the special military life; John Kennedy of the Eastern intellectual life. But it is a question whether Lyndon Johnson can be a product of Texas. It may be more to the point to say that he is a product of Washington, D.C., the first President in more than a hundred years of whom this could be said. He has spent no less than thirty-two years in Washington; that is more than half his entire life. No other man in our history has come to the Presidency with such a background. Robert Taft was called "Mr. Republican." Sam Rayburn was sometimes called "Mr. Democrat." One is tempted to call Lyndon Johnson "Mr. Government."

What is important right now is not his views on this issue or that one, but his fundamental approach to the art of governing. He has been the politician par excellence, and, as Harry Truman said, it is politicians who make the whole thing work. Politics is the art of the possible. With Johnson this is not just a cliché, it is almost his credo. He never supported lost causes. One biographer noted that his most frequently used adjectives are "prudent," "reasonable," "responsible." His favorite quotation is from Isaiah: "Come, let us reason together."

There is not much point in asking ourselves if he is a good administrator; he was, as Senate leader. But the Presidency is not essentially a matter of administration. As Franklin Roosevelt said, that is the least of it. It is an art, a personal art, not a science or a business.

This country has no national gods, no king, no Delphic oracle, no Platonic academy of the all-wise. We have only the President. We act sometimes as if opinion polls and committees and the mechanics or organization can find the way for us, but again and again we are thrown back to the old, simple truth that only a man—*one* man—can lead us.

But where do we want to go? Pretty certainly, to a new frontier we thought we had crossed long ago—to national unity, to the old sense of being Americans together. For we are badly divided, as recent events have shown, in our towns and cities. We are badly divided in the federal government, where the checks have dominated in our system of checks and balances.

Lyndon Johnson's special genius as Senator was as the conciliator, the man who got opposing men and ideas to go together. He is now the man *of* the hour. He could be the man *for* the hour.

He doesn't represent Texas anymore, he represents America. As Woodrow Wilson said of Presidents in general—"Let him once win the admiration and confidence of the country and no other single force can withstand him. . . . if he rightly interpret the national thought and boldly insist upon it, he is irresistible."

The difference between the men and the boys in politics is, and always has been, that the boys want to be something, while the men want to do something. The men, in other words, love power and the exercise thereof.

Under the modern conditions of Presidential government our system can only limp along without one of the men in the White House, and it is abundantly clear that with the possible exception of Theodore Roosevelt no Vice-President (and few elected Presidents) has ever laid hands upon the levers of power with such zest as has Lyndon Johnson. He's happy in his work, not merely in his new address. John F. Kennedy knew what he was doing—with more than the campaign in mind—when he chose Johnson as his running mate in 1960.

Those previously acquainted with the man knew perfectly well what a geyser of energy was bottled up in the Vice-Presidency; now everybody knows it. But how ludicrous are the workings of publicity! A couple of months ago the "Candid Camera" of television claimed to demonstrate that not a man or woman in the streets could identify the man called Lyndon B. Johnson. The other day an opinion poll had Johnson at the top of the list of "most admired persons" in the world. All that such polls really indicate is who has been getting the most non-harmful publicity; in no way do they reflect any careful weighing of virtues and faults, and their results change with rather hopeless rapidity.

The point about this, nevertheless, is its proof that Johnson has achieved a startlingly quick success in his first aim—the establishment of himself as a household name and face in a favorable manner. He must be master of the household before he can be master of the political battlefield. In the process the special characteristic of his identity or "image" will have to take form—already is taking form. It will not be charm, glamor or intellectuality, as with Kennedy. It will not be warmth of personality, as with Eisenhower, or the homespun characteristic of Truman. Simply put, it will be strength. If all goes well with him, his public image will be that of the "boss"—more so than with any recent President save Roosevelt.

It seems clear that he not only feels and wants this, subjectively, but that he understands objectively that this is the only posture remaining and appropriate to him. It is hard to escape the conviction that some time before November 22nd he had thought out his actions and his personal posture should fate shove him into the White House. If this is so, then Johnson, as well as Kennedy, possesses that curious, self-analytical quality of the "double vision." As he acts he observes himself in action.

Perhaps this is to say no more than that most highly successful performers on the great stage of public affairs are intensely self-conscious individuals. Not all, but most—certainly most of those who seek the heady wine of popular, electoral endorsement and have their consciousness of self fortified thereby. Those who end up in appointed positions on the great stage tend to have much less awareness of self—a Dean Rusk or a McNamara or a Dillon. Those who go the political route have, like actors, more than the normal allotment of vanity. This ought to bother no one, because it implies, first of all, belief in oneself. Our vainest captain in the great war, MacArthur, was probably also our ablest. We are not led by saints, after all, or even by Lincolns; and if we never again see the humble, chastened Lyndon Johnson that we saw in his first address to the Congress, so be it. He is what he is. Efforts by a President or by his advisors to change a President's normal and natural behavior are always mistaken and always fail.

In any case, the normal and natural Johnson is a considerable human bundle, bulkier than any present we had a right to expect under our tree this particular Christmas. It is perfectly clear what the basic strategy of the President and his advisors will be all the way to the November election. Under all circumstances they will nourish and fortify this impression of size and strength. Their present intention is to make the Republican opponent, whoever he is, look like a pygmy in contrast, as did Roosevelt three times running.

Of course, the best-laid plans of men, as well as mice, can go astray. If intervening events do cut Johnson down to life-size, they would almost surely have to be domestic events. Events abroad, no matter how distressing, nearly always fortify the incumbent President, as Eisenhower proved in the fall of 1956, when he had, in fact, lost control of the Alliance. The electoral effect of a shocking increase in unemployment or of the Negro "revolution" run wild in the streets could be something quite different.

The Johnson era formally began with his State of the Union address. It was not quite a speech as the term is usually understood for such occasions; it was a legislative shopping list of items the national household requires, in numbered sequence. It dealt with the quantities in American material life, not with the qualities of the American character, intellect, environment or dream. It was in the direct line of succession from New Deal, Fair Deal and New Frontier. But the Johnson Administration is apparently not to be identified with a caption such as those, but with a slogan, "unconditional war on poverty."

The President has said in effect that the number one problem in this era of unparalleled American wealth is American poverty. In the original New Deal Franklin Roosevelt spoke of one-third of the nation as ill-housed, ill-clad, ill-fed. Lyndon Johnson speaks of one-fifth of the nation as too poor to satisfy basic needs.

In thirty years, then, of enormous government-led effort, of an enormous increase in total national production, only 13 percent of the poor have made the climb from distress to comfort.

In almost every paragraph the President's address reflected the imbalance, the wild extremes in the American society: too many of the very old and the very young; too many now living in the sprawling cities, too few in the countryside; those who are rich getting richer, those remaining poor getting poorer.

The average American family income in this country is about $7,000 a year. One-fifth of our families have less than $3,000 a year, the poverty line by government definition. Their share of the national income is decreasing, not increasing, and they pay out a higher percentage of their income in taxes than does much of the middle class.

To improve this startling imbalance is, apparently, the special mission of the Johnson Administration. His approach will proceed on many lines, including housing, medicare, tax cuts, education and a domestic Peace Corps.

The address, prosaic and practical, had an intramural quality about it, directed not so much to the public or world at large, but straight to the legislators who sat before him. It was the ex-headmaster returning to the old school, laying down the line, wasting no time, appealing to common sense, not to the heavens, history or the founding fathers.

There are only about 200 politicking days before the next Presidential nomination, but here in Washington you get the feeling the last shall be first. It is the Democrats who lost their leader, but the Republicans who inherited the immediate problem thereby. The Democrats have an undisputed new leader while the Republicans are drifting toward their old leader—for advice, if not consent.

Mr. Eisenhower is acting as coach and sending a new platoon onto the field, a defensive platoon to hold and stall a while. The offensive platoon, captained by Senator Goldwater, is temporarily benched for repairs. The generality of Republicans will meet nationwide by closed circuit in January to raise funds, but their real problem is to raise a candidate.

The dimensions of the change produced by the Johnson Presidency and future candidacy are becoming apparent. The Republican problem is how to get at him, from either the left or the right. To resort to the standard metaphor, the Johnson bandwagon is not only occupying the middle of the political road —its wheels extend well into both the left lane *and* the right lane.

He has big labor pledged to his support and has already disarmed and reassured much of big business. Negro leaders are giving him the benefit of the doubt and Southern white leaders aren't exactly mad at him. If no large groups are wildly for him so far, no large groups are against him, either; he not only covers the middle of the ideological and social spectrums, but the age spectrum, too. To revise the war-time song slightly, he's neither too old nor too young, neither too gray nor too grassy green. The whole Republican problem is to find the man who can find the chink in all this armor. Any candidate with whom bronco-busters as well as coronary victims can identify is hard to get round.

The outlines of President Johnson's vital relationships—to his work day, to the American public, to the Congress and to the critical foreign problems—are already discernible and quite different from the circumstances that surrounded John F. Kennedy three years ago.

Mr. Johnson is a strong human being, but to his age of fifty-five must be added the few extra years that a past heart attack enforces upon a man in terms of his daily conduct. Here the new President is his own worst enemy. He is not only a driving, obsessive worker, but he engages strong emotions in his work, more than did any of his three immediate predecessors. The circumstances of succession to the Presidency are so disturbing right now that President Johnson's first and plain duty to the country, regardless of his personal wishes, is to carefully control his work compulsions and avoid exhaustion.

In these early days he has the overwhelming sympathy and support of the American people, as did Harry Truman in 1945. Soon his degree of popular support will be what he himself—and the enemies that will arise—make it. Manner is not so likely to be confused with matter. The eyes of the press, and therefore of the people, will be more on what he does and less on how he does it, because he will not benefit by the public fascination with youth, style and glamor that so strengthened Mr. Kennedy's hold on the people. Here his problem in following Mr. Kennedy is not entirely unlike Truman's problem in following Roosevelt. It is more severe in that Truman had four years in which to prove himself and Johnson has one.

For this reason, among others, he is bound to concentrate his considerable personal powers on the Congress, the chief block to action, seeking his biggest success where his predecessor suffered his worst failure—in the realm of domestic legislation. When Mr. Kennedy assumed office there was an electric feeling, at least around the White House, that a new day had dawned, that a sharp break with the past could be made. There was much illusion in this, but, acting upon the belief, President Kennedy poured upon the Congress an enormous cargo of proposals. President Johnson cannot do this and would not. The phrase "politics is the art of the possible" is not a cliché to his mind, it is virtually his credo. His whole behavior as Senate Majority Leader demonstrated this. He operated a two-track legislative highway. On the main track he pushed unceasingly at those matters he judged *could* get through. To the side-track he relegated all those matters he judged could *not* get through, no matter how many powerful groups thought they were of prime importance. For the present, of course, the priority of the tax and civil-rights bills has been settled for him. On these he will concentrate his full energies, and in my opinion will have more success than Mr. Kennedy would have had, not only because of the country's chastened mood, but because he will be much rougher in private on obstructive Congressmen. Here he will be like Franklin Roosevelt, save in manner; Mr. Roosevelt cut political throats with the air of one saying it hurt him more than the victim.

When President Kennedy took office he found some fluidity in foreign affairs. His creations, such as the Alianza and the Peace Corps, were imaginative, and his act of defiance over the Cuban missiles an historic stroke. But President Johnson now confronts an immobility in world affairs such as Mr. Kennedy confronted in domestic affairs. It is the great powers that have been losing their ability to act; it is the small powers that are creating what movement there is.

This is true in our relations with our major enemy and it is true in relation to our major allies. The Alliance cannot be held as it is unless the problem of sharing nuclear power is solved, and it cannot be solved without a common agreement on the German role. All present signs are that President Johnson will continue to press for the multi-national nuclear fleet, including the Germans, that he will give no encouragement to De Gaulle's nuclear aspirations or general view of the future Europe. The leaders are new—in America, Britain, Germany and Italy—but the old dilemma of the West is unchanged.

The oval-shaped office of the President of the United States is a lovely room: books, flowers, glass doors giving out on the lawns and magnolias. In Roosevelt's day thirty or forty of us would crowd in there for a news conference, using pencil and notebook, and inform the world, as best we could, of the Presidential mind.

That was B.T.—before television. The three of us who talked for an hour in front of the cameras with President Johnson consumed maybe a tenth of that room; electronic machinery took up most of the rest of it. But what a difference in the net result! The machinery, when a man relaxes with it, is his servant, not his master. Mr. Johnson made it serve him this time, and the result, I suspect, was that the American people got their first palpable, sensory feeling of the man and what makes him tick.

What is the essential Johnson? The tough and restless wheeler-dealer? Or the patient, soft-spoken gentleman humbly conscious of his grave responsibilities? Well, human beings are complex entities; Mr. Johnson is more complex than most, and I suspect all these items of characterization are part of the total character. The great office cannot put into a man something that wasn't there to begin with. It can, and almost always does, bring *out* his best characteristics, however hidden they may have been. In that sense, the office is transforming the man as the man is slowly but surely transforming the office and the whole tone in Washington. My own dominant impression was that of his force of personality. I had not met him in several years, and I did not remember him as quite this erect, slim and composed; in time the office will put lines of fatigue in his face, but if a middle-aged man ever can be said to bloom, he's blooming right now.

I don't know if my two colleagues, William Lawrence and David Brinkley, had the same feeling about the whole setting, but my feeling was that of being in the calm eye of the hurricane. The newsfilms each day are tense with the world's violence, page one black with the world's angers and dangers. But in that oval room, the focus of all these turbulent forces of a jostling humanity, there is quiet—not the quiet of the scholar's cluttered study, but that humming quiet of an orderly engine room where all the parts are oiled and working. The number one headquarters of the world seems under control, even if the world isn't.

Human beings are about to turn over the calendar page and say goodbye to that fraction of time known as 1963, but there is nothing much to suggest that in our individual or collective forms we are turning over a new leaf, that either sweet reason or senselessness will rule in 1964. Presumably we shall trudge along in our normal proportions of general goodness and general cussedness. Still, the atmosphere contains suspicion that affairs have been so arranging themselves that cussedness will have harder going in the coming year.

It is a little hard to believe that, at home, we will repeat a year in which a President, a Negro leader and several little girls were assassinated, the latter within a church, sanctuary even in the Middle Ages. It is easier to believe that in the world at large we can repeat a year in which the major forces for danger held pretty steady, in which the icebergs of the Cold War melted a little, at least above the water line. There is more reason now than for some years to feel that in the interactions among nations, especially the great nations, the forces for order are stronger than the forces for disorder. Like all hunches, this one could be proved wrong by an overnight event, but it happens to be very difficult to see just where such an event could develop. There seem to be no likely candidates—not even Berlin.

There was much wild talk among nations in 1963, but very little wild action, and no grand confrontations. Indeed, it seems fair enough to say that the outstanding behavioral characteristic of the nations in the past year was restraint. That is a long way from peaceableness, but one of its prerequisites. No adventure remotely comparable to the Soviet adventure in Cuba in 1962 was attempted; even the fire-breathing Chinese walked softly around the borders of India and made no noticeable effort to extend or intensify the war in Viet-Nam. At least for the time being they are going easy on Korea and Formosa, as well; whatever their talk, they seem to have no stomach for a real risk of nuclear war.

A *pax atomica* is by no means the ideal kind of peace, but it is the kind we have, and it is serving its purpose this side of a real spread of atomic weapons into irresponsible hands. The hands that now hold them are intensely, painstakingly responsible, and are likely to remain so, notwithstanding the efforts of overheated authors to imagine catastrophe by accident or panic.

There has been measurable cause for President Johnson's claim before the United Nations that, "The world has become a little safer, the way ahead a little brighter."

Quite clearly, the process known as the "depolarization" of the political world has continued in this past year, and almost, as it were, against the will of the great powers, America included. Small islands of political strength or at least stubbornness have emerged all around the world, and we have been less able to exercise our will within our system of alliances, as the Russians have been less able to exercise their will within their system. One cannot yet be sure, but there is the chance that the great lesson of this period will be that there is safety in numbers in a sense not originally intended by that phrase—in the sense of diversity.

Since it is the Communists who push and drive the hardest against diversity, who strive for a monolithic world, in their own pattern, it seems reasonable to look at this developing condition as a gain for the West and what it stands for. The strength of Western culture and its economic systems are proving far stronger than the Communists anticipated, and far more of a lure and example for the new little nations than they had thought. In any case, simple nationalism, especially the brand-new nationalism of the "emergent" peoples, is a more powerful motivation than any ideology. In the long run our interests can prosper under such conditions; the interests of Communism cannot.

Revolutions, coups, acts of aggression there will be in the year ahead; local Communist victories there may well be. But there is little reason to think that the paralysis of the great powers imposed by the atom will not continue. Great power adventures and confrontations seem less and less likely. Within this over-all straitjacket the wildest antics of small nations can be endurable. If this is so, then the chief item of business on the new calendar of reasonable men on both sides of the Iron Curtain is to see that other nations do not obtain the atomic weapon.

7

Governments
Are Not People

June–November 1961

I hope American nerves are strong; I know American heads are be-fogged.

The showdown with the Communist world conspiracy is on. We have entered the final stage of the long struggle to determine if we can hold our world position short of a great war. We are in that stage because Khrushchev has decided we are. He will act accordingly, which will force us to act accordingly—if we can clear our heads.

He did his best at Vienna to make us understand, just as Hitler did, time after time. It is wrong to think Khrushchev said nothing new. When he said, "No negotiations on anything unless it suits us tactically. No disarmament agreement, no test stoppage agreement, no U.N. save on our terms, no letup on Berlin"—when he said all this in effect, he was saying, "We have you. Why go on with the chess game?"

He has concluded that the Western Alliance cannot be pulled together; that North Africa will soon be wide open to Communist exploitation with Central Africa to follow; that Southeast

162

Asia is rapidly crumbling into Communist hands; that our Latin American flank is being turned. He is now sure that the great game of isolating the United States, then impoverishing it, then breaking its will is all over save for our helpless, thrashing convulsions, which will be interesting and from time to time dangerous.

No doubt there are after-hours parlor games in the Kremlin these nights. Betting pools, for example, on the precise month when the U.S., driven desperate by Castro's subversion of other Latin regimes, threatens to use force, whereupon Castro laughingly points out that he has short-range missile emplacements aimed at the lovely white city of Miami and would we care to test his will to use them?

I imagine they play an uproarious game of "Can you top this?" reading selected items from the British and American press. The passionate claims of British Socialists that Britain will have *more* world influence if she gives up her atomic weapons must be a consistent funny-bone tickler. These days they must particularly cherish the Whitehall–Lippmann theory that if we show willingness to re-negotiate West Berlin, the Reds will obligingly give us at the bargaining table a *stronger* position than we have now.

Surely they adore reading the worrying, hair-shirt arguments that the United States must not do this or that because it will offend "world opinion," knowing as they do that there is no such thing in the moralistic sense—the proof of which is that after all their crimes, including Hungary, they enjoy more influence and respect in the world than ever. They must love the British–American notion that the bosses of the new, "neutral" nations are somehow more high-minded and spiritual than those of the committed nations.

They must have shaken their heads in happy disbelief when they read that conservative newspaper executives, calling on the President, said "no," when he asked if they accepted his premise that the United States has entered the most critical period of its history. And they must love the large school of professional American liberals who assume that any given country, however barren and illiterate, however profound its background of violence and chieftainship, is capable not only of economic modernization, but of parliamentary democracy.

The liberals with social-worker mentalities do not grasp that illiteracy, low wages, concentrated land ownership and so on are not "social problems," but integral parts of a *system* of life and, therefore, enormously resistant to quick change by anything less than the "totalitarian disciplines" the same liberals abhor. The liberals assume that, because a Marshall Plan worked in modern Europe, a similar plan can work among those regimes of Latin America, where statistics are wild guesses, where trained economists hardly exist, where economic planning is finger painting, where, as between countries, there is very little background of communications, normal trade or even intellectual interest in one another.

The gamesmen in the Kremlin must smile in their sleep as they realize how deeply ingrained is the American illusion that a ton of wheat can offset a ton of Communist artillery shells, that a squad of Peace Corpsmen is a match for a squad of guerrilla fighters.

But I hope they frowned a bit when they read the angry retort of Defense Secretary McNamara when he heard, for the umpteenth time, the pious theory that the Communists were gaining in Laos and South Viet-Nam because the regimes there are "unresponsive to the people's needs." A burning sense of reality on a short fuse can make a quiet man shout (as I'm afraid it makes me shout these days) and McNamara shouted that the Communists are gaining in those countries for very simple reasons known as guns, bombs, fighters and threats.

Frightened people in a score of desperate countries want to be on the winning, not necessarily the moral, side; and we have to start winning soon. We are going to lose in several more places before we do. We may as well face the fact that we will also lose in places we cannot afford to lose, until and unless we are willing to fight no matter the reproving editorials in the Manchester *Guardian,* no matter what the temporary backlash of "world opinion" may be. The relations between nations are not the same as those between individuals. We can afford to lose everything—except respect for our strength and determination. Lose that, and Khrushchev won't bother to sit down and talk again, even to say "no."

Noting, but not examining General Eisenhower's ambidextrous performance in ridiculing the Peace Corps while accepting the chairmanship of the "People to People" organization, which is based on the same premise, we might look at the popular, chiefly

American notion that if only people alien to each other could "get to know one another," peace will be preserved.

History not only suggests but insists that while the by-products of personal and cultural exchanges across frontiers are many and important, peace is not necessarily numbered among them. If there were a direct relation between acquaintanceship and peace, then generations of a saturating intercourse through tourist travel, literature, science, music and the visual arts should have produced something else between Germany and her neighbors than three ghastly wars in seventy years. Then the American Civil War should never have happened. Its opposing participants were hardly strangers to one another; some were of the same family.

Physiologically, "all men are essentially the same," but in terms of ideas and illusions they are not, and it is illusions and ideas that set great movements in motion, including wars. Contrasting ideas do not always merge and soften by conversational contact. Indeed, the more contact I have had with hard-core Russian Communists the more inimical I feel, the wider the chasm grows, the more frightened I become of their prefabricated, mechanical minds; and, presumably, they feel the same.

As things now stand, the only form of "greater understanding" between Russians and Americans that is conducive to peace is the mutual understanding that if one tries to destroy the other, he will himself be destroyed.

We have to assume that Communism is not even remotely an alternative way of life, but is, in fact, a political weapon designed for the simple seizure of power. We have to assume that the likeliest—perhaps the only—practical road toward peace lies in the slowing and eventual halting of the Communist advance. Therefore, all person-to-person contact with the Communist world must be designed to weaken their resolve, which is exactly the design of all the contacts they initiate toward us.

Not always does the chasm widen. Occasionally they win a victory, as in the case of the nationally circulated columnist who recently informed millions of Americans that we must get used to the idea that "Communism isn't really all that bad." More often they lose; individual defections from traveling Russian delegations are a familiar story. They will continue to happen in spite of the severely hand-picked nature and the severe supervision of their cultural emissaries. They will happen in spite of the fact, discovered by American investigators, that one-fourth of their visitors are repeaters, returned here because of their proven trustworthiness and proven abilities as intelligence agents or propagandists. We have something to gain, little to lose, by continuing these exchanges, and we would gain more if all our own emissaries to Russia were trained debaters.

There is a certain amount of hunger for information about the West in Russia itself—and this is not true in reverse. But the assembly halls of Moscow University and the conference rooms at Black Sea resorts are not exactly soft spots in the Communist intellectual fortress. The soft spots are in the satellite countries. Historically, the Slavic peoples of eastern Europe provided the willing transmission belt for getting Western ideas into Russia. If East Germany is now a fenced-in intellectual desert, Poland is fairly open to our efforts, and there, if anywhere, should our efforts be concentrated.

Governments, for most countries, decide peace or war, and governments do not always or often behave like individuals, which is where so many well-meaning Americans get confused. But there remain governments on this earth which are subject to degrees of popular feelings conditioned by personal exchanges.

Thousands of "returned students" from America proved ineffective when the Communists conquered the mainland of China; all their training was a waste. Scores of devoted Western missionaries have been tortured and killed by the very African nationalists whose aspirations we had endorsed. Yet there can be little doubt that a generation's work by American schoolteachers in the villages of the Philippines had much to do with that country's generally good relations with us.

Nkrumah of Ghana was embittered by his experiences in America as a student and his present policies may stem in part from that. Yet a couple of hundred miles from his old Danish presidential palace Azikewe of Nigeria sits as governor-general in the old English palace at Lagos. He is equally black; he, too, was a young student in America, but for him the American experience fortified belief in democracy.

Personal exchanges cut the ice both ways; on the whole, I think, the larger portion goes to us. Even on a massive scale they could not guarantee peace. But they can slowly, bit by bit, weaken the force and attraction of Communism, the serious debilitation of which will be the ultimate guarantor of peace.

Until the other day when Khrushchev promulgated the new Communist charter and vision for his people we had been worrying exclusively about what Russian Communism was doing to other peoples, and it comes as a wrench to start grieving about what it is going to do to the Russian people. It is going to impose affluence and leisure upon them, and they ought to be warned.

In the same document in which Khrushchev declares that the United States and other Western societies are past their zenith and in decline he sets out a detailed schedule for the Russians to travel precisely the same route. It is the first time that Socialist planning anywhere has included suicide as a goal and named the date.

In twenty years, says the document, everyone will live in easy circumstances, all collective and state farms will become highly productive and profitable, the demands of the Soviet people for well-appointed housing will in the main be satisfied, hard physical work will disappear, and the U.S.S.R. will become the country with the shortest working day.

Obviously the Russian censorship concerning life abroad has left the Russian people in the dark, and the full horror of what is planned for them has not yet penetrated their minds. That is the trouble with their closed society—they are unable to spy out the secret weaknesses of enemy countries and fall right into the capitalist trap.

As is well known, the strength of the democratic system is that it forces its opponents to imitation. As soon as their farms become highly productive, they will realize an anti-Marxist fact: people can eat only so much bread or potatoes or rice a day. Ugly aluminum storage bins will deface the broad vistas of the steppes. Strawberries will rot on the ground, little pigs will be plowed under, but in Moscow restaurants and supermarkets the price of both strawberries and roast pork will continue to rise, leading to a furious campaign against middlemen who have been working a full eight-hour day, the traitors. Walls will be covered with posters saying the revolution has come and you'll eat strawberries.

This will do no good and black markets will develop, people secretly trading carloads of strawberries for valuable antiques like peasant stoves, icons, carts and village pumps. Dwellers in millions of well-appointed homes will spend their leisure time carting their high-fi and TV sets, their automatic toasters, washers, drippers and dryers and disposals to and from the repair shops—between trips to the garage to see how they're coming with the distributor on the sports car.

167

After a while wives will ask husbands to sit for a little talk after the children are in bed. Millions of couples will conclude that their life has become overcomplicated. They just don't seem to have the time for each other as they did in the old days when he worked the night shift and she worked the day shift—and why don't they all go on a long camping trip, learn to work with their hands again and get back to the simple life? A walking trip, of course, to avoid the traffic.

Other husbands will conclude that this business of sitting around the house half of each day is getting on the wife's nerves and losing dad the respect of his children through over-familiarity. Anyway, he's bored with the do-it-yourself set of tools, with the free lessons in Chinese on TV, and has discovered he's no good at water colors, let alone oils. So he decides on "moonlighting" and drives a taxi at night, shrinking under the "nyaahs" of the regular drivers as they deliberately brush his fenders at the stop lights. Leaders in dentistry will call all-Soviet conferences to campaign against children buying sweets with their large allowances because, as in Britain, they average about six cavities per mouth. The party itself will proclaim a physical-fitness campaign, because the age of the auto has softened the leg muscles of the youth, as in America, and football coaches and army instructors are viewing with alarm. A TV series will deride "The Fat Comrade."

A commission will be formed of leading intellectuals to define "The Soviet Purpose," and to set new moral and spiritual goals for their people. A new phrase will be invented, "The Lost Generation." Idealistic college boys will drink coffee all night while complaining that their fathers had all the fun—revolution, war, conquest, purges and slave-labor camping. The Kremlin (that part of it not torn down for new parking space) will be overrun with emissaries from backward countries demanding grants and soft-currency loans and threatening to turn to America if Moscow doesn't kick in. New schools will be set up to train foreign aid administrators, some of whom will be ridiculed in a book called "The Ugly Russian."

Visiting lecturers from Asia and Africa will inform uneasy Soviet audiences that "The trouble with you Russians is that you want to be liked, when you should want to be respected. You are trying to buy everybody's friendship and it can't be done. We suggest you make a small start by persuading your tourists abroad to stop throwing heavy tips around, which only earns

you the contempt of our people. Ruble worship, you must realize, is not an exportable religion to older cultures."

Khrushchev's new document opens the way for a brand-new
Western foreign policy called "self-containment." All we have to
do is sit tight for twenty years and the Russians will do themselves in.

London

In Berkeley Square the first of the crisp, yellow oak leaves
are sailing across the streets, tinkling against the showcase of the
Rolls-Royce salesroom and the windows of the old house where
Clive of India lived. Grouse and partridge, shot this week in the
heather and stubble, hang in the open markets. The morning
air is cool to the lungs. This reporter is leaving the muted tones
of old Europe in the loveliest of autumns for the hard colors, the
thrust and vitality of his homeland, and not without some pangs.

I suppose Americans who love not only their own land, but
their civilization, their heritage, will always feel this way, their
hearts always pulled a little, eastward and westward, as they cross
and re-cross the Atlantic. You want to be among your compatriots whose will and drive and competence you really trust, in
the land that is more than ever the "last, best hope" of man. But
somehow we have become the guardians, the trustees at long
distance of the cultural homeplace, this Europe, this garden of
the senses, this translucent meadow of grace and custom and continuity. You feel responsible, even when you leave.

All the arts of living are accumulated here, and life in Europe is very good. You feel the beautiful complexity of this marvelous work of man on this "extension of Asia." And then you
see that porcine Russian face squinting over his brick wall, cemented by human blood, enclosing the social piggery called "East
Germany." You hear the ranting voice announce that everything
on this side of the wall is decaying illusion, that the true garden
of progress is over there to the East, where live the "peace-loving"
in the true brotherhood of man.

Each time he speaks you have a sense of madness loose at
last. You feel almost paralyzed with incredulity, as when Adolf
Hitler roared of the master race from the *sportspalast* in old
Berlin.

Arguments rush to clog the angry brain. They do not know
how to live in Russia and they will never learn so long as that

169

monstrously unnecessary system prevails. Successful, they call it. Any system can be made to work after a fashion if all opposition to it is destroyed long enough, and forty-five years is long enough. Virtually everything was copied from the West. All Russia sweats to have precisely what the West already has, and yet we are told that the West is all wrong, unworkable by the laws of Marx and history. Russia has made a "remarkable recovery" from war's devastation under Communism—but one thinks of West Germany or Italy, both smashed even worse, proportionately, and now providing a higher average standard of life than the Soviet Union. Surely free choice has something to do with this. The whole debate is a joke, but only the gods can laugh.

On the facts the argument is closed. But we have entered a weird and frightening passage of history, where facts are not of consequence. Khrushchev knows the facts and their existence explains much of his rage. Communism as a doctrine is finished. It cannot advance another foot by the momentum of its own "unanswerable logic."

But Russian power advances because the thrust of it is now aimed, not at man's reason, but at his nervous system. This works, in fits and starts, but usually enough for each immediate Soviet purpose. We have thought of the "battle for men's minds" in terms of facts and persuasion. The Communists believe this battle can be more quickly won by instilling fear. Russia lies close and heavy upon Europe, Asia, the Middle East; America is far away, a modulated echo.

Some words of John Foster Dulles are most pertinent: "Few men in political life anywhere act without first thinking whether they will please or displease the leaders of the Soviet Union." Fear has done this, fear of mystery, unpredictability, amorality, ruthlessness, the fear that all normal men always have of the "special strength of the shameless."

Of course, Eisenhower and Dulles failed to "regain the initiative" in world affairs: Of course, Kennedy and Rusk have equally failed. Those driven by a profound, unshakable philosophy of deliberate conflict, those who seek not order, but disorder must always have the initiative. We shall view the world and our own capacities more clearly once we accept this simple law of human society.

But now an ominous thing has happened. The Soviets have acquired the greatest, indeed the ultimate weapon, in this battle for man's nervous system; the central engine for maintaining the initiative is in their possession. They have convinced much of mankind that the decision for peace or war is theirs, that they and they alone are the arbiters of man's final fate. At their indulgent caress the light will keep on shining, or, at their signal, the darkness will engulf us all.

They have convinced half mankind that they hold the mortgage on the earth and they expect a file of quaking tenants seeking terms to pay the interest charges. The principle will never be paid off, for Khrushchev expects to raise the interest rate, higher and higher, if and as his stratagem works.

Now the President anxiously seeks to know how we, too, can engage in "psychological warfare," as distinct from the standard image-creation of normal information and propaganda. I hope he finds a way. Other Americans have tried it in peacetime and failed.

We cannot instill fear of ourselves in others. Many people may dislike us, but fear us they cannot. We cannot work at instilling fear of Russia in others for that would only add grist to Khrushchev's mill. Nor can we become the youthful, dashing, unconventional leader of the worldwide "revolution of rising expectations." I dearly wish to be wrong on this. But we are not the America of Tom Paine, and I can think of no backward land likely to accept us in that role. As a generous, patient, richer uncle, yes.

For the moment there is only one thing we can do, but it is basic to everything that may follow. We can decide in our hearts that we will truly risk war rather than pay the kind of blackmail that would start a rush of tenants to Khrushchev's door. We have to decide this and somehow convince the enemy of our decision. There is no other way.

Berlin
June 24, 1963

The bizarre becomes the customary in time, familiarity breeds boredom if not contempt, so there are now one or two stations at the infamous Wall—including the place where President Kennedy stood—which Berlin friends will describe to one as "just a tourist trap."

History moves rapidly in this century; what may be the first city wall to be constructed in Europe since medieval times already looks old as sin, as well as ugly as death. Each stretch and turning of the gray cement is already invested with story and legend; the Wall has a sated air of permanence about it.

Still, it does not hint of the future half so explicitly as it calls up the past. To stand by it in the gray gloom of evening at the Potsdamerplatz, once the bright, busy heart of greater Berlin, to see the cement blocks, the tangles of barbed wire, the rows of steel-studded tank traps beyond is to be transported back to the war and the Siegfried Line. In the twilight and the rain the platz is an island of desolation, a sick dream from the past of the European insanity, hanging on in the rational present.

At American University, just before he came here, the President intimated that the Cold War might begin to end if men would begin to alter their habitual thinking about it—Westerners as well as the Russians. Our thoughts must be liberated before the world can be liberated, he seemed to say. But for Berliners the Cold War is the structure of their physical lives and no thoughts of theirs can make the Wall come down. The Berlin question cannot be settled until the German question is settled, and there can hardly be an end to the Cold War until that is accomplished, whatever the agreements on nuclear testing, however unbridgeable the gulf between Moscow and Peking. Where the first real breakthrough toward an East-West rapprochement will come no mortal man can say. The Potsdamerplatz in a drizzling twilight seems a poor candidate for the honor.

West Berlin has become a state of mind, to a surprising degree. When a uniformed soldier turned our car away from one western approach to the Wall, my Berlin-born driver, twenty-three years old, snorted. "Those Germans!" he exclaimed. I said, "Well, you're a German, aren't you?" "I'm a *Berliner*," he stated firmly. He was convinced the people of Berlin were different, superior to the generality of Germans, even those in the western Republic. He did not feel a spiritual identity with them. "Would they give up their TV sets and their new cars if that were the price of re-unification?" he said. "I wonder!"

I suspect he would be proved wrong were that test to come about. In spite of appearances the Germans are not essentially a materialistic race; materialism happens to be the only ism around for the following at the moment. They have shown their capacity for self-conscious sacrifice before, to everybody's sorrow, often enough.

This country is struggling toward a new role in the world, truncated though it is, and it feels its strength more and more.

It is perfectly aware that it provides most of the conventional defense against the East, that its bank balances are bulkier than any others in Europe, that it is shoving Great Britain out of her third place among the world's industrialized nations. It remains intensely aware of what it owes to the United States, even if Britain and France have forgotten, but it is not likely to continue for long as a completely obedient policy client and ward.

The American military presence is more intensely important to Germany than to France or Britain, but there is less worry here than there that the Yanks will suddenly decide to pull out one day. There is probably less worry about an American "deal" with Moscow and much less fussing about the so-called "Americanization of Europe." (America, after all, has been Europeanized for 300 years.)

It is impossible to think of this country submitting to a French leadership of Europe. Germany is becoming the most vital nation in Europe and knows it; she is becoming, willy-nilly, America's key ally in Europe, and she knows that, too. It remains only for an anti-nuclear Labour government to replace the Conservatives in England and for a patched-up political coalition— possibly Popular Front in structure—to replace De Gaulle in France, for Germany's new position in the Alliance to be revealed to everybody, the Russians not included, since they go to sleep with this thought on their minds every current night.

August 17, 1963

The extreme right wing in American politics is not likely to prevail in the debate over the nuclear test treaty with Russia, in spite of the respectable doubts of such open-minded men as Senator Jackson, in spite of the clear truth that the treaty by no means implies the end of the worldwide contest with aggressive Communism. The long reach of history is accomplished by such short, often unpremeditated steps; and this seems to be one of those times when it is better to move than to stand, however impossible it may be to identify the next move after that. What we are engaged in with Russia is a game of poker, not chess.

Before this current argument is over the United States will have again demonstrated to the world that if there is any basic flaw in the American world stance it is a leaning toward trust rather than distrust, a deep-seated predilection toward lowering our guard, not toward rigidly and ingrained hostility, in spite of the clamorous, guilt-ridden claims of all those groups which arrogate to themselves the desire for and the label of "peace."

No, if from here on we are led into policy errors by reason of domestic pressures, it will not be the pressure of the overly suspicious right-wing minorities but the pressure of the left-wing minorities, who persistently equate American with Communist responsibility for the dangerous condition of the world—those groups which would have us detach from Viet-Nam because its government happens to be nasty in right-wing fashion and which would have us draw closer to Cuba because its nasty regime happens to be left-wing. Brutality itself does not bother these groups; they are concerned only with the words of the torturer's chant as he wields the whip.

One can hope. One can hope, for example, that the tenor and outcome of this debate on the test treaty will demonstrate to these groups and their counterparts in Europe that, while the "military-industrial power structure" of which Eisenhower warned is indeed worth worrying about, it is not determining the foreign and defense policies of this country. President Kennedy and Secretary of Defense McNamara are doing that, as much, if not more, than ever.

One can hope that the tranquilizing effect of the treaty agreement will not put the efforts to reorganize and strengthen NATO, already half-paralyzed, into a coma. It is entirely permissible to believe that this prospect was one of Khrushchev's various purposes in welcoming the agreement.

One can hope, also, that behind Khrushchev's corollary desire to isolate the nuclear ambitions of the Chinese there is not something far more immediate and frightening than a doctrinal disagreement about the worth, in Communist terms, of risking big war. With no hard evidence to support it the nagging thought persists that the Chinese may have been pushing, not merely for doctrinal support from Moscow, but for support of Chinese plans for immediate, overt aggressions, whether against Viet-Nam or South Korea or Formosa or India. It may not be merely the Chinese ideologues who left Moscow in disgust last month, it may be also representatives of the Chinese general staff.

It is a scary notion. Whether or not aggressions do come on such a dire and drastic scale, what we cannot realistically hope for is an end to small-scale Communist aggressions in the Far East or an end to Communist-created alarms and excursions in Latin America, which could easily snowball. The coexistence

Khrushchev has in mind is an intensely competitive coexistence, both political and economic. There is no reason whatsoever to think that he, any more than the dogmatic Chinese, has revised his declaration that "Socialism is working for history," which is a program of action, as distinguished from the old Marxist slogan that "history is working for Socialism," which was an intellectual abstraction.

It is generally and historically true that tyrannies do pass away in time, that doctrines are always diluted by realities, that any church militant tends to become, with prosperity, the established church. And it is also true that these processes, like all social processes, move through their cycles at a faster rate than they did before the modern revolution in communications. But the worst mistake we could make would be to assume, on the evidence of the test ban treaty, that these processes have come to completion, even with the Russians. With the Chinese, of course, the processes have scarcely begun.

São Paulo, Brazil
May 8, 1961

The young Cuban Democrats who fell on the beaches of the Bay of Pigs did not die in vain, nor has United States leadership of the Latin American bloc of nations been wrecked by the double image of aggression and incompetence that we projected in the tragic invasion affair. The more one travels, reads and converses, the more the evidence demonstrates that the mad, defiant gesture of those youthful Cubans won the hearts of millions among the essentially humanistic peoples of Latin America.

Great numbers, especially among the young, have turned furiously and definitely anti-Castro. The former picture of the overbearing Yankee colossus bullying a weak nation is fading, and now the dominating mental image is of a brutish, bullying Castro slavering over the anguish of his victims. By long conditioning most Latin Americans resent the top dog no matter his name or nationality, and Castro, not Kennedy, now suddenly appears top dog here in modernized, industrialized South Brazil.

I have observed the same backlash against the Communists I saw in feudalistic northeast Brazil. For the first time in years the local Reds are openly, even physically, challenged. For the first time anti-Communist students and intellectuals are organizing. After the expected Communist march on the American

175

Consulate here, students broke up a Red rally. Eighteen-hundred of them signed an anti-Castro statement. Leaders of a hundred labor organizations signed another. High school boys marched into the USIS offices demanding pro-American films to be shown in their schools. A band of law students began shaping plans to organize other students in every Latin American country for a continental anti-Communist congress, and from the fire in the eyes of those I met I believe they will do it.

Castro blundered in making a Roman circus of his captives. He has made a more far-reaching blunder in formally proclaiming Cuba a member of the Communist bloc and refusing elections. By this move, as the *Jornal do Brasil* has put it, "Castro burned his ships."

Four leading papers in São Paulo immediately endorsed the Kennedy proposal for joint Latin American sanctions against Cuba, and great numbers of individual liberals, land reformers and generic anti-*Yanquis* are getting off the burning ships as fast as they can. Like the C. Wright Millses and Kenneth Tynans and other "Let's-be-fair-to-Cuba" first-guessers in New York and London, they cannot defend the regime in Cuba now unless they are equally ready to defend the regime in Hungary or Czechoslovakia.

The same phenomenon apparently is occurring in every major South American city. As of right now Castro is not splitting the Latin bloc—he is pulling large parts of it together. Himself he will pull down sooner or later. He is bound to by the uncontrollable drives of his own psyche, even if outside pressures do not touch him, for his is unmistakably the psyche that can exist and feel alive only in crisis and drama, that cannot plan or build or tolerate peace and normalcy, and that has within it the martyr's drive and death wish that forces such a personality to pull down the temple upon himself. He has the emotional structure of the late Joseph McCarthy—brilliant, fearless, bulldozing, heedless, utterly reckless and without plan and impervious to the feelings of others.

The other night I sat in a Brazilian patio with a Cuban lawyer who had gone to school with Castro. He told me the story which I cannot relate in its full maniacal flavor of sixteen-year-old Fidel and the mountain:

"So the professor said to me you go and talk Fidel out of this crazy notion to climb the mountain. So I went to Fidel and in thirty minutes he had talked me into joining his expedition.

So two of us rode the train with Fidel three, four hours. We got off at a village. 'Where is the mountain, Fidel?' we asked him. 'This way,' he said. 'Just follow me.' So we walk, we walk all night. In the morning there is no mountain. 'Just follow me,' Fidel said.

"We walk all day. At night there is still no mountain and we have to sleep. 'How do we sleep here in the jungle?' we ask Fidel. 'We have these tents,' said Fidel. We struggle with the tents and say, 'Fidel, how do we make the tents work?' And he shrugs his shoulders and says, 'How do I know about tents?' So we lie on the ground with the canvas over us like blankets. In the morning we have no more food and Fidel says, 'We find food some way, I guess.' So we eat some fruit on the way, but we are very hungry. We walk all day again and sleep the same way, hungry, all bitten by mosquitoes, filthy, but we find the mountain."

"Did you climb it?" I asked.

"Of course we climb it. You cannot stop Fidel, you cannot argue with Fidel. We climb it, and the Fidel Castro expedition gets in the papers and everything, but the thing was, when we get down, we find there is a smooth road right from the railroad to the foot of the mountain and we could have found the mountain in three, four hours of walking. What a leader! This Fidel he gets where he is going, but I tell you, he never know how, he don't care how, to make plans is a bore to Fidel. He just goes, goes and you got to go with him, or too bad."

October–November 1962

An hour after President Kennedy had delivered his ultimatum to Soviet Russia, in those moments when the human spirit was everywhere numbed, I happened to be standing with a group in a Los Angeles street. One man said, "Well, this proves that it really can happen"—meaning Armageddon, "the great day of God."

A few minutes after Khrushchev capitulated, six days later, I was with a group in a New York office, and one man said, "This proves it really can't happen"—meaning that no government, however irresponsible, will set it off.

Would that there were some alchemy by which to analyze all the factors of human motivation and response in the Cuban affair and produce a finding. But proof or disproof is not there to be found, I am afraid. The minds and the factors involved over Cuba will not necessarily be the same, one, five or ten years from now. Not even the Cuban crisis revealed a governing rule of human behavior for this age of overkill.

Nevertheless, various less apocalyptic but vital truths to guide our conduct were revealed by those six days of quiet terror. Among them, so I at least believe, were these:

Khrushchev, leader of the more open, supposedly "status-quo-minded" Russia, can be quite as conspiratorial and reckless as Stalin, if the stakes seem important enough.

Russia remains the weaker in the continuing struggle by both sides to gain an uncatchable superiority in strategic positions and tactical power. No true plateau of nicely balanced power is likely to be reached, and therefore there is no chance for true disarmament unless we hold our superiority in power.

There might be under that condition, if prolonged enough, some chance that another generation of Communist leaders will give up the contest, recognizing and accepting at last that Western societies are unaggressive by the nature of their position at this point in time. To this generation of Communists no political status quo is acceptable because, in their view of history, evanescent. Indeed, to the younger ones of this generation, the Castros and Guevaras, the violent process of revolution remains the goal and the joy, not the fruits of revolution.

All this means, I am afraid, that the "equity" argument—if we satisfy their security requirements, they will satisfy ours, and the contest can continue by peaceable means—falls once more to the ground, to be picked up yet again, I am also afraid, by the neutralists, the British Socialists and their intellectual compatriots everywhere.

We are reminded that we must not simply assume that this world contest is a "battle for men's minds" or that the winning side will be the side that "proves it can do the most for people." The winning side may be the one that holds the strongest power positions.

We are reminded that with predominant power goes predominant responsibility and that this includes the responsibility, when our case is sound, to create Allied solidarity by acting, not by waiting for it to solidify first; that "world opinion" is also created, like consumer wants, and does not have an independent existence of its own anymore than it has an operating edge.

We are reminded of the usefulness of the United Nations,

not in terms of initial or independent action of its own, but in terms of its capacity to deflect, absorb, justify and legalize the actions of great powers. It appears to be, in these terrible wars of nerves, as utterly necessary to all sides as was Switzerland in two conventional wars.

Finally, most of us learned, I suspect, from the great fright that we would not, after all, prefer to "die with dignity" than live among ruination. Very few there must have been who did not give anxious thought to means of escape or protection from possible blasts and radiation. The survival instinct is simply too powerful to be reasoned away. Since this is so I believe it the plain duty of government to aid the chances of survival by the most thorough planning and most detailed instruction of every citizen in civil defense. I do not believe for a moment this would make us either more "warlike" or more complacent. In our time we have seen great cities, in fact whole nations, unimaginably shattered and yet seen their life gather and flower again.

This is what would happen with us should my pessimistic Los Angeles friend have sensed the true meaning of those six days in October.

I cannot get Major Rudolph Anderson, Jr., out of my mind. The thought will not go away that a time may come when it will be a tradition for Americans—and foreigners as well—to place wreaths at the grave of the U-2 pilot shot down over Cuba, our one casualty in the showdown, our "known soldier" representing hosts of others who did *not* die in one of history's most decisive victories.

It is too soon to be sure. The balance of power has been preserved, but the Cuban threat is not entirely liquidated. Russia's long-overdue setback and her alarm over the Chinese attack on India have not yet yielded evidence of a reorientation of Soviet policy and the herald of a new world equilibrium with Russia essentially on the side of the West, fulfilling the prophecy of De Gaulle. Should this miracle come we would then think of Cuba as its point of origin; John F. Kennedy would surely be immortalized as one of our greatest Presidents and Major Anderson as the martyr who died for us all. Let his present grave be well marked.

That is for the future. For now, we know that a clearing of the fetid, confused intellectual air has started in Europe, in Asia, in Latin America. What has begun to begin is a new sense of reality, an end to innocence, an understanding at long last that neutralism, if not "immoral," as John Foster Dulles claimed, is a worthless stance for many countries, devoid of safety as well as of the "moral power" so long and so spuriously claimed for it. I omit the new African regimes. They will not soon abandon their notion that singly or collectively they can somehow affect the course of world power, because without this notion they would commit political suicide on the international scene.

I am thinking chiefly of India, Brazil and Britain, our most important friends in Asia, Latin America and Europe. Nehru has already shown the courage and candor to admit that he and his people have been living in "an artificial atmosphere of our own creation." No additional comment is necessary or tasteful, save to point out that Nehru was the chief carrier of this intellectual infection to other regimes.

Because of the same illusions, plus domestic pressures, Brazil had started down the road to what seemed to me neutralism, however insistently labeled independence in foreign policy. It began under Quadros and continued under Goulart. Perhaps, now, Brazilian politicians will release us from our unmerited role as chief whipping boy for their tribulations and recognize that we have no designs on Latin America save its stability and security.

The British government quickly grasped the importance of the Cuban crisis and stood fast behind President Kennedy. Yet I must include Britain as one of the three critical countries needing an intellectual housecleaning, because most Americans, so instinctively inclined to respect and reliance where Britain is concerned, have never understood the British state of mind in recent years. They have not grasped the extent of the pro-neutralism (or isolationism) forces, the anti-American, anti-Alliance, "plague-on-both-your-houses" attitude concerning the great powers.

An American in London could endure the envy and resentment of United States wealth and power, expressed in endless condescending, if witty, slurs, even in Conservative circles, knowing that the Conservative government would stand up and be counted in the test. But what was alarming was the deep hold of the vague, unrealistic but serious belief that American and Russian policies were equally noxious, that our diplomacy was dangerously brassy and bumbling, that if we would stop shoving at Russia, she would stop shoving at everybody else. The hold of these pathetically obtuse notions was profound in the universities and grammar schools, in the labor unions, in the press and television. Some sincerely believed that Britain could find safety only by opting out of the power struggle. Others wanted it both ways—the protection of American power but without the risks involved; others were simply fellow travelers, consciously or unconsciously.

I left England a year ago reluctantly convinced that Communists and pro-Communists were wielding influence inside some of Britain's most important publications and broadcasting offices. There is at least one regular television program of national following which has not yet had a good word to say about America or a bad word to say about the Soviet Union. When the President delivered his ultimatum to Khrushchev only two of Britain's major publications, the *Telegraph* and the *Express,* grasped the historic necessity of driving the ultimatum through. All the others wavered, niggled or carped, so disorganized is British opinion.

A Labour government under Gaitskell could come to power in England one day soon. He and his closest colleagues would try to stand steady within the Alliance. But the contrary pressures upon him from within his party's ranks would be tremendous— one reason for hoping that the intellectually sanitizing effects of Cuba and India have really taken hold among our strongest-hearted allies.

Key West—This is where freedom comes to a point.

The southeastern tip of this southernmost fragment of the United States is a low stone seawall curving from the Navy installation, along the George Smathers public beach, past the Howard Johnson emporium, the long row of stabled fishing boats and the Food Fair, until Roosevelt Boulevard becomes Truman Avenue. At the corner of Truman Avenue and Margaret Street stands the Margaret Truman Launderette.

Key West, part Spanish, part Anglo-American, is an architectural mish-mash of lovely, balconied New-Orleans style frame houses lost in a neon-lighted nightmare of gas stations, shops and joints. The tourists are few, middle-aged and Middle-Western. Youth consists of pairs and trios of bored U.S. sailors drifting along Duval Street under the eye of the Shore Patrol. The cars move at sedate speeds, the pelicans glide very slowly and even the gulls seem rarely to scream. It is the frequent jet fighter planes on patrol that supply the vigor and the sound.

181

The tip of freedom points toward Cuba, which is closer than Miami, and easily penetrates the azure curtain of sea and sky. One has only to switch the television knob to channel five and Castro, Communism and the new songs of old Cuba, lyrics by ideologues, suddenly fill one's motel bedroom with clamor and tense reality. Nothing but the sea and the sky separates this place from the tragedy, ever present in the faces and the conversations of Cuban waiters, chambermaids, drivers and fishermen all over this raddled spit of land.

From here the refugees are scattered, all the way up the Keys, through and to the north of Miami, their Mecca of desperation, their gathering and their festering place. There the complete agony is assembled out of its tens of thousands of human parts—the pride, the soul-sickness, the blind but urgent hopes, the shapeless plans to somehow plan. The joy over the returned heroes of the Bay of Pigs was short-lived; the fiery, promising words of President Kennedy in the Miami Stadium fade from the conversation or are repeated in ironic echoes. The demurrer of the Attorney General on the question of the air support came like a whiplash in their faces.

The fact that they may be truly lost is beginning to penetrate. They are a passionate people; they speak their bitterness as readily as they spoke their gratitude. The State of Florida and the federal government have an enormous and growing problem on their hands. Every living Cuban here asks himself and his friends the daily question, spoken or unspoken: Are we going back? There is no answer. If an official answer does come and it is affirmative, with evidence to support it, they will remain together and live only for the day of their return. If the answer is negative, they would explode, but sooner or later they would begin to dull the pain and to think in terms of assimilation to North American life. One way or another their life would go on with some meaning and purpose. But today they exist in a state of suspension, their feet not on the ground nor their heads in the clouds. Prolonged, this will prove unendurable.

The other side of this coin is the dilemma of the U.S. Government. It can issue general assurances, as the President did in Miami, but it cannot support the assurance with public proof of specific plans. There is a difference between an official attitude and an official policy. For this slowly festering pool of displaced humanity here in Florida an attitude very soon will not be enough. A positive policy, even if short of armed invasion, but promising a specific schedule of pressures severe enough to realistically foreshadow Castro's downfall, would seem to justify the idea of a Cuban government in exile. It would serve a host of useful purposes, including Cuban cohesion in Florida now and limitation of the anarchy and fraternal violence in Cuba later.

It would also permit and inspire serious advance thinking here about the nature of the post-Castro Cuban political and social order. It is these formulations for the future that responsible Cubans here now wish to get on with. It is a new vision of Cuban life in liberty and social justice, thought out in some detail, that ought to be crackling through the airwaves now to the ears of all within that island fortress. They ought to hear it night after night, as they now hear the mechanical drumbeat of Communism's slogans, insults and alibis. Where the vision is unstated, as where there is no vision, people perish, whether in their homes, or abroad and seeking to find their homes.

January–April 1963

Cuba may well be, as now predicted, the prime issue in the national politics of 1964. But unless the issue is clarified far beyond its present state it will be a rhetorical question, not a question for true debate. Alternative policies are required for true debate and all we have on either side, so far, is attitudes.

With justice, President Kennedy has insisted that his critics show more precision in their prescriptions for handling Cuba; but with equal justice his critics can insist on more precision from the Administration. What we are now witnessing is a collision of two fog banks. This never clears the air, in nature or in politics; it merely produces fog of double thickness.

However uncertain the future course, there can be little uncertainty about what the immediate past has produced:

1. The Russians now possess a military, political and propaganda base in the heart of our area of security and influence.

2. Their troops in Cuba constitute a "trip wire," paralyzing to American action, as our troops in Berlin constitute a trip wire there.

3. Cities and installations of the United States mainland are now open to damage by conventional weapons, and have become, therefore, in some degree hostage to Communist purposes. Theoretically, at least, the Russians could damage us by proxy, their method elsewhere, without themselves being directly involved.

183

4. Castro's physical hold on the island is complete, with the underground movement facing probable extinction.

5. The mass of Cuban manpower in exile is now a "blown instrument," a handicap and thorn in our side, not a weapon for our uses.

6. A foreign policy quarrel of serious proportions is engulfing an Administration which has not yet found its feet in the area of its domestic policies and programs.

7. Once again, world Communism had succeeded in choosing the point of conflict and crisis in the Cold War, and once again, as with South Korea or South Viet-Nam or West Berlin or Laos, the locus of contention is inside the realm of the free world, not in the Communist realm.

Whatever the precise degrees of blame to be placed on American Administrations, past and present, or on Cubans, past and present, the net result is as described above; and in spite of the trade restrictions and the partial efforts of the OAS at diplomatic "isolation" of Cuba, no persuasive evidence has yet developed to justify optimistic assumptions about the future effects of Castroism in the Caribbean and in continental South America.

Quick reversals have been a hallmark of the volatile politics of Latin America, and it strains credulity to assume that a general era of stability is now beginning. For countries like Peru and possibly Brazil it is hard to convince oneself that the fundamental forces for integration are stronger than the fundamental forces for disintegration. Latin-American Communists believe the contrary, and are relatively quiescent right now only as a matter of strategy, waiting for the time when the United States will relax about Cuba, take its nervous finger off the trigger, and gradually slip into a state of de facto coexistence with Castro. As we drift in that direction most Latin governments, as well as those European allies anxious to resume trade with Cuba, will try to force us further in that direction.

When northern opinion is adjusted to accommodation Communist strategies will change again, and with the present electricity dissipated we shall find it far harder to rouse ourselves to forceful action in the case of some attempted uprising in Cuba or in the case of Communist coups in nearby nations. This is the prospect unless somehow we find a way to increase our present pressures on Cuba. If they are not increased, they will decrease; it is not in the nature of these things that a status quo can be indefinitely maintained.

Wise and good men are reminding us that a Communist Cuba is not a mortal threat to our vital interests. In and of itself, of course, it is not. But that opens, it does not close, the argument. A Communist Viet-Nam or a Communist Laos or Indonesia or Venezuela or West Berlin would not be mortal threats, either—in and of themselves and separately considered. But the Communist world strategy of protracted conflict is a strategy of the piecemeal advance. There are only so many pieces on the board. With the capture of Cuba they have taken a tremendously important piece. Dozens of Russian ships would not be plying the Cuban trade and thousands of Russian citizens would not be turned out to cheer Castro if the Kremlin didn't think so.

September 16, 1963

It is nearly a year now since there occurred the first of the two great events whose consequences have altered the structure of the world power balance as well as the dynamics of the Cold War. We shall all be busy for a long time trying to trace out the blueprint of the new structure and to take the temperature of the new dynamics. All one can say for sure is that either one of these events would have marked the twelvemonth in capital letters of red; their concurrence has made both definition and prediction hazardous in the extreme.

The first event was the establishment, at long last, of the credibility of the American deterrent. Credibility had been the vital but missing ingredient for all the seventeen years in which the deterrent had physically existed, and the ingredient was supplied in the affair of the Cuban missiles by the uncommon boldness of the President's ultimatum.

This event accelerated and helped to produce the second great event of this unusual year—the formal and apparently irreparable consummation of the break between China and the Soviet Union. And both events together have produced, as their first tangible fruit, the treaty for the limitation of nuclear tests. This much we have; no one can yet be sure that it will prove productive of further specific steps in a momentum toward a detente between Russia and the West.

The desire for alliances is an instinct as well as a calculation in the biology of nationhood—even the professedly non-aligned seek to band together in their own *ad hoc* alliances—and the bare bone of the matter is that each of the two great Communist

185

nations is now isolated. Each faces, in the far reach of its strategic thinking, the distinct possibility that, if it found itself in war, it would face a war on two fronts. That is the oldest nightmare of all among governments.

It could be that the whole postwar world system of alliances is breaking up—General De Gaulle may provide the final answer to that. The strains within the military framework of the North Atlantic Alliance are great, with no relieving reforms in sight, yet the community of culture and common interest among the Western nations is such that one cannot conceive of a break so clean as the break between Russia and China.

Russia's position is not enviable. She has tested the nuclear will of the United States and has found it a reality. She has lost her one important ally in the world. Her diplomats are now her most important leaders; they have a whole new course to chart and every day's front page shows them to be busy about it. Her current opening bids for successive steps to the nuclear treaty must be viewed less skeptically than ever before, but always with the concern that these steps might lead to the ungluing of the Western Alliance, an outcome Moscow must logically hope for to alleviate her nightmare.

Developments in the world of politics simply produce further developments. Two new themes are now emerging. Their capacity for contagion is very hard to judge; if it is a real capacity, we are in for an interesting time. Both themes are being stimulated by the now isolated Chinese.

One theme proclaims the natural identity of interest between the non-nuclear powers as against the three nuclear powers, and to the current of this theme General De Gaulle adds a freshet from time to time.

The second new theme is the more consequential because its seeds lie in the nature of the human being himself, not the nature of governments; because it is all but permanent, while nuclear alignments shift; because recent events nearly everywhere in the world, America included, have given it a dynamic of its own. This theme is the racial theme. The Chinese are boldly and blatantly interpreting the break with Russia in racial terms to the rest of Asia and to Africa and Latin America. This is the most elemental and inflammable of all great animosities. It is, so far, no bigger than a man's hand on the horizon of the future.

It has, nevertheless, a certain frightening potential. The new, aroused racism lies close behind the new nationalism in parts of this world. I am one who takes seriously the warnings of race war in Africa coming from Sir Roy Welensky of Rhodesia. The potential in Southeast Asia is considerable and there are places in Latin America—Peru, for one example—where the class war has audible and disturbing overtones of race war.

The Chinese will try to identify the nuclear power that hangs over the world with white power. Few can now accurately guess at the possible consequences of this; but one may logically suggest that in this pregnant matter we could use the help of our psychologists as well as that of our diplomats and spies.

June–September 1960

Twenty years ago this weekend Paris was surrendered—or, rather, left behind—to Hitler's armies. There is some dignity in formal surrender, but the gracious city was not accorded that. Clouds of dark smoke from downriver spread over the skyline like a gathering shroud; stillness moved from street to street as the life of the city flowed away through the southern arteries. Paris was in a coma before the first German invader touched it. The most marvelous complex of urban brilliance since the Athens of Pericles was given over to the barbarian without a struggle, without even a parting cry of defiance from its rulers.

Months of post-mortem followed: "France is decadent," or "The British let them down," or "Their generals were stupid," or "The French Revolution was never finished," implying that for Frenchmen class-against-class, peasant-against-city, ideologist-versus-ideologist were more meaningful battles than those between the nation and its enemies. It is *chacun à son goût* in theories of history and any number can play; to me it always seemed that 1918 was the cause of 1940. World War I broke the spirit of implicit nationalism among the French people. That victory was purchased at too high a price and became a spiritual defeat. I believe it crystallized the ancient Gallic tendency to distrust one another, to give confidence to very few outside of family and self. One need not be historian or psychologist to perceive this in the French. As Suzy Parker, actress, said the other day: "France is a nation of critics. They are critics of everybody, including one another."

The critical mind is not usually the constructive or cooperative mind. How then does one explain the French scene twenty years after the dreadful proof of what the non-cooperative society

187

can come to? We now see a French economic renaissance at least the equal of Germany's; France has created more industrial output in the last fifteen years than in all the previous 150 years since industrialization began.

We see a professional army with a veritable thirst for battle. We see a totally new constitutional system, permitting an effective executive for the first time. We see the French, with more cause than any Western people to hate the Germans, going further to embrace them politically than anyone else. We see France taking the aggressive lead in creating the joint organs of the new "Europe."

Clearly, we all underestimated French technical and organizational capacities. We had forgotten that the tradition of the French professional soldiery is a living thing and quite different from the mores of a people's army. Massive financial infusions from America helped produce in France the same prosperity that all Europe now enjoys, and prosperity dulls the discontent of any working class. The undiminished French intellect, personified in the genius of Jean Monnet, truly the "first European," moved into the vacuum left by Britain's refusal to lead postwar Europe, and began to fashion the economic institutions that may one day lead to a politically federal Europe. De Gaulle himself and his executive system were products of crisis and vacuum, last-ditch alternatives rather than consciously constructive acts in a fit of co-operative common sense.

France has established a kind of intellectual hegemony in Europe; it would be rash to deem it more than that. It would be unwise to believe the new French army will forever keep its disciplined place in society if the Algerian War goes on and on. It would be unwise to believe that a serious dip in employment and living standards would not break the armistice between economic classes, and unwise to assume that an effective but still democratic executive system would survive the passing of the man who now broods and presides upon it.

The new house of France is not yet a welded structure, as is the house of Britain. It is still a mosaic held together by new rivets of remarkable design, and all depends upon how seriously and how soon they loosen. This is one reason, though only one, why the British hesitate to commit their fate—in trade, in atomic science, in defense—to the Continental framework.

They are not yet convinced that the ingrown nature of the Frenchman has basically altered, and they suspect this spirit will come into play the moment the binding rivets seem to loosen. And yet, in the longer view, one must acknowledge that societies change and achieve cohesion only by fits and starts and that the movement of France these past few years is remarkable by any accounting. What we have been seeing is not the restoration of French "glory" in the Gaullist sense, but restoration of free play for the French genius, our creditor often enough in the past.

An "agonizing reappraisal" of President De Gaulle is going on in the private minds of public men, brought about by De Gaulle himself, who has once again descended from his mountain and handed out graven tablets containing his commandments for the conduct of nation states.

Even many of those most admiring of his character, most relieved by his restoration of discipline in France, now realize that what Gaullism implies for the West is almost total repudiation of the grand design for peace and security as conceived and labored at for fifteen years by the best and bravest of Western statesmen.

The basic assumptions in the grand design were these:

1. That Europe is too crowded and inflammable to permit a relapse into the national competitions that produced two world wars.

2. That Europe can never reach the American standard of living unless the thickets of investment, technological and trade barriers between the countries are cleared away.

3. That in the age of titans and mass weaponry Europe can neither deter nor win a war save by a closely integrated defense system and one to which the United States is fundamentally and permanently committed.

4. That European defense is fruitless without Germany, always the heartpiece of European power, as part of it; and since Germany herself contains seeds of menace, her military power must in large part be contained within a joint command.

5. Since the implementation of these assumptions could (and did) produce a Western balancing of Soviet might, there must be an over-all world forum and instrument for the airing and cushioning of conflicts between the two sides.

From these assumptions have flowed these fifteen years the most sustained, imaginative and promising works toward unification that Europe has known for several centuries. These efforts

189

have created the Coal and Steel Community, Euratom, the Common Market, at least the facsimile of a European Parliament, the NATO defense and command structure and, in the world background, the United Nations.

Now General De Gaulle reveals that he is not impatient with the slow forward movement in this broad advance, but fundamentally opposed to it. He would tear away everything in the edifice that restricts national sovereignties. That means he repudiates the basic assumptions themselves, the lessons we all thought history had so painfully taught us. He wants a *"Europe des Patries."* If this means anything different from the old system that was the affliction of Europe and the world, it is hard to see what it is.

He would reduce all the supra-national agencies, including that now operating the Common Market, to purely technical and advisory levels. He would grant, apparently for window dressing, a new European Parliament, but one with no more authority than the existing Strasbourg assembly. He would change the basic structure of NATO and put the great defense decisions in the hands of a triumvirate composed of America, Britain and France. He would end the integration of armies, navies and air forces, and be content with the old system of consultation. He would extend the co-operation of the triumvirate to foreign policy decisions involving Africa and Asia. As for the United Nations, he simply sneers at it, and in its greatest moment of crisis.

What are the probable effects of a De Gaulle world policy in action? Certainly these, at least: A slipping back by European countries toward economic autarchy; victory for those forces in Britain now preventing Britain from coming into Europe; further compromising of bases and facilities in those small and already nervous countries such as Norway, which would have little enthusiasm for an alliance in which they had no vote; an end to the containment of German strength and the virtual certainty that Germany would become the dominant military power in West Europe.

For France it would mean merely an increase in prestige, not in strength or safety. As for joint, three-power co-ordination on African and Asian policies, there is not the slightest reason to believe there would be any more of that than there is at present. Nor could such co-ordination replace the vacuum left by the elimination or diminution of the United Nations, for no big-power policies on Africa and Asia can ignore the aspirations of African and Asian leaders, and the United Nations is by all odds their chief avenue to prestige and world identity.

Finally, the De Gaulle "plan" would fairly surely accelerate the partial withdrawal from Europe of the United States. No American President or Congress could willingly submit to the reversal of our most basic convictions about Europe, upon which we have lavished billions of dollars and years of effort.

President De Gaulle is a great man, but chiefly in the purely nationalist context; that is to say, in the context of a bygone age. Historians of our time will measure greatness by twentieth century terms; and this is the century whose mission it is to bridle nationalism if the world is to live.

January 15, 1962

In its relation to the modern miracle of continental Europe the United States and its Congress stand today in the same painful position of urgency combined with confusion in which Britain and its Parliament stood a few months ago.

The implacable facts of life forced Prime Minister Macmillan to make the try to take Britain into the astonishingly successful European Common Market while there was still time to avoid serious economic injury to his country and a trade war that could undermine the Atlantic Alliance. Yet he made the move when the British people remained uneducated as to its necessity and significance. The speed of events had upset all orderly planning; he was forced to jump first and explain later.

Now, one year earlier than the original thinking in Washington had called for, President Kennedy has asked for the broad tariff-lowering authority that would enable the United States, not to "join" the Common Market, but to maintain a constant, matching association with it. The fight in Congress with the infinitude of tariff lobbies will be savage and must be won, if not in this session, then in the next. Should this fight be lost Europe's common external tariff wall—enclosing, soon, a 300,000,000-consumer market, bigger than our own—will tend to be a high, not a low tariff wall; a slow throttling of our export trade would develop and the Atlantic Alliance would suffer truly terrible strains.

Like Macmillan, the President has been forced to decide first and explain later, but he knows that the real educative process

191

will occur in a protracted series of open Congressional committee hearings, an instructional institution the British Parliament does not emphasize. World trade is no less dismal a study than other branches of economics, and we are all of us in for a semester's heavy saturation in the "dismal science."

In the process those who do more than read as they run will learn why it is that charming, archaic Europe is suddenly a hard-sell, up-and-at-'em economic duplicate of America; why, to paraphrase Coolidge, "the business of Europe is business," and why Communism is a lost cause in Western Europe. History does not always repeat itself and men do learn from experience.

The Europeans of the post-World War I period had learned nothing. Country after country returned to autarchical, isolationist economic structures; business leaders clung to high-profit, low-production, closed arrangements, trying to preserve, among other things, their social class systems; for twenty years Europe was thought of as the tired continent.

The destruction of World War II was even greater than that of the first war, yet in spite of this—partly *because* of this—the industrial production of this postwar Europe has already more than doubled; the Continental area has become the most dynamic economic engine on the world scene; Britain with her Commonwealth and the United States, though in lesser degree, are obliged to seek terms of mutual existence from Europe.

European leaders had learned their lesson and they took their cues from the example of the United States. They made two profound changes in the material life of Europe: they opened their borders to one another's produce, power, currencies and ideas; they set out to redistribute income, not only by state-managed social welfare measures, but by building the American type of mass-production, low-profit, low-price industrial unit which basically rests on the purchasing power of the consumer, not on the earnings of the investor.

A "consumer society" in Europe was bound to mean the withering of the old class society, and this is happening, even in stodgy old England. The other side of this coin is, inevitably, the vast expansion of the middle class. With this, the historical prophecy of Marx—and the conviction of all Communists—has been proved wrong. In the continuing expansion of the middle class lies Europe's great hope for stable democracies, in spite of the past political record in Germany, Italy and France.

192

Along with general literacy, the existence and growth of a middle class have come to seem prerequisites for the free, democratic societies that America's prodigious efforts and expenditures everywhere have as their ultimate aim. This is why our hopes for African nations must be long deferred and why success in some Latin-American countries is by no means assured.

It is also why we—and various African and Latin-American political groups—should cease the foolish argument on private capital investment versus government-to-government loans and grants. These are false alternatives; the choice is not one or the other, but both. Private capital invested abroad is not going to build the schools, hospitals and highways everywhere needed; but it can and constantly does by its presence and practice show and lead the way toward consumer-based, mass-production, mass-distribution economic societies in which a middle class can grow and political democracy has some chance of growing.

The middle-class system is what virtually all of Latin America, consciously or unconsciously, has been so bitterly struggling for so long. But in Cuba the middle class is being destroyed because a man named Karl Marx said in a book that middle classes everywhere would disappear. Whatever the sins of the Cuban upper class, they cannot have justified this tragically stupid reversal by force of history's manifest course.

January–July 1963

The last time Prime Minister Macmillan visited Washington he said to an American dinner partner, "Every country has its particular nightmare. Ours is unemployment. What's yours?" The answer was, "Another Pearl Harbor."

Anyone keeping this exchange in mind will better understand the essence of British foreign and defense policy and the real nature of the present squabbling about nuclear independence and American leadership of the Atlantic Alliance. He will understand why the United States willingly faces a federal budget of a hundred billion dollars; and why Britain dropped her Bluestreak missile for the virtually free Skybolt, went into an uproar when Skybolt was canceled, will not undertake a truly independent modernized nuclear arsenal, and fails to bring her Rhine army up to strength; and why part of the British press openly accuses the United States of using the U.N. Katanga Operation as a cover under which to grab economic concessions away from Europeans.

The maintenance of her present prosperity is an obsession in Britain and the fulcrum on which her governments rise or fall. Whatever regime occupies Whitehall finds itself caught in the Procrustean bed of the implacable interaction of rising domestic consumption and falling exports. Britain must still "export or die," her room for maneuver is slight and she must live by her economic wits.

What will determine whether Britain "falls to the status of a third-class power," to use the phrase Tory backbenchers now cry aloud, is not the question of her nuclear independence from us or from NATO, but the questions of her joining the Common Market and what happens after that.

Inside the market she has still got to compete in production and sales with the other members, and this means a profound renovation of British industrial equipment and methods. In a certain, ironic sense British industry was not destroyed enough in the war; the new plants in France, Germany and Italy are far more efficient than much of Britain's. The great port of London is sluggish and archaic; labor union feather-bedding and wildcat strikes make matters worse; even in shipbuilding, the Germans, Dutch, Swedes, to say nothing of the Japanese, equal her in quality and beat her in construction and delivery times and in prices.

Only a fool would underrate the British people in any crisis, but when they say, as so many do, "Ah, well, we have a way of winning the last battle, you know," one is obliged to wonder if they are not fooling themselves. This kind of slow war of economic attrition has no dramatic last battle. Salvation depends on what was done yesterday, is being done today, as well as what will be done tomorrow.

The problem goes deep and involves, I'm afraid, the mores, values and habits of a whole society. We, the Germans and the Japanese seem to live in order to work, and it makes life tense and exhausting. The English seem to work in order to live; this makes their life infinitely more pleasant and leaves room for the human graces. But history will not stop, only the fittest will survive and the business life of the British remains essentially Victorian. The truth is that they are not a hard-working people in this era of "I'm all right, Jack," and the tax rates scarcely encourage the shedding of sweat, to say nothing of blood and tears.

The trouble is pandemic and includes management. A leading London public-relations expert said to me, "In America public-relations firms essentially handle publicity for an industry. In Britain we are also consultants on management, because British business, like her sports and her politics, is largely run by amateurs—by sons, grandsons, nephews who have had a literary education and for whom precision, punctuality and detailed expertise are regarded as bad form."

(My first friendly admonition upon joining a London club was that to be overheard discussing business at lunch might well bring a polite note from the club secretary.)

Anyone who loves London as it is, who loves the long week-ends, the country visits, the tea breaks, the fusty offices and the handwritten notes, contemplates their conquest by the frenetic spirit of Madison Avenue with sickness in his stomach. But to contemplate the withering of Britain as a political and human force in this harsh world is to feel a lot sicker. They have a choice, but they all have to see and accept it, down to the last stenographer, though this may require a peacetime Churchill, if there be such a thing.

If Charles De Gaulle is crowning his giant's career with a gigantic mistake, it will be because his sense of time, not timing, is out of joint with that of his contemporaries. His mind inhabits the far-distant past and the far-distant future. He wishes to resurrect the European hegemony of the Mediterranean culture which passed with Napoleon's defeat. He envisages the end of the Cold War and the rapprochement with Soviet Russia, although most of the current evidence surely means that what he has now done to the West's grand design will encourage the Russians to intensify the Cold War in order to expand the breach.

Near the taproot of De Gaulle's cosmic thinking lies a profound distrust, not only of Anglo-Saxon civilization as a civilization, but of the Anglo-Americans as statesmen. As translated from De Gaulle's past writings this means, simply, that Britain and the United States will always, in the test, combine together, whatever the loss to France. And what he has now done is surely to bring about what he dislikes the most in the postwar pattern of alignments.

This attitude was crystallized in 1942 when De Gaulle concluded with resentment that Winston Churchill had decided, once and for all, to bow to the imperious necessity of the American alliance" (*War Memoirs of General De Gaulle—The Call to Honor*). Macmillan's compliance at Nassau in December with the Kennedy nuclear plan for Europe merely confirmed De Gaulle in his conviction.

But he did not deliver his blow to Britain because of this, or because his treaty with Germany was signed, or because Russia's falling out with Red China has been crystallized. He did it *when* these things had happened, as he has always serenely expected them to happen. No doubt he now waits with equal serenity for the fulfillment of his prophecy that America will leave Europe. This thought is the child of a wish, and his actions to come will be children of the thought. He will do his best, in many ways, to bring this about.

What we had forgotten about General De Gaulle was his capacity, as former Secretary Dulles once privately put it, "to wait." And so we are surprised and shocked at his smashing blow at Britain's hopes. Yet, two and a half years ago I wrote—and I could not have been alone—"what Gaullism implies for the West is almost total repudiation of the grand design for peace and security as conceived and labored at for fifteen years." I added that if De Gaulle's *"Europe des Patries"* means anything different from the old system that was the affliction of Europe and the world, it is hard to see what it is. It remains quite as hard today, for there is no implicit reason to believe the French-German alliance is made of more durable stuff than the American alliance with Europe; no overwhelming reason to think that France will not again become politically disorderly when De Gaulle departs, or to think that France can permanently lead a Europe that contains the German race, fundamentally more disciplined and more militant than the French.

In a sense De Gaulle still uses weakness as a weapon, a stratagem of which he proved himself master in World War II. At one point, quarreling with Britain over the Levant and East Africa, he broke off relations between the Free French and his allies, though he possessed but a few battalions, supplied by his allies, existing through their agreement. At another point in those quarrels he threatened to take the Free French out of all fighting and use them to hold down French territories he believed the British laid covetous eyes upon. A man that bold is a man bold enough for anything. He understood perfectly well his own operation; it was not purely emotional reaction, as many then thought, but coldly conceived. In one passionate interview with Churchill, he made it plain. His memoirs include this passage:

"We spoke of Roosevelt and of his attitude toward me. 'Don't rush things!' said Churchill. 'Look at the way I yield and rise up again, turn and turn about.' 'You can,' I remarked, 'because you are seated on a solid State, an assembled nation, a united Empire, large armies. But I! Where are my resources? And yet I, as you know, am responsible for the interests and destiny of France. It is too heavy a burden and I am too poor to be able to bow.' "

One cannot call this stratagem irresponsibility; De Gaulle is quite convinced that his present ends fit the tide of history. But it remains true that the manner of his doing what he has now done is a manner available only to a small power. This is why President Kennedy, tactically weakened by the inescapable responsibility of great power, cannot act against De Gaulle in like manner.

The governments of the West, our own included, have been gazing with wild surmise at the limitless expanse of Gaullism since he announced France's freehold claim to the future of Europe on January 14th. In these two months the cries and criticism have concentrated on his threat to undo the Herculean labors of fifteen years for European unity and on the future dangers of a Europe once again living and acting from the nationalistic instinct and nothing more.

Save in private, almost no one of public consequence has tried to answer the question of whether France has, or will have, the capacity to provide consistent and lasting leadership for a "Europe of Fatherlands." It is a seriously debatable question. If the present French government can entertain dreams of such an elevated role, it is not only because Charles De Gaulle has a stronger will than any current European statesman, but because there is "a role wandering aimlessly about in search of a hero to play it"—to quote Gamal Abdel Nasser from another context. Nasser, however, in what may have been a fitful gust of modesty, added that he did not mean the role of leadership but of "interaction and experimentation." De Gaulle means leadership.

The role is there by default. Britain chose not to seize the leadership of Europe at the close of the war when she alone wore the hero's mantle, though whether she had the strength to do it at that time is another debatable question. Italy has renounced any role of power whatsoever and, indeed, remains uncomfortable as a spear carrier in the wings. Germany is not only amputated, but still on parole, obliged to report her behavior to the constituted authorities at intervals.

There is only France. It is a France blessed by some individual leaders and thinkers of brilliance, a France finally cleared of an unmanageable and unmanaged empire, a France with the beginnings of modern military power, with a modernized, efficient industry, but, underneath all this plaster, a France that may still suffer hemorrhage at any moment from social wounds unhealed since World War I and possibly since the French Revolution.

One generalizes about a whole people, especially a people as gifted as the French, at his own risk, but it seems to me from considerable French residence that there exists in France a deepseated social disorder. It was shockingly revealed at the time of the Dreyfus case, again in the squalid defeat of 1940, again in the incredibly messy panorama of Algeria, with Frenchman against Frenchman; and the organized plots to kill De Gaulle still suggest implacable hatreds between groups and classes. Can this poisoning of the blood be cured in the ten years De Gaulle reportedly allots himself? One is entitled to wonder, and to wonder if the nation which has oscillated so very long between political authoritarianism and semi-anarchy, which has never achieved internal peace, can preside over the external peace of Europe.

It has always seemed to me that France is not much more of a true community of men with a common sense of identity and general purpose than is, say, Greater New York—a human melange which, I suspect, would come apart at the seams under heavy shock, as France has come apart in the past.

De Gaulle has said that he cannot conceive of a France without glory. I had thought he meant that such a France would not be *his* kind of France. But perhaps he meant something very different—that unless France rides the crest in "grandeur," it comes apart; that it lacks the social cohesion to endure adversity or mediocrity, which Britain, for example, can endure and yet remain Britain, a homogeneous people.

A few great men of generous vision like Jean Monnet excepted, most Frenchmen, from peasant to Paris intellectual, are spiritual isolationists; they are driven by centripetal, not centrifugal, emotional forces, many of them to the point of undisguised contempt for the American "do-good" psychology and tradition. Rightly or wrongly, any number of visitors to France share the impression that they distrust and dislike foreigners because they distrust and dislike one another. For the most part they seem profoundly disinterested in other lands and peoples.

That is their privilege; and this is not to say that our own quite different faults work less hardship on others. It is to say that a people so constituted are not nature's choice for the sustained leadership of a common alliance. It is to say that a man who believes power is everything in diplomacy has a long way yet to go before he can convince others that the political power of France rests on social foundations dependable in all weather and built to last.

Rome

In the realm of ordinary life—traveling, doing business, sitting in the sun or inspecting one another's lovely vistas, museums and antiquities—Europe and the Europeans are thawing out. The winter of their physical discontent is ended.

In the realm of high politics the freeze is still on. The winter of Allied discontent, dated for the history books by De Gaulle's renunciation of the whole post-war grand design, has become the spring of restless perplexity. With what sometimes appears to be the single exception of De Gaulle himself, even responsible Europeans have no firm idea where their countries, singly or collectively, go from here.

Within the safety zone made possible by the American deterrent and commitment Europe has surpassed its former prosperity, itself made possible by American capital infusions. Yet today more and more of political Europe looks on the American presence with a more and more jaundiced eye. But emotional reactions of resentment on our part would be childish. Gratitude rarely plays a leading or lasting role between nation-states; gratitude toward France didn't govern the foreign policy of the American Founders once the Revolution was won.

The Alliance is now blanketed in dense fogs of dilemma and paradox. For every European—and they were numberless—who once criticized isolationist America for not being committed to them there is now at least one who criticizes America for being

199

committed too deeply and dominantly to them. For every one who fears American bravado will bring war upon them there is another who fears that if war should come upon them from other causes, America will not have enough bravado to defend them.

On the general wish to remain free there is, of course, universal agreement within the Alliance. But on no specific issue, whether Berlin or Cuba or Africa or East-West trade, does pan-Alliance agreement exist; and it is out of such issues as these, not out of the general philosophical weather, that war would come, if it comes at all. On top of this, coincidentally, there remains that wonderfully illogical psychological phenomenon involving the inverse ratio of fear to proximity—when war seemed possible over Berlin the nearby Europeans were calm and the far-off Americans scared; when war seemed possible over Cuba the far-off Europeans were scared and the nearby Americans calm.

In diplomacy European governments want to be treated with more equality by America, but the cohesive "Europe" that would make that not only possible, but inevitable does not yet exist. In the interim European governments disagree as to whether they should even try to provide themselves with the military power that must underlie diplomatic equality.

A fundamental, if obvious, flaw in the Alliance is that the majority power is held by one nation, able quickly to make vital policy decisions, while the minority power is diffused among several nations whose individual decisions are, for the most part, extremely limited in effect. Yet the conventional wisdom more and more thinks and speaks of the Alliance in terms of America and "Europe," an essentially false apposition.

It can be argued, indeed, that the very concept of "alliance," as history has shaped the common concept, is essentially false in the era of nuclear power, which has basically altered not only the nature of war, but the nature of sovereignty. Until our time the final act of sovereignty was the declaration or the acceptance of war with the risk of defeat. Now, for the crowded countries of industrialized Europe, if not necessarily for our own spacious land, it is the acceptance of suicide, of non-existence. No European government can voluntarily make that choice for its people. None is likely to make it if America should be hit and Europe left alone.

Present speculative talk about who would remain faithful to the Alliance commitment and who betray it in case of war seems pointless. Atomic weapons have meaning only in their deterrent capacity, as keepers of the peace, not as winners of a war. More specifically, it is the credibility of the deterrent that matters. We have established our nuclear credentials in the issues of Berlin and Cuba sufficiently to make the Russians give over. It is too hard to believe that fractional nuclear power in any independent European hands would be credible to Moscow.

Short of universal disarmament or the over-arching detente with Russia that De Gaulle envisages—either one a long way off—there is no substitute for the American nuclear presence. This seems true even though the question of "whose finger on the trigger and the safety catch" appears insoluble. Better, perhaps, that the European powers throw away their atomic weapons than that they continue the drive for independent arsenals— and that could happen in a post-Macmillan Britain and a post-De Gaulle France. Washington has no power to bring this about. It is, therefore, stalling and hedging against proliferation of atomic arsenals by its successive—and confusing—schemes for "inter-Allied" and "multi-national" nuclear strike forces. Waters as opaque as those in which the Alliance now drifts can be muddied even more, but not much more.

London

Kennedy and Khrushchev have gone home, the foreign policy carnival of crowds and banners and speeches is ended, but the Wall that divides not only Berlin, but the deepest beliefs of Western man, remains. The "immobilism" of the two great powers since the Cuban crisis continues. Moscow hints that it wants accommodation, but does not clearly indicate where; Washington does more than hint, but finds no piece on the chessboard it can pull back of its own volition. The most sensitive human antennae sense that something should give, but no one knows where, and in this interregnum what hopes exist fasten on the nuclear test ban talks.

NATO, the formal arrangement of the great Alliance, which the French with some justice differentiate from the Alliance itself, remains stalled at its center, the United States fumbling for practical ways to share the leadership with allies, no two of which agree in their immediate interests or their long-range view of political and military strategy.

One could easily despair and conclude that no peacetime

alliance of nations equal in sovereignty but vastly unequal in power can hold together minus the goad of frequent threats from a common enemy. Yet one feels as he makes his inquiries around this new Europe, where life is so good, that even if the machinery dissolved, this Alliance itself will remain intact in heart and spirit until and unless the East makes some overriding, self-enforcing accommodation that would obviate the necessity of this Alliance. That time has not yet come, as the President warned, but China and proliferation of the final weapon could yet make it come. A "third force," so often predicted, can arise in the Far East before it arises in Europe, with the whole world balance and alignment just as profoundly altered.

Time, after all, is life; life is good in the West and getting better in Russia, and there may be a certain inborn, unconscious but instinctive human wisdom involved in the painful forward motion of common policy through the incredible cluster of national obstacles. Speed of decision somehow does not comport with the awful finality of the stakes, at least in this part of the globe.

Perhaps this is much too comfortable a sensation, but it is the sensation one acquires in the new Europe. It is a question of one's sense of pace and of historic continuity, and this contest of visceral attitudes can be applied to internal, national societies as well as to the external, international scene. Britain today is a prime case in point.

The average Englishman, I would think, has a sensation of living better than he has ever lived. Employment and wages are high, the shops are full, the new cars pour out of the factories, berthings for sporting boats are as hard to come by now as parking space for automobiles. New houses, new colleges are going up. The Englishman, as a private person, is doing very well; but England as a nation competing for trade and prestige with other nations is doing very badly. Britain's share of world trade has dropped precipitously in the last ten years. Her productivity per worker is near the bottom of the Western list. Rule of government and industry by the vaguely educated amateur continues—there is but one scientist in the Ministry of Science and one in the Treasury, and outside Treasury and Agriculture there are exactly four full-time economists in government service.

So reports *Encounter* magazine, its entire issue devoted to this question: "Suicide of a Nation?"

If Britain is dying, as so many of its intellectuals fear, its common people are enjoying the process and, indeed, feeling intensely alive herein. They have an instinctive aversion to defining "the national purpose," an instinctive fear that efficiency is the natural enemy of tolerance and kindliness. The world scientific revolution may have made the British system old hat, but they happen to like old hats and find them comfortable.

One's heart is with them in this, but one's reason is obliged to believe that kindliness is not and must not be incompatible with efficiency, or this democracy, like our own, is in for the deepest trouble.

In the very long view it may be, indeed, that Britain's solution of her internal problem will prove more important to this Alliance and to American world interests than any new weapon and command machinery within the Alliance. Germany is the immediate key to the Alliance, and she may become, by the book figures, our number one ally. But not by the final accounting, that of the spirit. There Britain is surely secure.

April–July 1963

Miss Christine Keeler is not likely to stand in the big league with Claudia the Roman or Madame Pompadour or even Lola Montez, but she, too, has affected the political command over millions of people and, like Claudia, she will have her page in history because of a Parliamentary convulsion, even though the accusatory orations of Harold Wilson in the fogs of Westminster are not likely to stand with those of Cicero in the hot sun of the Roman Senate. Mark down a net loss for posterity.

For the present all manner of thinkers are trying to find "social significance" in this current example of the sexual ingredient in high politics, and one joins the effort with trepidation. But what recurs is a remark made to me by a well-known English writer at a London dinner party not long ago—"My friend, you'll discover one day that right under the surface, this is a nation of sex maniacs."

Beneath this remark, overstated for effect, lies a considerable cargo of meaning. There is no doubt that what has been going on in London since the war, especially among the teen-agers and the social upper classes, is in violent contrast to the middle-class stereotype of a puritanical ethos. There is no doubt that, as so much English literature attests, the British were a dancing, singing, hard-drinking, lusty people until the Industrial Revolution simultaneously produced a middle class, the necessity to keep the working class sober and punctual and the smug and forbidding visage of Victoria as the public symbol of the new puritanism.

There is no doubt that the supposedly direct relationship between poverty and crime and vice is very much to be doubted. Marx, alas, preceded Freud, and only recently have British Socialists frankly faced the fact, so painful to their doctrines, which reflected little knowledge of human nature, that affluence and full employment have brought more, not less, crime and prostitution. One suspects that the reason is simple enough: there is more easy money around for the having.

There is no doubt that a large segment of the British upper class, like a large segment of Hollywood, has long considered itself exempt from the accepted rules of personal conduct. Indeed, the public in both countries has encouraged this, as if most morality-bound people in their routine lives need an escape hatch, however vicarious, for their unconscious longings to bust loose. In New York thousands seek tickets for "Cleopatra," chiefly motivated by Miss Taylor's uninhibited sex life; in London the popular press virtually makes its living on sex and is now engaged in wholesale pandering with the Profumo case, whatever its piously hypocritical editorials may say.

What gives this case its cutting edge, of course, is the security aspect—a Minister of War has shared a call girl with a Soviet officer-spy—and it is here that I would, somewhat hesitantly, add another interpretation to the many already offered. It seems to me that the social and psychological effects of a sudden loss of national power in the world are akin to those of defeat in war.

I would not equate London today with the cesspool that was Berlin in the early twenties, but in Britain, even in the realm of government, certain stays and fastenings have surely come loose. Neurotic resentment against America is part of this instability in a people once famous for their steadiness. I think there is also a general slackening of efficiency and personal dedication in British government. This was probably inevitable for the simple reason that what British leaders do, say and think no longer affects the whole world; they are no longer an example for everyone. Bereft of a great role the severe standards required of greatness must wither; the best men of a generation must relate their lives to something bigger than themselves if they are to be big; where the puddle grows small the frogs, with few exceptions, will shrink in size.

This is the core of the malaise in the British Establishment, whose very reason for existing is vanishing. A Wellington, whose class as well as whose fame was secure, could say, "Publish and be damned" to a blackmailing ex-mistress. No British leader today could do that.

Even twenty years ago a Profumo case would not have happened—not this way. The man would have been instantly out, or the case successfully smothered and the damage repaired in private; too much would have been at stake. There would never have been this bumbling and fumbling, with events getting entirely out of hand. The wrong mistresses in the wrong place have shaken the governments of various comic-opera Ruritanias. If this is something new for Britain, it is because this is a new Britain.

Responsible Englishmen, masters at criticizing their own institutions—and who fiercely resent criticism from foreigners—are getting weary with the sex aspects of the sex-and-security crisis. Daily servings of sex stories have the same effect as daily servings of pink champagne—the stomach rebels.

Security is what interests them now. What they really want to find out is whether the accepted tradition of masterful British super-sleuthing, fictionalized and enshrined in a succession of folk heroes from hawk-eyed Sherlock Holmes to steely eyed James Bond, 007, is itself a fiction. Editors and politicians who have been crying "What's going on in this country?" now want to know if the supposed geniuses of M15 know, themselves, what's going on in this country.

Reluctant admission by Macmillan's government that the man who tipped off the escaped British diplomat-traitors, Burgess and Maclean, was indeed another British diplomat, Harold Philby, although Macmillan himself once denied it—this has been the last straw. Whether it will break the back of the Conservative regime is uncertain. What is certain is an overwhelming demand for a renovation of the personalities, procedures and—this seems fundamental—the attitudes and values prevailing in British security services. Embattled authorities were pleased to have the television testimony of Mr. Allen Dulles, who said British security was efficient, but this will satisfy almost nobody here.

The purpose of counter-intelligence is not just to catch spies, but to prevent their spying. Macmillan claimed the identification of Philby to be a security success, not a failure, to which the furious opposition retorts that the man, like Burgess and Maclean, not only got away with his spying, but got away himself.

If there is a gross slackness in British security, it concerns every government allied with Britain; what remedies shall be applied, and how, concern Britain alone. Her political procedures and traditions are very different from ours, and what is appropriate in the context of Washington may not be appropriate or workable in the context of London. Whatever is done, we may be quite sure that nothing resembling a "witch hunt" is going to develop in Britain; guilt by simple accusation, which is essentially what happened to many Americans in the McCarthy period, is not likely to get out of hand. Nor would a British policeman, even one as highly placed as the counterpart of Mr. J. Edgar Hoover, be permitted to act as his agency's press agent, admitting never a failure, or be permitted to indulge in homilies and lectures on the political philosophies of those to the left of center.

All this Britain will certainly spare herself. But the painful problem of reconciling the interests of the state with the rights of the individual will not go away. Almost certainly British authorities in their security procedures are going to have to move, however cautiously, in the direction of giving less benefit of the doubt to the suspected individual. It will be difficult, almost as difficult as altering the pattern of a physical reflex; so homogeneous and deeply patriotic a people have a hard time crediting the existence of such a thing as treason; people so passionately jealous of their own privacy and personal dignity find it excruciatingly painful to invade the privacy of anyone among them.

In the realm of security many Englishmen now concede they have been tolerant to a fault. Item: when Foreign Secretary Harold Macmillan eight years ago accepted without question the assurances that Philby was all right, he said to the House of Commons, "We must take care that in protecting our way of life we do not destroy it." Item: when Miss Mandy Rice-Davies, the second little doxie in the Profumo affair, had testified, the first angry questions in the House were demands to know by what right the government had prevented her from leaving the country. Item: the private incomes of traitors Burgess and Maclean are still regularly forwarded to them from Britain.

But the moral and intellectual climate in which British security people must work is not exclusively composed of native and ancient traditions. Two other, latter-day influences have played a part. One was made in America—McCarthyism—and the profound revulsion it created in British minds. The other has been the intensive, if not extensive, effect of intellectual Marxism, beginning in the universities and extending into some areas of the civil service. A bona fide Communist would be hard to find today in the British government. Others, from the habitual fellow traveler, to the kind of person who equates American policies with Russian policies, to the simple, "let's-not-be-beastly-to-the-Russians" fellow, are not so rare. Nor are they rare in some areas of press and broadcasting. Whatever history in the remote future may prove about their attitudes, present history merely proves that the Russians try to use them and sometimes succeed.

8

The Poor Nations
Ye Have With Ye Always

1960

Politically, this is black Africa's season in the sun. Country after country is erupting into independence and Britain's Prime Minister Macmillan symbolically represents, not just Britain, but the whole white race on his journey. Into his ears are poured the hopes, fears, denunciations, the praise, the big visions, the petty recriminations.

The first British Prime Minister ever to visit black Africa while in office has undoubtedly been told all that is wrong with the Western white man, his past record, his present fumbling. And much of this he cannot gainsay. There is not much point in trying to argue back; the climate is not propitious for telling the newly educated, excited Africans that when the Lord shared out faults among mankind he did not exempt them any more than the whites. But if Macmillan did choose to meet their advice with counter-advice, we suspect he would feel an urge to say the same things that other Westerners of good will have often desired to say to the new

Africans. Such things as these:

A whole race cannot be condemned, not even the white race. Guilt is individual; you cannot hold me responsible for the slave trade conducted by my ancestors any more than I can hold you responsible for the slavery conducted by your ancestors long before the white man came to Africa.

Most of you are getting your independence at the negotiating table; many Western countries had to fight for it in most terrible wars. Self-pity is not among the noblest traits of man.

Remember that democracy is the most difficult form of government that ever existed. Freedom from white rule will not guarantee that you as individuals will be free men. Already in your parties and groups you give signs of turning upon one another with most repressive measures. Many of you, especially the educated, suffer from what psychologists call the "illusion of the central position." You think the future of mankind depends upon what happens in Africa. This is doubtful. Relax. You try my temper when we talk because yours is out of hand before you open your mouth. I am not the white race, the British or American government, or the United Nations. I am an individual wishing you well. Stop addressing me as though I were an institution. If you would learn, do less lecturing and more listening.

The good life for Americans or Britons was earned the hard way. They developed their countries by study, work, self-denial; but you sound as if you want the fruits before the tree takes root. You want a social-welfare state, complete with minimum wages, medical insurance, pensions, before you have created the capital to pay for it.

Don't all of you try to be politicians or administrators in the civil service; they run countries, but they don't build them. I admit love of red tape is an acquired characteristic and you got it from your white overlords, but it isn't worth such passionate devotion. Having a junior clerk around to scold as your superior scolds you is not the highest goal of human endeavor. Don't grow out of your own tribal status symbols only to take over ours. Make room in your social pecking order for scientific farmers, civil and mechanical engineers, chemists, veterinarians. You need them, badly.

Secure your own country for democracy and stability before you try to rouse a whole continent in what you call pan-Africanism. First, you're bound to go through the era of nationalism, like every other continent; don't expect to be exempt from the hostilities, aggressions, maybe even the wars that go with nationalism. Most of your people are still tribal-minded, not yet national-minded and a long way from international-minded.

I guess that one phrase would sum it all up: Begin at the beginning.

On June 30, 1960, the 500 tribes within the immensely long, arbitrary and almost meaningless borders of the Congo become legally "independent" of Belgium. Supreme political power is to be put into the hands of men totally without political experience, almost totally without serious education and saturated to their marrows with the psychology of tribalism.

Africa, as an Englishman has observed, is producing far more history than it can consume locally. The coming spectacle of the Congo should oblige sentimental liberals in the West to drop their excess baggage of illusion about Africa, which may be its only beneficial result. For what we shall likely see is not only no true independence but no Congo.

The official policy of the American State Department is to avoid the Balkanization of Africa. It is a vain hope, for years to come. The inner-directed drive of tribalism is still far stronger in most of Black Africa than the outer-directed drive of nationalism, to say nothing of international pan-Africanism. Africa is being Balkanized before our gaze. It will be good luck if the far more advanced Nigeria remains in one piece; the Congo has virtually no chance to avoid a breakup that could last for decades. I have a hard time believing in "African Federation" for any big section of that enormous continent and an easy time believing that the talk of Africa coming to hold the "world balance of power" is airy nonsense.

Nor can I believe that national freedom will equate with individual freedom in a single new black state. Why we continue to think that political democracy is exportable or even teachable in less than generations of fortuitous conditioning escapes me. Nearly every one of the post-World War II states from Indonesia to Morocco has continued under or reverted to strong-arm control. In a century and a half of trying not a single Latin American nation has been able to sustain a true political democracy for more than a few years at a time. The highly educated Germans, Japanese and Italians periodically fail at the effort. That many Westerners expect it in black Africa is one of the more impressive examples of the human capacity to stare down the facts.

None of this is to say that African freedom from foreign rule should be opposed; opposition is wrong because it is fruitless, among other reasons. Nor, of course, is it to say that Africans are intrinsically inferior to other people. It is not even to say that they cannot run their own affairs—they ran their own affairs for thousands of years. But it *is* to say that they cannot run the bureaucratic-technological systems built and imposed upon them by white men without revolutions, tribal wars, breakdowns, stifling red tape and periodic dictatorships of the most tyrannical kind, even though they have heavy infusions of technical and administrative assistance from white men. Without that assistance the jungle would grow over various African cities. If we can imagine the American founding fathers in 1780 waking up one morning to find themselves confronted, through the magic malevolence of a time machine, with Detroit's assembly lines, modern mental hospitals, the stock exchange, electronic computers and Cape Canaveral—theirs to operate lest the new nation founder—then we may grasp what the new rulers of the Congo are taking upon themselves.

The true and terrible indictment of colonial rule in Africa is its failure, nearly everywhere, to educate the people to understand the twentieth century at a pace equal to the pace with which colonial rule introduced the apparatus of the twentieth century to their lives. And in recent years, of course, both processes have been far outpaced by the spread of fervent nationalism.

The Western white man does have an obligation to the Africans, chiefly because of this failure to teach them to master the life we insisted on bringing to them. Beyond that the white man is not so dreadfully guilty as neurotic African undergraduates shrilly claim that he is. Their hot convictions that white rule "held them back" are mostly self-serving nonsense. But we bear enough guilt, we share enough responsibility to make it imperative that we aid them as generously, judiciously and patiently as we can. We have, in fact, no other choice, since the Russians and Chinese are ready to travel Africa by the busload, as we already see them by the busload in the new and "free" island of Cuba.

Thousands of Congolese went semi-berserk after their Independence Day, June 30th, for the same reason that hundreds of simple Italians crawled down from Mont Blanc in a state of shock after their Judgment Day, July 14th.

The Congolese followers of Lumumba had believed that their personal world would be born anew on June 30. The Italian followers of Elio Bianco had believed that the world itself would end on July 14th. Man can endure war, pestilence and poverty, but he cannot endure the sudden exposure of his illusions.

Western diplomats, intelligence agents and—let us admit it —journalists, repeatedly fail in their prognoses of human behavior, whether it be in Hungary or Cuba or the Congo. They fail because they are trained in the social sciences of politics and economics and do not possess the tools of modern psychology. Those few who do hardly dare employ them for fear of being judged slightly queer by their superiors or their readers.

We blunder on. The new African states are currently crawling with earnest American experts in political institutions, economics and social welfare, many sent by the well-meaning foundations. To one of them in equatorial Africa last winter I said, "You can help these people with your surveys and statistics, but don't expect to understand them and, therefore, don't expect to influence their behavior. What is happening in Africa is not an exercise in political science or economics. It is an expresson of tangled human emotions. Only psychologists and artists—novelists, say like a Joyce Cary—can grasp what the new Africa is all about." I only offended the man, a political scientist.

This week I received a long letter from a perceptive American novelist and playwright who traveled in the Congo just before Independence Day. Let me share parts of it with you:

"The prime factor in the puzzle is that not until *after* Independence Day was there a single incident involving Europeans, to my knowledge. In East Africa and Rhodesia Europeans were absolutely convinced the murdering of whites in the Congo would begin well before Independence Day.

"Yet when it came it did *not* represent the long-heralded boiling over of suppressed African resentment against whites. Africans have short memories and they don't bear grudges very long. They have always been kicked around, by blacks as well as whites.

"What happened was very different. The Congolese leaders betrayed their people with promises that in America would be normal election procedure, but in the Congo were believed. They did it out of their own ignorance and because of election pressures. Thousands of Congolese believed literally that with independence all would change and wages would double. Thousands believed they could go to the bank and get all the money they wanted.

"But no miracles transpired. The Congo troops found themselves taking orders from the same Belgian officers. That the Belgian officers were themselves now taking orders from the Congo government was unimportant to the troops. You remember Britain after the nationalization of coal. It was the basic disaster of the Labour Party. The miners found they faced the same bosses, whether ownership was private or public. All they knew about was bosses. And the socialist dream collapsed.

"But one must not take any such parallel too far, because there's another point. I am now positive that the cry for freedom in Africa is soundly based on the African belief in magic, and 'freedom' is the magical word. They expected a true *magical* change. When it did not come, something happened inside the Congolese that neither you nor I will ever comprehend because we don't accept magic.

"This is the basic point in the Congo terror. God betrayed them. Magic went wrong. And everybody, black and white, is going to catch hell in consequence.

"This is the way it looks, but I don't know the final answer about this most impenetrable of continents. All I'm sure of is that the fellow who finds the answer had better be on good terms with his local witch doctor. In fact, he must to some degree believe in him."

These observations on the Congolese psyche do not, of course, explain the whole spectacle since June 30th. They do not account for some of the weird expectations and reflex actions of the Belgian government, nor for whatever hidden strategy may have been employed by the financial octopus, the *Société Générale,* nor for whatever international game either Lumumba or Khrushchev may think they are playing. But at bottom what matters in the Congo is what the Congolese believe and do. And these observations surely explain as well as any we have had the emotional chemistry of the spark that ignited the political, military and diplomatic fireworks display now hideously illuminating the African night.

The distant observer has the impression that the head of the family-elect jumped up from the Sunday lunch table and exclaimed, "Anyone for a fast game of touch-Africa?" Whereupon Brother Ted ran to the closet for the butterfly net in which to snare the "facts," and G. Mennen Williams sent out a rush order for a polka-dot pith helmet for the historic moment when he would say, "Mr. Lumumba, I presume."

Mad dogs and New Dealers go out in the midday sun, which has been a good thing for most people; but it has not diminished the sun. It might be wise for all latter-day Tugwells, rolling up their sleeves to make Africa over, to understand that the infestation of Africa's political, economic and emotional mosquitoes is old, in places immune even to patented American DDT, and loves fresh, exposed flesh, however muscular.

What I am expressing here is not the spirit that built America, but it is, I think, the spirit of the wisest Europeans and Africans who are trying to build Africa. And if Mr. Kennedy's New Frontiers lie in equatorial, not North American climes, as it begins to appear, I hope Mr. Williams will let the earlier scouts trace at least a rough map in the dirt by his campfire before his safari treks toward the hinterland.

I am glad there is at least one enthusiastic, unwearied democratic country left in this world so stained and soiled with public problems, and I am glad it is my own. Most other peoples, if forced, would confess they, too, are glad. But let us not risk the fate of another Children's Crusade.

Let Teddy understand that the "facts" about modern Africa already fill volumes and innumerable wiser heads than his, that statistical methods will not lay bare the hidden source springs of much African behavior. Let Mr. Williams avoid the gossip fate of the lady emissary to whom Pope Pius supposedly said, "But, Mrs. Luce, I *am* a Catholic!"—and not be told by some African chief equipped with Oxford accent and degrees, "But, Mr. Williams, we *have* been discovered!"

I am troubled by the President-elect's judgment that Africa (like Asia and Latin America) has been "short-changed." I do not like the suggestion of guilt and moral responsibility in this. Africans have not been short-changed by America, and only in degree and in places by European colonists. Africans were short-changed by fate, according to the iron law of anthropology by which the weaker races of man continued to reside at the poor addresses, whether equatorial Africa, the Aleutians or the Australian bush.

I am troubled by the concomitant reports that Mr. Kennedy tends to regard Europe and Africa as two separate sets of problems, that American energies and ideas can, in large measure, be switched from the former to the latter. This is surely illusory. The American road toward massive amelioration of the dangerous African chaos runs through London, Paris, Bonn and Rome.

The direct and exclusive American opportunities for effective work in Africa are sharply limited. Americans in Africa must move through the corridors and around the obstacles of European investment, institutions, procedures and attachments almost everywhere they set foot; and they will find that nearly all, if not all, their brightest ideas have been thought of and often tried before.

What Americans can do and must do, first of all, is to make African nationalists abandon their comfortable hatreds and acknowledge that the British and the French, if not yet the Portuguese, truly *are* moving out of Africa, truly *do* seek free and viable African states. By no means must they be given to think they can play off the United States against its European allies.

The ex-colonial powers of Europe are now getting rich. Their politics are now dominated by a whole new attitude toward Africa. African leaders ought to rejoice at the thought of what a combining and co-operating Europe could do with its new money, its old talents and experience to lighten the gloom and griefs of the Dark Continent.

For this reason—this midwifery at the birth of the new peoples into the twentieth century—as well as for the fateful reason of the world's power balance, the overriding objective of the sixties must be to accelerate the movement toward a new and unified *Europe*. This movement is now endangered by the growing trade split between the continental "Six" and the British-led "Seven."

Let Mr. Kennedy, and all of us, remember the anxious words of Gladwyn Jebb upon his retirement as British Ambassador to France: "Unless a real effort is soon made to achieve the politico-economic unity of Western Europe, we shall *all*—and I mean without exception—go into a slow decline in comparison with the bloc of the Eastern countries. And we know in our hearts where such a process must inevitably lead." It will lead, of course, to the remorseless spread of Russian influence and control, with the new Africans among the earliest and easiest victims.

1961

The richest nation can help all of the world some of the time and some of the world all of the time, but it cannot help all of the world all of the time.

If I have learned any one lesson in travels through four continents it is that the United States has spread not only its money, but more obviously its trained personnel, techniques and concepts far too widely and, therefore, far too thinly. We are trying to defend everywhere to some degree and so we defend nowhere to a high and convincing degree. Our lines are so extended that we find ourselves vulnerable to the Communist guerrilla tactics of the task force and the selected target in this economic and propaganda war, as well as in the military combat.

This has happened gradually over the years in the absence of a carefully defined strategy, and as policies and policy-makers have come and gone. Of course, every project and every area come to seem not only important, but critical to the dedicated Americans charged with each one, and slowly the disease of "localitis" has dispersed our forces and our attention. General Marshall fought a continuously bitter fight to prevent this kind of waste of the armed forces in World War II. His success has not been duplicated in the great political war of the last fifteen years, save during the dramatic engagement of the Marshall Plan in Europe.

So, strange anomalies have developed—high-priced drama troupes, for example, sent over to improve our cultural image in noncritical Europe, while one lone American with a jeep, a few films, publications and radio programs has been expected to combat Communist agitation among 13,000,000 people in the extremely critical northeast region of Brazil. This particular lapse, I believe, is being corrected, but corollary conditions exist in all backward countries, in respect to engineers, teachers, agronomists, as well as propagandists.

Many critical areas have experienced newly arrived Americans endlessly duplicating the interests of present or departed Americans. They represent different agencies of government, foundations, universities, religious societies and a legion of cause groups. To all of these we may now add the Peace Corpsmen.

In both Africa and South America I have heard local administrators confess their weariness with the process of explaining the
same facts over and over again. The world is our sick oyster, all
right, but someone, somehow must discipline the horde of doctors, professional and amateur, before the helpless patient dies
of kindness and confusion.

We have not only accepted our responsibilities around the
world, but we have fallen in love with them. Love feeds on itself and we constantly create new love objects where none existed before. So we endlessly expose ourselves to new hurts, jealousies and embarrassments as this mania grows. Exactly why the
United States government must "take a position" on Portuguese
Goa, for example, or on the legal status of Dutch New Guinea
escapes one's comprehension. The thin red-white-and-blue line
of our prestige can only thin out to the point of invisibility if
we cannot curb this compulsion. Our inability to let anything
alone, anywhere, is a matter of despair among our experienced
diplomats, and, one might add, a matter of alarm and ridicule
among British diplomats.

(It is also, of course, of frequent advantage to the latter.
When the British quietly take leave of their formal responsibilities in the West Indies next May I have no doubt that the West
Indians will ask us to add their economic problems to our present grab-bag, and I have no doubt we will do so.)

The occupation of Washington's command post by the intellectual frontiersmen has added impressive energy and imagination to the national leadership, but it has also deepened and
institutionalized this particular American compulsion. Leading
historians or journalists are generalists by nature, with an insa-
tiable, world-ranging curiosity. But the scholar Bacon, who took
"all knowledge for his province," was one thing; the Bacon in
office, trying to take all areas and all policies for his decision and
action, must have been quite something else again.

I'm afraid it is in the nature of the professional intellectual
to feel that ideas are self-enforcing, that a problem defined is a
problem solved. The conceiving of ideas and the stating of ideas
is the beginning and end of an intellectual's function in private
life. It is merely the beginning if the intellectual holds public
office, and the rest of the job is much the harder.

The Eisenhower years seemed almost barren of men of ideas
and, therefore, barren of ideas. Today the White House seems a
hot stove hopping with crickets. (Some are already scorched.) If

anything, there are too many men spinning off too many ideas on too many subjects, and the President himself must be included. There is a dispersal of mental energies apparent in the headquarters, as there is a dispersal of personnel, money and equipment in the field.

The showdown period in the bloodless war for the world has begun. The hour is late, but perhaps not too late if we can now learn to concentrate our forces, from Washington to the remote Viet-Nams of this earth, cut our losses and bear upon critical targets of our own selection.

The American social-worker mentality that regards the world as our sick oyster has probably done more good than bad. But I am relieved that President Kennedy is trying to get his ducklings in a row before dispatching the proposed Peace Corps of eager youngsters to work among the mud huts of Africa and the tin-can shanty towns of Latin America.

It is faintly possible that they can accomplish something, although it will have nothing to do with peace.

To the restless and large-hearted young, of course, distant misery is always more attractive than misery close to home. I have just met the lovely daughter of a British statesman, who is setting sail to do social work in the West Indies. Ten blocks from her London home thousands of West Indians live in the sordid tensions of North Kensington. I know true believers in Washington, D.C., who travel 10,000 miles to be moved by the sufferings of the black men Dr. Schweitzer is trying to help, but who never set foot in the Negro ghettos of southeast Washington.

On their way to black Africa the young American corpsmen and corpsgirls will pass hundreds of African boys and girls heading for Europe and America for study and work. Many of them will be equally selfless, but many others of them intend never to return if they can help it, or to return equipped to make as much money as fast as they can. African society, I would guess, is the most profoundly materialistic on earth.

The young American idealists are going to be shocked to find a high percentage of their black counterparts in African colleges totally inured and indifferent to the sufferings of their own countrymen and interested in freedom, not as individual freedom, but as the political reshuffle that will give them the jobs, big houses, cars and servants, their true goals in life.

The Peace Corps recruiters must rule out two types at the

start—the romantics and the eager beavers. Both will simply get their hearts broken and return as cynics, a posture the young carry off but awkwardly.

I suggest the administrators seek counsel, as far as Africa is concerned, from Ernest Montgomery. Ernest is a red-headed, easygoing boy from Connecticut, still in his twenties. On the grassroots, backwoods level he was the most effective representative of America I've run across in years.

Until the government lost him—alas—to the Rockefeller outfit in Ghana he was, as information officer, the only official American among the millions of Ibos in eastern Nigeria. There he was America all by himself.

He never preached; he never tried overtly to improve the people. He never expected gratitude or even results. So he often got both. I lived a week in his comfortable bachelor house in Enugu, and every night it was the gathering place for Ibo politicians, journalists, doctors or just friends who wanted to play his records and shuffle around in the "benue" or "high-life" dance steps. He was the type who could drift around the countryside in a station wagon equipped with sleeping bag and digest the native food. On one trip this lanky youngster took to demonstrating the hoola hoop in village squares, and created adoring pandemonium everywhere he went. He knew more about what was really happening in that big section of Nigeria than any foreigner there. In another African district there was another young American, a highly trained sociologist and social worker. He was full of drive and idealism. On housing problems, for example, he harried the local authorities, demanded action daily, cried aloud at the built-in corruption, sloth and inefficiency, and ended up disliked and isolated and useless. He was an eager beaver. He also happened to be Negro himself.

The Peace Corps administrators must realize that it takes a very special kind of foreign youth even to become accepted in any backward, ingrown, semi-primitive society. They must also realize that it takes years for any individual to accomplish anything worth accomplishing. A system built on brief tenure and rotation will, I freely predict, become an expensive joke, a sequel to *The Ugly American*.

São Paulo, Brazil

American businessmen abroad are as blunderingly innocent of the sharper political arts as they are at home, and because of their innocence they have just been made to appear Machiavellian and guilty by the South American Communist apparatus, which attributes mass suffering on this continent to "Wall Street's conspiracy" with various national governments.

It all began with angry urgings in the Hearst press and the columns of Mr. George Sokolsky that the United States ought to penalize Brazil economically for the gestures of friendliness extended by the enigmatic President Quadros toward Cuba and the Iron Curtain countries. These comments disturbed American business leaders here much more than the Quadros gestures, which they believe to be a finesse to weaken his domestic left-wing opposition.

So on April 24th officers of the United States Chamber of Commerce here sent a circular to all members explaining their reasoning and expressing their own conviction that Quadros is "solidly with the United States and the free world and against Communism and there is no danger of his becoming another Castro." In their innocence they labeled this circular "strictly confidential," although it went to 1,500 persons.

The predictable happened. Banner headlines in the left-wing press the other day accused Quadros of faking his foreign policies and of sealing a secret agreement with Washington and "Wall Street." Quadros is furious. The American effort to keep strategic Brazil aligned with the West has been injured to some degree, and the myth of "dollar domination" of Brazilian life has spread further.

It is a myth in economic as well as in political terms. The picture of South America as a continent "plundered" by North American capitalism, so widely believed in the states as well as here, certainly does not apply to the biggest of the Latin countries, even though American private investment in Brazil is greater than in any southern country except Venezuela, and in this one state of São Paulo is greater than in all of pre-Castro Cuba.

There is American domination in a few minor industries such as pharmaceuticals, and American and Canadian domination in the major and basic electric-power industry, but otherwise the picture is startlingly unlike that constantly painted and believed by both nationalists and Communists in Brazil.

The truth, as pieced together from Brazilian-American and international statistics, is that the total U.S. private investment in Brazil amounts to $3\frac{1}{2}$ percent of the gross internal product of the Brazilian economy. This is less than the American investment in foreign countries averaged over the whole world. America's "cold-eyed bankers," to quote the *New Statesman* of London, have a bare toehold in Brazil. All foreign banks put together do no more than 5 percent of all Brazilian banking and, what is more, they hold strictly to the legal 12-percent interest rate on loans, while 30 percent is about normal for the big Brazilian credit combines, some of which blithely loan out ten, twenty or thirty times their capital resources.

American companies here would do well to spread shareholding further among Brazilian citizens. Indeed, there is a voluntary campaign to do so among American businessmen right now. But the notion that vast and disproportionate profits are being sucked out of the country is highly questionable. Extreme left-wing and extreme right-wing deputies are demanding that President Quadros produce the figures on remitted profits, but it is hard to see how he can produce anything other than the statistics compiled by one of his most trusted financial advisors, Roberto de Oliviera Campos, who has recently stated that less than half the annual American profits are sent out of the country, the rest being re-invested in Brazil. Though no effective law makes this obligatory, Oliviera Campos demonstrated that remitted American profits total less than the annual spending of Brazilian tourists abroad!

How high do Yankee profits run in Brazil? Ten per cent on the average is the latest official estimate, up about $2\frac{1}{2}$ percent because of the hair-raising Brazilian inflation of the last few years. This is ludicrously small by traditional Brazilian practice, and in this contrast lies the fundamental difficulty of American propaganda here, both private and governmental. It is the same insurmountable embarrassment that American propaganda encounters all over Latin America. It is both socially and politically impossible for American guests in a country like Brazil to publicly reiterate the truth that their business practices are not only more efficient, but more socially constructive and more honest in terms of profits made and taxes paid than the traditional, built-in practices of their hosts. The considered judgment of one accounting expert with many years experience here is that nine of ten Brazilian concerns keep two sets of books, the rigged one for the benefit of the tax collector. An annual profit of 30 to 50 percent is considered normal. (One new Brazilian concern making washing machines showed a profit of 70 percent its first year, and its dissatisfied directors ordered salary cuts all around.) There is no capital-gains tax save on personal real estate sales, and that is but 15 percent. The hypothetical maximum on individual income tax is 54 percent, as compared with 94 percent in the United States. Yankee cupidity and hijackery are by no means unknown here, but the fact remains that American profit taking and re-investment practices are on the whole more beneficial to the future of this magnificent, barely exploited land than most Brazilian practices.

This is true in other Latin countries, but not because North Americans are more virtuous by nature than South Americans. It is because North American businessmen function out of a totally different tradition and psychology. They have been taught in the United States to assume political and economic stability. Expansion and the future are their natural themes. South American businessmen have been taught by their entire history to assume both economic and political instability. It has always been impossible that they do anything else but take the cash and let the credit go.

But insistence upon a fundamental change is becoming stronger every day, and no voice is more insistent that that of Janio Quadros of Brazil.

Rio de Janeiro

This, I'm afraid, is written more in anger than in sorrow, which may in itself be something to be sorry for. But the more one travels during this spring of our discontent, the more he reads in the American press, the more *mea culpa* open letters he is asked to sign by high-minded American professors deploring the principle of the Cuban invasion attempt, the more impatient one feels.

I am impatient with myself, first of all, for having had to leave the self-conscious masochistic atmosphere of Washington and undertake two middle-aged years of travel in order to see clearly that the generous humanitarian American formula for saving underdeveloped countries from Communist-oriented upheaval cannot work in a good many such countries.

I feel impatient about the crippling confusion still being sowed by so many of our most respected voices, who write off the peripheral nations so easily, who believe that cloak and daggering or use of force is beneath our virtue and who seem to believe that any given land of human wretchedness can be saved by our money, technicians, more exemplary conduct at home, in our racial policies for example, and by ceasing to support the local dictator.

I believed that this over-all recipe would work. I wish to heaven that it would. But I know now that in many critical countries it will not. There isn't time. Laos is going. Thailand and South Viet-Nam are likely to go next. Venezuela, even under liberal rule, is shaky. If he is not already at it, Castro is preparing to run guns to his co-conspirators in every likely Caribbean country. Nkrumah, a Marxist at heart, is reported to be running guns into the Congo. In Portugese Angola the advance of Communism is measured in years. The advance toward free societies based on developed economies must be measured in generations. A short-lived attempt at progressive rule in South Korea has given way to a military coup. In the vast arc from the Far East to North Africa some of the new postwar nations that tried the free political system have abandoned it. There is little chance that a single new black nation in Africa will achieve a real political democracy based on economic justice in this century.

Latin America is doing much better in these past few years. It made somewhat the same kind of convulsive leap toward democracy in the early part of this century, only to lapse back into strong-man and rich-man rule. The chance that most of Latin America will hold fast to progress seems better now than then, but there can be no guarantee that it will be, especially not in some countries, if Castro breaks into the open with the ball.

I can no longer believe as an inclusive formula that a different United States policy would have prevented all of this, or even very much of this.

I can't believe as a general principle that we are losing because we have placed the weak countries in a dilemma where they must stand still with us and our client rulers or start moving with the Communists, to quote one of our most respected writers on public affairs. Of course, it must be our persistent policy, as he says, to offer a third option—economic development without the totalitarian disciplines of Communism. But in more places than he seems to realize we have too little time and too little to work with on the scene. This is what has dawned on me after many sweaty nights of hard talk with economic planners, engineers, agronomists, landowners, peasant leaders and politicians in northeast Brazil, a fair example of those regions in the world where no amount of American advice, machinery or money can make an effective dent in the illiteracy, disease, land system or explosive rate of population growth in the time that may remain—in this case, before the entirely enlightened government at Brazilia has a second and Communist-led Brazil on its hands.

The problem is not just to develop what is. It is also to break up what has been for centuries, and this is fantastically difficult for the most progressive government without resorting to totalitarian disciplines.

We underestimate these conditions and we overestimate our own powers. It is beyond my vision to see how the liberal societies that we pose as the ultimate answer to Communism can be created until middle classes are created. That means industrialization and/or systems of small landowners on a vast scale. It also presumes general, if not universal, education. Even in Brazil, with four centuries of civilized culture behind it, a child goes to school only three or four years on the average, and about half never go at all. If one applies these requirements for defeating Communism to Africa and most of Asia, the heart sinks.

Do I have a formula then? Nobody can have a single over-all formula for dealing with this wildly varied, this rending and tearing world.

Of course, we must keep on with the development formula in those countries where it has a real chance, and it will have more chance if we demand with a loan-shark's ruthlessness that collateral be posted in terms of measurable social reforms, as President Kennedy asks. But let us also devise a better cloak-and-dagger operation, not throw away what we have. Let us train far more men in the Mao Tse-tung tactics of guerrilla warfare. Let us look through twentieth century lenses at the principle of non-intervention, which not only plays into the hands of the Communist interveners, but which is contrary to our historic tradition of acting to keep men free.

Surely this does not mean abandoning American principles or imitating our opponents to our own moral corruption. We are intelligent enough not to confuse ends and means, and informed men everywhere know the difference between our aims and those of Russia. We lost ground in Latin America with the Cuban invasion, not so much because we *tried* it as because we *bungled* it.

One is obliged to observe, whatever its moral implications

about men and governments, that, in spite of all its crimes, including Hungary, the Soviet unit enjoys more world respect and influence today than ever. History and our own conscience, which now makes fools if not cowards of us all, will fail to forgive us but one thing—the loss of this mortal combat.

Once again, the American foreign economic aid program has been reorganized at the top, re-titled, and this time, we are told, recast in its fundamental principles so that the days of the *quid pro quid* shall be behind us.

Under the principle of the *quid pro quid* a foreign regime would accept our aid, but it had to give a concession: it had to agree to accept more aid later on. The Kennedy Administration fails to see the charm in this, and by all reports is now switching to the *quid pro quo*—a foreign government will get our help only if and as it exhibits workable plans for actual social reform. Someone seems to have noticed that in many countries the peasants and working people never see or feel the benefits of our money, and Communism marches blithely on.

The New York Times tells us that we will now put "new emphasis" on low-cost housing, sanitation, schools, public health, farm-to-market roads and rural development. Ignoring for the moment the hard fact that economic plans as prepared by the governments of most backward countries are merely sketches by our standards, let me inflict on you some brief mental images of Brazil and Peru that re-lighted in my mind as I read the *Times'* categories of expectation.

The only new low-cost housing I saw around Lima was built for army personnel. There was plenty of no-cost housing, made of mud and straw matting, clinging to the dusty, rocky mountainsides as shelter for the Indian peasants who had drifted in from the valleys looking for food and work. There are no sanitation facilities whatsoever. Lima has 103 churches and one children's hospital. Farm-to-market roads? They have built roads linking Lima with the western farm valleys, and the half-starved farmers promptly took to the new roads to pack into the city.

The same thing has happened in northeast Brazil and in Venezuela. (For that matter, this is what is happening all over Africa, too.) Rio de Janeiro now has a third of its population, some 900,000 people from the country, living in the wretched *favellas* above the creamy beaches, existing by begging and stealing and odd jobs. Here are the true centers of Communism, these universal shanty towns where the once passive, inert peasantry are massed together and subject to all modern stimuli, including the bitter contrast of the rich villas a stone's throw away.

Schools? Brazil has developed new roads, railroads and many new industries the last few years, and her educational system is going to ruin. Even in the richest city in South America, São Paulo, elementary children now go to school in two and three shifts a day. Brazilian kids stay in school an average of three years. One-half the school-age population never sees the inside of school. Teaching standards are steadily falling as the proportion of "certified" teachers drops. President Quadros will try nothing substantial about schools until he has the national budget closer to balance.

Public health? In Recife and other Brazilian cities there are "re-hydration centers," where babies dying of gastric diseases are pumped full of fluid to keep them alive—those few whose parents understand and bring them in. Rural development? In northeast Brazil they are starting to irrigate some drought-stricken lands and will turn them over to peasant ownerships. This will touch but a fraction of the 20,000,000 northeasterners. They have plans to move some families out to humid areas further north and west. But they must have something to move to; there is no sense trading pure subsistence in one mud hut for pure subsistence somewhere else. And local politicians fight bitterly to keep their constituents where they are.

In Peru the peasants on the western slopes already own their own plots. They are starving just the same. Not even the United States government can make rain to fall where it rarely falls.

In northeast Brazil a foreign agronomist said with anger, "I tell you it won't work! Divide up all the land if you want— every family would still have no more than two or three acres and they know nothing about farming. They're not farmers, they're cane cutters. You will have to move two or three million families right out of the northeast, and God knows where or how they will live."

In Lima one of the biggest businessmen of Peru said this: "I know it would mean the end of everything I have, but this country is finished unless some kind of tough, socialist government takes hold and forcibly moves hundreds of thousands of people in the south over the mountains into the eastern valleys where the rain falls. Otherwise it will be the Communists one day. They will do it, and of course I'll lose everything, anyway. I'm sorry to have to conclude that the slow methods of development are too slow."

In northeast Brazil, in southern Peru, in many other areas of Latin America the Malthusian law is in operation. The population increases right up to the edge of the available food supply. Every year the dry, rocky soil of Peru has to maintain an additional quarter-million people. Every year flood-stricken, drought-stricken, feudalistic northeast Brazil has to cope with an additional half-million people. So the schools are swamped, worse each year; the hospitals are swamped; sanitation breaks down; the new employment created by new industries is quickly soaked up. Birth control is scarcely a discussable topic, and for it, too, years of teaching and learning would be required.

Of course, Communism increases, not because of any intrinsic attractiveness of its own, but because people are desperate and will try anything at all. The bitter irony is that not even Communism, as the history of Russia and China gives evidence, can increase the total food supply per capita short of decades of intense planning and work, and in that process many millions would die just as young as they are dying now.

1962

The Kennedy Administration is moving with hypnotic sureness toward a most painful psychological defeat in its foreign policy as applied to Latin America. I say "psychological," as distinct from a realistic, defeat, because at no time was there a real chance that the Alliance for Progress could bring about the political and economic reformations which the Administration itself advertised in the whole of the target area and by the official target dates. It is now obvious that the admirable effort is going to fall far, far short of its own goals.

Peru has made clear to the semi-informed what Argentina, many weeks ago, had already made clear to the well-informed. This is, first of all, that exterior influences in the form of American economic threats or economic promise cannot determine the internal course of events in Latin countries to anywhere near the degree we have so fondly thought they could.

Argentina stands at the top of the Latin American list in literacy and close to the top in per-capita income, and it has a big middle class, one of the requisites for democratic stability.

Peru stands near the bottom of the list in both literacy and income and has a tiny middle class. Yet both countries were unable to maintain legitimate rule and both have fallen under military control.

It has been our dream and our effort to bring underdeveloped countries like Peru up to the level of well-developed countries like Argentina, and we have automatically assumed that a rising level of literacy and income would automatically bring a rising level of democratic stability. There is certainly a relationship between the two phenomena, but it is a general and long-term relationship; we are naive to apply it for the short term and to any specific country. Woodrow Wilson's warning remains true: "Self government is not a mere form of institutions, to be had when desired if only proper pains be taken. It is a form of character. It follows upon the long discipline which gives a people . . . . the habit of order and peace and common counsel and a reverence for law which will not fail when they themselves become the makers of law."

Among the illusions to which Argentina and Peru have given the *coup de grâce,* one may hope, is the illusion that since the war it has been American "support" of reactionary and dictatorial regimes that has prevented many peoples from progressing economically in democratic stability. For we have "supported" a long list of democratically inclined regimes, including those in post-Rhee Korea, Burma, Pakistan, Turkey, Sudan, Ghana, pre-Batista Cuba, Ecuador, Argentina and Peru, only to see them fall under military and/or dictatorial rule. Nor are Brazil, Chile or even Venezuela out of danger.

But what matters is what we now say and do in respect to Latin America. We must no longer talk about the Alliance for Progress in the cheerleading accents of an emergency task force which can, and in a few years, peaceably manage from Washington, D.C., a massive social revolution among 200-million people who must, in hard truth, double their real income in the next thirty years even to maintain their present miserable standards of life—so explosive is their population increase. We cannot continue to talk this way because the inevitable disillusionment will be too harsh and our national prestige, as well as the President's prestige, will suffer too painful a blow.

We are obliged to lower our sights and our voices, to talk of economic growth in terms of a generation, not a decade and to uphold parliamentary democracy in Latin America as an aspiration, not as a requirement. (We have already made the latter change in regard to the African states.)

Privately, if not publicly, our policy-makers may very well have to concede that in some areas of Latin America, including Peru and perhaps Chile, we are too late and cannot halt the forces of disintegration now at work and the violent revolutions now fairly certain. This implies drastic alteration in the present scatter-gun approach with our efforts, and much heavier concentration on a few places, among them Argentina, Venezuela, the Dominican Republic and Brazil. For myself—and I hope I am wrong—the chance for Brazil is poor, but her size and position, as well as her long history of amicable relations with us, make it mandatory that the attempt be made.

A few months ago, I was talking with a United Nations medical scientist as we slapped mosquitoes in the dank heat of a hotel lobby in northeastern Brazil, the biggest area of human blight in the Western Hemisphere. He had been making the rounds of the local dietetic experts and inspecting the "re-hydration centers," where vacant-eyed peasant mothers walk in every day carrying babies already half dead from malnutrition and gastric diseases.

He said, "I'm getting so I wake up in the morning with the thought that should never pass through the mind of anybody with the job of helping human creatures. I wake up thinking, 'What are we saving the children *for?*' They just go back to the mud hut in the ocean of sugar cane on the feudal estates to die a little later from the swamp water they must drink."

These are pictures indelibly stamped on the mind of Westerners who travel through Latin America and Asia in these years of the mid-twentieth century. Such a traveler has a choice of obsessions these days. He may return with a burning urge that America plunge into these places and these miseries with all its energy, money and talent; he may feel the opposite urge that we get out completely and leave the mass tragedies to God and nature; he may, in thinking about certain regimes and bosses, indulge the fantasy wish for a return to judicious assassination as a diplomatic stratagem. But for many the obsession easiest to come by is the desire to shake by the shoulders all those ignorant of the need to check the rate of human births and all those who wish it to be ignored.

Americans who do not travel in these regions speak and write of "what will happen" if the world increase in population continues at the present rate of 50 millions a year; if India, "that dust of people," as De Gaulle has called it, continues to add 8 million more human beings each year; if Pakistan grows at a rate which has added 18 million people in the last ten years; if Latin America makes its projected leap from 200 million to 300 million in fifteen years; if the intense overcrowding continues in the small and increasingly desperate West Indian islands.

But "what will happen" is already happening in some of these areas and in others. The Malthusian law is in operation; people are living to the edge of the available food supply, then dying. We speculate about how many tens of millions might die in an atomic war and whether cultures could survive such a shock. But nature, with the help of human science, has already loosed a war on the world, tens of millions are dying now, and it seems to me a present question whether many ancient cultures and social structures may not crumble before this storm of life is brought under control.

For India and Pakistan, for parts of Latin America, North Africa and the mid-East, there is, so I have come to believe, no chance of the stable economic growth and progress in enlightenment that our foreign-aid programs are designed to help achieve, without direct recourse to birth-control practices on a massive scale. I am aware that such a statement gives offense to many, that many intelligent Americans believe highly intensified efforts in irrigation and scientific farming, land ownership reform, industrialization and education can and will be the successful as well as the morally superior alternative. I can only say that from what I have seen I cannot share this belief. After a half generation of extraordinary effort, India's long-run prospects seem no better than they were when the effort began, even with the direct encouragement of birth control by methods now widely practiced in Western countries. Nasser's ten years of effort with land sharing, irrigation and industrialization ought to have transformed Egypt, but each year some 400,000 additional Egyptians wipe out the over-all gain with the regularity of a tide blurring over castles of sand.

He has hoped, he told me in August, that eventually education will bring about smaller families. Yet educational structures and standards are themselves diluted and blunted by the same tidal wave, as one sees in Brazil, where one-half the total population is now under nineteen years of age and where, even in the booming areas of modern prosperity, children must attend school in two and three shifts a day.

The arguments on the morality of artificial birth control are as familiar as they are fierce and sincere. But there are signs that the premises involved may be slowly shifting. In our own country there are Catholic intellectuals now making a sharper distinction between what is morally wrong and what is legally wrong. There is developing a new round of argument on the morality of the new "oral pill" for women, with some prospect of a broader area of agreement on the whole subject, so painful for so many on both sides of the discussion.

It is not beyond possibility that history will one day record the invention of a safe, effective anti-birth pill, cheap and simple enough for use by the most ignorant Asia peasant, as this century's great contribution toward peace and order, more important than any missile, "anti" or otherwise.

———————

The massive American "foreign aid" program is moving through the Congressional labyrinth, but it is highly likely that this is the last year the program will emerge in roughly the shape and size outlined by the President.

Something has happened. Responsible members of Congress, including some of the most liberal and enlightened members, are simply losing their illusions as to what money, food, arms and exported expertise can and cannot do in and to "underdeveloped nations." The privately growing suspicion that every President from Truman through Kennedy has wildly oversold the prospective economic and political results from America's generous interventions is now becoming a conviction.

Sooner or later we are going to witness a public reappraisal of the foreign aid concept, fundamental in nature, and on the highest levels, as we began to witness this winter in regard to the United Nations, when Senator Jackson first sliced deeply into that forbidden fruit. As one House Democrat, quoted on foreign aid in *The Reporter* magazine has warned, "Next year, unless we see some results, it will be pure charity if we keep it going."

This may come as a shocking sentiment to many high-minded American citizens. If it does, it can only be because they lack firsthand experience of Africa, Asia and Latin America, or because they are unaware of the hard re-thinking about the "backward" societies that is going on in universities and private study groups by men who cannot be thought of as reactionaries, isolationists or tightwads.

The pendulum is making its inevitable backward swing, and our best minds are beginning to ask themselves what the purposes of foreign economic and military aid really are, after all. It is a fact that in Washington's recurrent agonies with spot crises around the world, in it's acrimonious involvement with the personnel, budgets and methods of the foreign-aid agencies, Washington has not in years asked itself this first and fundamental question.

It has merely assumed. It has assumed that charity is materially good for the receiver and morally good for the giver—the most defensible of all arguments for foreign aid. But it has assumed, more importantly, that foreign aid produces economic growth in backward lands, that economic growth produces trends toward democratic freedoms, that democracy tends toward peace and that peace in these areas enhances America's national security.

These concepts have been articles of unquestioned faith—until now. Without adding unqualified endorsement to the arguments made, I do wish that every interested citizen and every Congressman could study four essays on foreign aid recently published by the Public Affairs Conference Center of the University of Chicago. They might pay particular attention, at least for intellectual exercise, to the cold logic of Edward C. Banfield, who goes so far as to suggest that a policy of no foreign aid at all would better serve the hard-core interests of our national security, if not our moral sensibilities.

We are all obliged, it seems to me, to take an unblinking look at the estimate of P. N. Rosenstein-Rodan, who assumes for purposes of forecast absolutely optimum conditions and then concludes that if the backward countries got all the aid they could absorb, used it well, and if their populations increase by one-fourth in the next fifteen years, the average personal income in those countries would be increased by no more than $50 a year.

We have to ask ourselves why we assume that intervention by foreigners in totally alien cultures can produce economic levels, political institutions and social mores in ten or twenty years of the kind produced in Western societies only after many generations.

We have to ask ourselves why we think we can produce even a respectable fraction of such results in lands where we have no enforcement powers when we cannot elevate life in the West Virginia mining areas or get on top of the problems of poverty, illiteracy, crime and crowding that are swamping welfare planners in our own urban sprawls.

Our illusions about economic growth and social justice in backward countries date, I suspect, from our successes in Europe and Japan. But we must ask ourselves if economic development from scratch is not fundamentally different from economic rehabilitation. Whatever the Senate and House may vote this year, the true examination of foreign aid has hardly begun.

Americans rush in where angels fear to tread, an occasionally endearing trait which has probably done more good than harm in a bewildered world. But we are also the people who invented the phrase, "check and double check," although we require an astonishingly long time to practice what we preach.

After a dozen years of fabulous expenditure of money, efforts and reputations we are finally to have a severe double-check of our foreign-aid programs by disinterested inspectors, presided over by the sharp, if not lofty, mind of Lucius Clay, whose instincts as well as whose face bear resemblance to the hawk that sees and pounces quickly and never lets go unless dragged from his quarry. As a carefree gesture I would predict that his major exercise in blame-laying will not question the competence of administrators or field workers so much as the capacity of many societies to *be* developed in our time and by our methods.

To say that the initial enthusiasm over foreign aid has gone yellow in the leaf is the understatement of the policy season. But while this massive double-check is put in motion we remain in the stage of "initial enthusiasm" about foreign aid's eager helper, the Peace Corps. Here again the cycle will repeat itself, though we shall all, ourselves, be much yellower in the leaf before a realistic appraisal of the Corps comes about, let alone reappraisal. There is nothing so irresistible as pure intentions backed by pure publicity, and I am aware that in the current atmosphere of euphoric reverence an expressed doubt about the Peace Corps will receive the same treatment as a doubt expressed about virginity.

Amid all the false starts and semi-failures of our manifold

world missions the Peace Corps, at least, is a solid success—so we tell ourselves in vast relief. Senator Humphrey, one of its sponsors, has sat in judgment on his own handiwork and finds that the Corps has done "an outstanding job," even though its first wave of recruits have barely had time to get the feel and grip of their various tasks abroad.

Of course, it is a success by the criteria so far employed: young men and women flock to join it, foreign governments welcome it (they should; it comes postpaid) and Communists attack it. I would go further and say that giving frustrated American youth a sense of mission and adding to our supply of comprehension of other societies fatten the credit side of the ledger.

Important as are these returns on our investment ($60 million this fiscal year) they remain fringe benefits. In the first place, the work of the corps has very little more to do with producing peace in this world than with producing war. The long history of peoples heavily interpenetrated culturally, frequently waging war on one another, undercuts the whole notion of peace preserved by "folks getting to know one another."

More importantly, while the Corps has something to do with spot benefits in a few isolated places, whether in sanitizing drinking water or building culverts, its work has, and can have, very little to do with the fundamental investments, reorganizations and reforms upon which the true and long-term economic development of backward countries depends. Perhaps the most fruitful field is in the teaching of skills to future agronomists and civil engineers and the like, because no development structure can stand without such underpinning of knowledge. But the end results of such efforts lie far beyond the mistiest horizons; it is impossible, as well as ridiculous, to start proclaiming them now.

If fringe benefits were all that the Corps' originators had in mind, then this should be made clear to the country. If they truly believe in solid, practical, measurable results, then we ought to have a preliminary accounting one day soon, always bearing in mind two things: the cost to the taxpayer and the proportionate good to the country involved.

So far, any taxpayer is entitled to wonder how much, if at all, a country like Brazil, for example, can be changed for the better by the presence of a handful of American youngsters in the face of an advancing sea of inflation, population tides and hunger among its tens of millions of people. The corpsmen now number about eighty-five or ninety to a country across the vast, unmeasurable human swamps of Asia and Latin America. Some awareness of the world's size might aid our assessments.

On the argument that the Peace Corps has proved a success the government now approaches the idea of a domestic corps for service in our own slums and blighted regions. I won't argue that we should have started there in the first place—this would not have happened, given the absence of glamor. But here at home, in the Harlems, South Chicagos and Kentucky coal regions, momentum will not be maintained by publicity, every constituency concerned will soon teach its Congressman the difference between fringe and measurable returns and the double-check will run from the beginning concurrently with the check. It won't require a dozen years and a General Clay to show the stockholders exactly what has happened to their investment. So maybe it should be tried.

June 1963

Political silly seasons are not confined to North America and the way of the aggrandizer is hard, as Nkrumah of Africa, like De Gaulle of Europe, is discovering. The quality of political common sense is not promiscuously distributed in the new African states because of sheer lack of experience, but the majority of their prime and foreign ministers can tell a can of fishhooks from a pot of gold, as they have just demonstrated at the Addis Ababa gathering of thirty-one independent African nations.

They have politely told Nkrumah to save his oratorical pleas for "union now" for his own political clambakes back home in Ghana and have departed Addis Ababa showing no signs whatever of a stricken conscience over Nkrumah's threat that Africa's 250 million people would never forgive them if they did not unify Africa under "a strong central government."

It may be argued whether 2, 3 or 5 percent of that quarter-billion population is even aware that the meeting and argument took place, but it is an unarguable proposition that a politically unified African continent is an impossibility, as unarguable as the proposition that Nkrumah himself dwells in a never-never land of paranoid fantasies more completely than his Western detractors supposed.

A love of steaming hot oratory has been a common characteristic of African politicians; with them, the word spoken was the deed done. How much of this came from a background of belief in magic and how much from the simple fact that they had never held practical political power would be hard to say; in any case, this psychic condition is altering as more of them struggle with the stubborn facts of governance. It is not surprising that the chief exponent of realism at Addis Ababa was the Prime Minister of Nigeria, Sir Abubakar Tafawa Balewa. He is a Moslem from the Northern Region of Nigeria where, under the "indirect rule" system to which the British consigned that area some sixty years ago, strong and able men like Sir Abubakar continued unbroken the art and tradition of governing their own people. They did not come fresh and starry-eyed to self-rule, like the Nkrumahs; in a real degree they had had it all the time.

The threads of unity that cross African national frontiers are emotional in nature, the remnants of the common desire to see the end of European rule. This is unity *against* something and there is still something to be against since areas of European rule remain. But it is not unity *for* something, as is the feeling and the effort in Europe, for example.

The new African states are a long, long way from the coalescing stage of their history. Indeed, it is probably true that they are approaching the fragmenting stage. The potential tribal and territorial disputes within national boundaries are many, and at the best there is bound to be a period of pure nationalism, with its concomitant international disputes and wars. Some will have to learn they can't lick each other if there is ever to be realistic thought of joining each other.

The psychology of political power is the same in Africa as anywhere else. It is hard enough to diminish the scope and authority of any government bureau, let alone a sovereign government, in the name of a larger whole. No African prime minister could tolerate diminution of his own power; if Nkrumah is the exception, it can only be because he sees himself, in his dreams, as leader of the "union," as prime among all prime ministers.

But there is much that can be done to arrest the Balkanization of Africa, which has gone far enough. Regional groupings for specified, limited purposes ought to be, and perhaps can be, brought about. There ought to be customs unions, common currencies, common visa procedures, common rules and standards of education, ground rules for private investments, mutuality in the promotion of airlines, highways, river traffic and electric power; intellectual and cultural exchanges of all kinds can be encouraged.

Sooner or later, most embattled Africans will have to settle down to the prosaic and onerous business of daily living under self-rule, and the rest of the world will regard Africa through clearer lenses. It will see that this is not going to be the "century of Africa," in spite of the late Dag Hammarskjold's prophecy, because Africa contains no real power centers.

PUERTO VALLARTA, MEXICO
February 1964

The lady, the lover and their attendant court have departed. Tourists are now ferried across the bay of beauty to visit the cove where the Hollywood set was built, unnecessarily and incomprehensibly, and at a loss to the local contractor. The iguana remains behind, its lazy spirit stealing over the place as much as outboard motors and the brasses and strings of the "Ultra Moderns" under the midday sun will allow.

Twenty-five years ago Acapulco must have had the simple peace that still reigns in this tropical Eden. Then the determinedly progressive Mexican government built the big highway and the big airport. The hotels designed in dental-clinic modern went up, to be immediately occupied by the white-on-white gents from Sixth Avenue and Sunset Strip with their mink-on-mink women. The inevitable semi-permanent colony of expatriates developed, and one more area of peace was populated by those who have no peace in their own hearts.

The government, defiant of political imperialism but determined to co-operate with the imperialism of money, is pushing a new highway in this direction; the telephone is coming. Surely, Mr. Hilton must have this lovely stretch of earth filed away for future reference. Then the lady and the lover, among others, will have to pull up their fragile roots and a-wandering go again. So it is; so be it. The Chamber of Commerce ideology of progress was invented by Americans, is making the American landscape hideous and who are we to complain if foreign governments have taken it over as one of their "rising expectations?"

It would be convenient to dismiss these thoughts as travel-snobbism, selfishly indifferent to what tourist money can do to improve the lot of the barefoot local Mexicans, who now appear smiling and happy in heretical rejection of the C. of C. and its implacable plans to make them happier. But what bothers me (I have never understood the chemistry of money, anyway) is that

237

all the tourist money poured in seems to vanish, to re-appear somewhere, but not here.

Two or three miles away, off the road and along the jeep trails, you come upon villages where the peasants live in brushwood shanties with dirt floors. They are dressed in rags. A few pigs root about. A few hounds lie in the shade. Save for their machetes and an occasional old bicycle, there is no article of value to be seen. This is bare subsistence living, on the African or Asiatic level. If the people are smiling and robust, it is because of the prodigious fruitfulness of this tropical soil. (Even the wild ducks, which I pursued, require no hanging before they are cooked, so rich is their natural diet here.)

But Mexico progresses as progress is commonly measured. The country seems a miracle of hope compared with most of Latin America. Peasants are moved about in the latest of the land reform schemes the Mexicans have experimented with for over a hundred years—but in what country is the agricultural problem ever really solved? The universal, apparently inexorable imbalance sets in, both money and people pouring into the big cities, the pattern in all Latin America, in Africa and in the great plains of the United States. The whole world is going urban, because money does not "filter down" to the peasant masses; they filter away in search of it.

Foreign money comes into Mexico because Mexico is politically stable. It is stable, not because it has solved the democratic process, but because it is governed by a responsible one-party rule, a condition we would never settle for, but which is the aspiration of many new countries. Under this kind of rule a considerable middle class has developed, the indispensable requirement for lasting stability without dictatorship, and the ingredient Castro has so tragically destroyed in Cuba.

Mexico is not only a marvelous piece of God's earth to enjoy: its story in modern times is, or should be, an object lesson for those who think the democratic political process must somehow march hand-in-hand with economic development. It is also an object lesson, incidentally, for those who don't understand that the rural poor can be rich—in sun and air, freedom and beauty —while the poor of the urban slums are generally condemned to poverty of the spirit as well as of the purse.

9

Self-inflicted
Wounds

December 2, 1955

Every four years we get to wishing for variety in the sounds that politicians make. This year we're not so sure; so many *other* sounds, traditional to America's aural landscape, are changing that there ought to be something to which members of the anti-progress society can cling. We charter members never thought we'd end up clinging to political sounds, but it looks as if we might have to.

The latest blow to anti-progress is the news from the northwest lumbering country; the "whistle punk" is doomed to extinction. The whistle punk is to lumbering what the printer's devil is to printing, the waterboy to football, the copy runner to the city room. He is the low man on the totem pole, on whose frail shoulders rests all the higher structure of categorical ego. The whistle punk blows the whistle to signal the donkey engine to jerk the logs. But he is about to be replaced by an electronic device called by the outrageous name of "talkie-tooter," thought up by some damnable vice-president or boss's son back in the head office. One veteran logger is quoted as saying, "At least the whistle punk knew his place. This gadget even talks back."

If logging can get along without the whistle punk, printing can get along without type lice, plumbing without the left-handed monkey wrench. But it is in the salient of sounds that our defense line has been giving way. We have already alerted an unheeding, ungrateful country to the decline of the loco-motive whistle in the night, being replaced by the absurd honk of the Diesel, which does not call to faraway places, but only echoes the shrill and anxious here and now. We have warned that in Texas the singing of the lonesome cowboy is being re-placed by the Cadillac saddle, equipped with a radio, now used by Texans who ride the fence line inspecting their oil wells.

But nothing has so disturbed our members as the news from Gettysburg. We were quite shaken when we heard that the new $4,000 tractor President Eisenhower's just been given carries an FM radio. Long ago we wrote off our books the clopping and snorting of the workhorse; we had settled for the chug of the tractor so long as it was accompanied by the song of the larks and the mourn of the doves. Know what came out of the Presi-dent's tractor radio the first time they turned it on? A hard-sell commercial with the words, "pick your suit right off our rack and save yourself some jack."

As if this were not enough, the President has accepted an-other gift named a "Kattle-Kaller." Both words begin with a "k," terrible news for another anti-society we belong to. This devilish thing is operated from the left-hand side of the steering wheel on the farm Jeep. Apparently it makes a sound like a bull. Anyway, the first time it was sounded the whole herd of cows came at a gallop and two of them tried to climb the fence, which, merci-fully, is of chain link, not of barbed wire.

It is time progress watches it step. Duck calls, crow calls, turkey calls—now cow calls. One day all wild and domestic creatures will discover that their mad dashes lead them not to their heart's desire, but only to a gadget and a two-legged crea-ture, probably the President of the United States. They will quit responding to any calls, and the whole balance of nature will be in jeopardy.

But everywhere the old sounds are disappearing. Since travel-ing in Europe this summer we've been meaning to send a report to Frank Sullivan, the sage of Saratoga, to inform him that his favorite sounds in both England and France are scarcely heard. His favorite sound in England was the throaty drawl of duchesses snubbing persons in trade; his favorite sound in France was the low hum of models posing in the nude.

November 1956

As the man said, birthdays aren't what they used to be. When the latest one pushes you up close to the mid-forties you not only get to wondering what you've done with all that time, but what all that time has done to you. For one thing, we find it harder to adjust to new ideas, such as the weekend information that the United States is still voting against its only real allies in the U.N. and that a woman had an operation done on her prize pigeon because it was pigeon-toed.

So it was comforting to find in the day's mail, among the birthday cards, handouts and dimly typed schemes for world salvation, the 140th issue of the *Farmer's Almanac;* comforting because the *Farmer's Almanac,* we're quoting, "for the year of our Lord 1957, being first after bissextile, or leap year, and until the Fourth of July, the one hundred eighty-first year of the Independence of the United States," end quote, hasn't changed a jot, to say nothing of a tittle. It still has the hole punched in the top left-hand corner, handy for hanging on the nail over the kitchen range, or on the string by the wall telephone in case you're engaged in weather prognosticating on the party line and want to prove your point in a hurry.

Of course, the first thing we turned to was the weather forecast, and we were faintly surprised to see how casually the *Almanac* regards the weather question, considering that its fame rests so much on weather wisdom. "The outlook for 1956–57 winter weather," says the *Almanac,* "is fairly mild, but the following winter will be somewhat more rugged. No one should worry about the weather changing," it goes on to say, "since it moves in cycles and we'll get back no matter which way the weather is at the moment. Remember someone is always pleased, weather or not." Maybe somebody composed a sly pun there—they have long winter evenings up in Maine—but no doubt when you've been dealing with weather as long as the *Almanac* people you get philosophical about it.

Another steadying and comforting thing about the *Almanac* is the woodcut on the top of the page for each month. In March the farmer, wearing a leather vest, is still pitching manure from a bullock cart. You don't feel the slightest doubt that *he's* going to get a crop. A fellow pushing the mid-forties just doesn't get the same feeling from that eye-patch farmer in the Hathaway shirt driving a spotless, bright-red machine while the weekend visitors pour cocktails in the patio, which is where the back stoop used to be.

The verses haven't changed much, thank goodness; most still seem to come from Edgar Guest, Author Unknown and his associate, Anon period. The advice is just as useful as ever, on just about everything a person needs to know, from how to lead a happy life to how to silence squeaky shoes. For the first, you keep your heart free from hate, your mind from worry, expect little and give much; and for the second you punch three or four little holes in the sole, right back of the ball of the foot; incidentally, a 100-watt light bulb gives 50 percent more light than four 25-watt bulbs, but uses the same amount of current.

Well, you move through the 1957 Hebrew calendar, the movable church days and holidays, and the '57 planting and garden calendar (in January, set eggs between the 9th and the 23rd) and you find out there will be a total eclipse of the sun on next October 23rd. You can see it if you can get to South Africa.

You leaf through the "Fisherman's Prayer," "The Editor Regrets" and you get to the lines that always made grandfather slap his leg and say, "Ain't it the truth." Like, "The best thing about spring, it comes when it's most needed," or *"All* marriages are happy; it's the living together afterward that causes the trouble."

Of course, this being a birthday we stopped at the horoscope, even though the *Almanac* editors print their own disclaimer about astrology, and were relieved to know we are impulsive, honest, quick, confident and fond of sports—mid-forties or no mid-forties. Altogether, it's pretty remarkable the way the *Farmer's Almanac* can take a person's mind off John Foster Dulles.

February–June 1958

It's been nearly three years since the Western Union Telegraph Company has added sweetness and light to this dark world. But you can't keep a good company down, and the board of directors that gave to mankind a Mother's Day telegram form smelling of the carnation was bound to be heard from. And, sure enough, Western Union has done it again; their Valentine's Day telegram form not only shows a lace-embroidered heart and a curly-haired Cupid, but guarantees that if you put a check mark opposite certain verses, their phone operators will *sing* the sweet song to the telegraphee.

They have composed three verses that will be sung over the phone to the tune of "Oh, Susanna" and two verses to the tune of "Clementine." Like:

> "Oh, won't you say that you'll be mine
> Cause you're the boy [or girl] for me,
> And if you'll be my Valentine
> How happy I will be."

What we mean is, Western Union has gone to a lot of thought here, and think of the troubles that could be cleared away if others took up where Western Union leaves off. Suppose, for example, Khrushchev got one signed "Foster" or Harold Stassen got one signed "Richard." Here's work to hand for somebody with a phone box and a lot of coins.

They let George do it, and George has done it. We mean good old George Oslin, the Western Union publicity director. George is a real two-gun man in the field of *belles-lettres,* which is French for "pretty words." George can write prose that sounds like poetry and vice versa; what we mean is, he can make with the language.

Three years ago Ol' George opened up with those Mother's Day telegrams by saying "Western Union has added scent to sentiment." The rest of us may be getting stodgy, but not George; he still has the old touch. This time his publicity release begins, "This Valentine's Day it's woo by WU"—"WU" for Western Union, get it? The company, he says, "will again belt out a burning ballad to your beloved."

"The young in heart," George writes, "will have a choice of five peppy, pre-fab proposals, all in four-line rhythmic rhyme." He thoughtfully adds, "if someone is searching for off-beat, heartbeat verse, a sort of tiptoeing-through-the-dew-at-dawn effect, the company will do its best to assist." And George concludes by saying, "Give your saccharine sentiment some extra socko with a sweetheart sing-o-gram."

We have been saying that throwing chunks of iron to the moon is all very well, but that a little progress in advancing the human spirit would be better. We underestimated both the machine age and the American genius. From the brochures collecting on the dusty, or southwest, corner of our desk we learn that machines are now available to reproduce the arts and pleasures of dining, to create personal history and pride of ancestry, to produce the miracle of close friendship and the exclusively human reflex known as laughter.

Washington journalists have been invited to a luncheon that will be served, from the soup, we are assured, to the nuts, by vending machines. The host will be, appropriately enough, the Vendo Company. The Secretary of Agriculture, we are also assured, will be there to make "a major statement" about June Dairy Month; dairying is also done by machines. Cabinet officers' speeches are not, though they sometimes read like it.

The next brochure comes from a concern in South Carolina, a place notoriously full of ancestors. This concern has decided that other Americans should be permitted to enjoy the soulful satisfactions of ancestor worship. With the return of the postcard and $10 in modern money it will, therefore, send you your family's ancient coat of arms, obviously machine-made. If they can change their die stamp to produce, not lions or shields, but crossed codfish on a field of sagging sardine nets, we'll consider giving them our business.

The next one is from a New York concern called the "Scientific Introduction Service, the exclusive registry (we're still quoting) for the above average adult." It works this way—you're above average, see, in fact the common clay around you don't begin to appreciate the subtle, sensitive workings of your intellect and heart. You are a flower among weeds; lonely, of course; where, but where, will you ever find a kindred soul in the teeming, common herd? The Scientific Introduction Service will fix you up. First a personal interview, then the information about you is compiled, coded and punched onto tabulating cards, then this cardboard image of your personality is fed into an electronic computer; it grinds, flashes and whirrs, and out comes the cardboard image of another human soul with attributes just like your own. *Voila!*—your dear friend to be.

The last brochure promises the production of humor and consequent happiness, not by a physical machine, but by the machinery of organization. It announces a national humor clinic to be held in August; this will seek, the paper says, to "increase humor production and forestall laugh shortage." It asks psychiatrists, comedians, cartoonists and, of course, gagwriters to attend. We always knew the reflexes of laughing and crying lie close together, but till now we never knew what fills that space between them; it is the reflex known as gagging.

February–December 1958

Paris is headquarters of the worldwide women's fashion conspiracy, about which we have long held two theories. The first is that women's fashions are designed by members of a third sex who are not interested in the interests of women or men. We have just made our first visit to a Paris fashion show and the theory holds up. The second is that all fashions are described in a secret scrambler code understood by females everywhere, but forever inexplicable to males.

So what follows is a Paris fashion show from the man's point of view, which in our case was a teetery little gilded chair in a polite semicircle, from which our knees protruded almost to the center of the ring. But first the historical perspective. Last year Paris went wild with excitement because woman's form had been lost. Dior's heir, a callow youth named Saint-Laurent, was the hero of Paris, save in places like Harry's New York Bar. This year Paris has gone wild with excitement because woman's form has been found. But they didn't find it precisely where it was last seen. Woman's waistline, for example, has moved in the meantime and is now right up under the bust. All designers have moved the hemline right up to the knee—all but Saint-Laurent, that is; so this year he is the bum of Paris. That's the way the cookie crumbles.

Now that you have the background, let us get on with the show. First it was lounging pajamas; these were worn by girls built like hockey sticks, who came out, in the words of Lou Holtz, "minsink on tippy-toes." The footies are part of the whole pajama; they look something like Eskimo muk-luks. The girls must have skipped gym class in high school; they walk with their stomach out and their chest in, but since they don't have much of either it doesn't matter.

All fashionable women this year will look top-heavy. With the help of hairpieces the hair flares out on both sides like baby elephant ears. Some of the hats look like oversized shower caps.

Some are big derbies made of fur with a cavalry strap under the chin, for windy days in the Waldorf. Some hats are made of beaver. The great days of Mike Fink and the river men on the upper Missouri died out when the gentleman's beaver hat died out, and for a moment there we had a wild hope; but women's fashions change too quickly. Next year it may be peach fuzz, and a rush for Georgia.

Where were we? Descending the chinline—well, the coat collars are as big as shawls; they lie down or they stand up; in the latter case, they collect rain like a bird bath, so the well-equipped woman also has an umbrella with a fur handle. These wide collars leave a skinny woman's neck looking like the flagstaff at the North Pole, so the space is filled up with what they call "jeweled bibs"—chunks of rock crystal, mostly, matching the clothes in color.

The dresses, we thought, were pretty squarish, often made of loose, heavy stuff, and all short, stout women may as well get themselves to a nunnery for the year. One outfit featured a fuzzy orange hat that looked exactly like the cedar mop of the twenties, and an orange dress made of minnow netting. A lot of dresses looked like half-opened parachutes.

The sensation of the show was a collection of evening coats of Japanese flowered silk on the outside and mink on the inside. This is very daring, with the French Communists in their present mood. As we left the wife of a movie producer was trying on one of these coats and he was giving us a queer look. It was much too late when we realized he was signaling for us to create a diversion, like yelling "fire" in the street.

We survived Thanksgiving, too. And as soon as we get a second wind, we intend to issue a double-dare to Christmas. We've managed Christmas before, and we can do it again. But no more last-minute frontal assaults; that's for youth. We intend to spy out the land first and infiltrate Christmas by degrees. As the old Yuletide saying has it, "He who shops and slips away, lives to go broke another day."

We have begun our reconnaissance operation by studying the television commercials and the writings of recognized scholars in the field. This year everybody has to tie up his gifts—gifts almost too pretty to open—in striped ribbons. Striped toothpaste will not do—too squishy. This year the art of packaging has become a little complicated. You have to re-package packages; you have to buy boxes to contain boxes. It is all part of the American love for disguise. And here we are citing the authoritative work of Mr. Philip Stoddard Brown, neighbor and economist, who shops earlier to avoid the crowds that shop early to avoid the crowds.

The Brown monograph is replete with evidence of the trend toward disguise. A whole house entirely furnished so that everything looks like something else is now within reach, no longer just an American dream. To wit: candles now look like oranges, salt shakers like pineapples, flower holders like sleighs and thread boxes like seashells. Practically everything else comes in the form of books, and bookends are in the shape of anything animal, vegetable or mineral. Of course, he notes in a footnote, not all disguises are perfect. The clock in the form of a ship's wheel, with the hands in the form of golf clubs, actually works like a clock and will frequently give the right time, a glaring failure of American enterprise.

This is going to be a very personal Christmas; things have gone far beyond the simple "his" and "hers" stage; also beyond initialed cufflinks and tie pins. This Christmas you can give monogrammed phone-dialers, Christmas tree balls and shoehorns, to say nothing of monogrammed pipes and—Brown will have to take personal responsibility for this—pipe cleaners. He also points out that you can now buy monogrammed gold and silver toothpicks, which we thought was thoughtful, the way people borrow things these days.

Suppose you have a friend who has everything. Don't give up. He hasn't got everything; American enterprise is still one jump ahead of him. Has he got a jeweled bottle-opener? Has he got a mink-covered can opener? Chances are he hasn't; this country is full of the underprivileged, in spite of those statistics from the Department of Commerce. Of course, some statistics are reliable and we can surely all take comfort in the knowledge that in the production of mink-covered can openers we are still ahead of the Russians.

It seems to us that Mr. Brown loses a bit of his Christmas spirit when he gets to some of the more expensive durable goods. The durable goods from Detroit, he suggests, don't look very durable, especially the dual headlights set in the outer edges of the exciting new grilles. This seems overly fussy to us. Lots of Christmas presents get busted by New Year's.

He also notes that certain services aren't catching on well this season. Such as Community Chests. In some places, like the State of Virginia, some services—schools for example—are actually being withdrawn from the market. But, as he says, those were just for kids, anyway.

Mr. Brown refrains from ending his monograph with the old rallying cry, "Yes, Santa, there is a Virginia," but we haven't.

The lovely and luminous moon has become a public issue. For quite a few thousand years it was a private issue; it figured in purely bilateral negotiations between lovers, in the incantations of jungle witch doctors and Indian corn planters; poets from attic windows issued the statements about the moon, and they made better reading than the mimeographed handouts now being issued by Assistant Secretaries of Defense.

The moon was always measured in terms of hope and reassurance and the heart pangs of youth; it is now measured in terms of mileage and foot-pounds of rocket thrust. Children sent sharp, sweet wishes to the moon; now they dream of blunt-nosed missiles.

There must come a time, in every generation, when those who are older secretly get off the train of progress, willing to walk back to where they came from, if they can find the way. We're afraid we're getting off now. Cheer, if you wish, the first general or Ph.D. who splatters something on the kindly face of the moon. We shall grieve for him, for ourself, for the young lovers and poets and dreamers to come, for the ancient moon will never be the same again. Therefore, we suspect, the heart of man will never be the same.

We find it very easy to wait for the first photographs of the other side of the moon, for we have not yet seen the other side of Lake Louise or the Blue Ridge peak that shows through the cabin window.

We find ourself quite undisturbed about the front-page talk of "controlling the earth from the moon," because we do not believe it. If neither men nor gadgets, nor both combined, can control the earth from the earth, we fail to see how they will do so from the moon.

It is exciting talk, indeed, the talk of man's advance toward space. But one little step in man's advance toward man—that, we think would be truly exciting. Let those who wish try to discover the composition of a lunar crater; we would settle for discovering the true mind of a Russian commissar or the inner heart of a delinquent child.

There is, after all, another side, a dark side, to the human spirit, too. Men have hardly begun to explore these regions, and it is going to be a very great pity if we advance upon the bright side of the moon with the dark side of ourselves, if the cargo in the first rockets to reach there consists of fear and chauvinism and suspicion. Surely, we ought to have our credentials in order, our hands very clean and perhaps a prayer for forgiveness on our lips as we prepare to open the marble vault of the ancient moon.

February 1959

We want to warn Mayor Wagner that for New York the zero hour, the nothing hour, is approaching; the time when that one more vehicle will be added to the traffic stream and nothing will move, north or south or across the town. We refuse to offer any solution, since he has already turned down the most practical ideas so far suggested—a plan for everybody on the West Side to shove cars into the Hudson River, everybody on the East Eide to shove them in the East River; and a second plan that at the next jam-up all vehicles would be paved over with cement and the city then start all over again.

If the mayor persists in his refusal to try either of these plans, he has only one alternative. He can declare New York City out of bounds for rain or snow. The little raindrops from heaven and the little snowdrops no longer fit into the New York scheme of things; they must be ruled out, with a firm hand.

You take Monday night. A sweet, soft rain was falling around six o'clock. The population was terrorized. People scurried, heads down. Policemen frantically tried to unscramble intersections where cars were locked together, their drivers having lost their heads. High up in office buildings lights dimmed low where vice-presidents bedded down for the night on the Bigelows on the floor rather than try to make it to the ranch house in Connecticut.

We hailed a cab. It sped by. In fact, forty-three cabs sped by. Seven buses crawled by, groaning with their cargo of homogenized humanity. The eighth bus stopped; the accordion door at the front struggled open and expelled a female shopper like a pip squeezed from a grape. We took her place, in a hard fight. By some kind of osmotic process through the next twenty minutes we seeped down the aisle until we were halfway between the front door and the back door—an ominous position, since our destination could not lie far ahead; and by a careful inch-per-minute-per-block calculation we realized we would be beyond Harlem at midnight before we had seeped all the way to the rear door. We read the bus ads. The one in front of our eyes said, "Avoid worries; ride public transit."

We were hemmed in by women. It was impossible to bend to either side without risk of a breach-of-promise suit, but we could bend forward toward the window. New York bus drivers refuse to call out the streets they stop at; they can count, but they just refuse, that's all. Now, the height of the bus floor from the street in relation to the height of the street signs on the corners is such that one can bend down and peer up through the window to see where he is, providing he is not over 5 feet 1 in height.

At our best bend we could just see the merchandise in the lower part of the shop windows as we crawled by. This is the way experienced New York straphangers check their position as they ride the buses. Those live lobsters on the ice, they mean street number such-and-such is coming up. That pink lower edge on the Playtex girdle, that means number so-and-so. For visitors to the city this system is a failure. We could feel panic rising in our breast.

Then a miracle happened; a massive surge, like that of lemmings nearing the sea, seeped us right to the back door, where we, too, were expelled like a pip from a grape, and found ourselves only four blocks from our destination.

That is the way New York works. You wait for miracles. *Only* miracles could make this city work. But, after all, Mayor Wagner isn't named Eisenhower and one day the miracle won't happen. He needn't come running to Washington; he's had his warning.

This is Eric Sevareid, leaving New York, if he can get out.

July 6, 1962

As the world knows the American people are not renowned as a contempla'tive people—or contemp'lative, depending upon where you went to school. Practically nobody in the world regards us in the same light as Buddhist priests, that is. We believe in action as the solution of ills and the right road to both happiness and heaven.

I suppose that since Teddy Roosevelt we haven't had in the White House a profounder believer in the mystique of action than John F. Kennedy. *All* the Kennedys are activists. It is clear where the philosophy of action gets the Kennedys; where it gets the country is something, of course, that future historians will decide.

The President's latest demand for actions came this week with publication of his speech to the foreign service, when he told our assembled diplomats that from now on they must drink deeply of life in foreign countries, involve themselves in the activities of students, workers, artists, etc., to make the American presence known in each country and to keep themselves up to the minute on what is *really* going on. Personally, I have found nearly all our embassies abroad pretty busy already, and I won't pursue this specific question further.

There was a commercial on television the other night—at least it occupied the time usually given to commercial announcements—which scolded the daylights out of a happy, pleasant-looking fellow who was relaxing in his hammock. *He* wasn't dashing out to make sure he'd registered to vote; *he* wasn't organizing a squad to collect contributions for the community fund; *he* wasn't spending his evenings working for the local library or hospital money-raising drives. And the scornful voice of the announcer made it pretty clear that such a citizen was no good, lazy, a detriment to the community, state, nation and world, and that *you,* the listener, had better avoid his example if you knew what was good for you.

I wonder. Maybe we better think about this non-active American more carefully. Maybe in his inertia he's achieved a condition of personal happiness, which is something that evades nine-tenths of us and is supposed to be the great goal of the American system, along with life and liberty according to the Declaration of Independence. Maybe he just writes a check for his community fund, knowing that he'd be all thumbs at trying to raise money. Maybe he's wise enough to realize that if *every*body got in the community act, nobody would feel virtuously superior anymore and the activists would find their fun completely spoiled. Maybe he doesn't always vote because he doesn't always approve of *any* of the candidates; the right to vote must involve the right to withhold one's vote or it doesn't mean much.

Maybe he's what I'd call a constructive daydreamer. Most great poems and plays, most philosophical concepts that have changed the world, most great practical inventions involved quite a lot of hammock thinking—that is, physical idleness. Carl Sandburg had another phrase for it, "creative loneliness." Not everything in this world requires the act of togetherness and some things are hindered by it. That's something I once wanted to say to a college graduating class, but never had the chance.

I sat on the gymnasium stage, listening to a businessman alumnus tell graduating seniors of a Midwest college what they had better do with their lives. They had better give what he called "service." They had better not forget their duty to be of service to the college which had done so much for them. At that point, I began to sweat a bit under my honorary cap and gown.

I was thinking, "these young men and women don't exist to serve this college; the college exists to serve them and those like them to come. If they want to help the college later on, that's fine, but it's no *duty*." The gentleman went on in his commencement address to say, "most of you understand that in most cities a central organization keeps tabs on the citizen's financial credit rating. What you may not know," he said, "is that in many cities a citizen's *service* credit rating is also kept; be sure you keep yours on the plus side."

At this point I broke out in a rash. This was pure threat— you be a good citizen, as we, the activists, the organizers, define it, or you'll end up in our black book and your life won't be so pleasant.

A lot, it seems to me, is owed to the activists and organizers in any community—but not deification and not unwilling submission; tyranny, even under a fair name, is still tyranny. There are a lot of ways to be a good citizen, and for some people the best way is simply to do their best at what they're best able to do—even if that requires a lot of hammock thinking or plain daydreaming.

August 17 1962

The other day our strapping, crew-cut Secretary of the Interior, Mr. Stewart Udall, said he was alarmed at physical unfitness in America. He said, "I was out in a farm state a few days ago and I found that the women generally had a firmer grip in a handshake than the men," and Mr. Udall thought that was a sad commentary on our fleshly condition.

A postscript to this view-with-alarm in *Time* magazine tells us that the farm state Udall was talking about is my native state of North Dakota, and I have therefore felt compelled to contemplate this allegation.

Looking for a caveat, I was tempted to raise the jurisdictional question. Does the Secretary of the Interior have any statutory right to speak about North Dakota? North Dakota is not an interior state, not even an interior state of mind. It is an exterior sort of state, way out on the edge, and if the country were shaken hard, it would probably break off along the dotted lines on the map that now attach it to Minnesota, Montana and South Dakota. It is, I am told, the only state Mrs. Eleanor Roosevelt has never visited, and I might make the argument that dealing with North Dakota properly lies within the jurisdiction of the State Department, Division of Northern Peoples.

But let us grant Mr. Udall's jurisdictional rights, and consider the early environmental influences (he's only forty-two) that shape his emotional outlook. He is what one may call a total product of the New Frontier. Like other appointees he represents the political invention of the New Frontier called Instant Eminence. He also represents the new Statecraft by Muscularity—he climbs mountains. He believes in the steady, direct gaze as well as in the firm, manly handshake, and probably in touch-football as the truest expression of the American Way of Life.

But what is required here is a return to thinkmanship, and if Mr. Udall will exercise his brain—though science says the brain is not a muscle—he will recall that Thomas Jefferson was a shifty-eyed, non-direct gazer, and that Napoleon's handshake was reputedly limp in the wrist action. I might inform him, indeed, that I once shook the hand of Winston Churchill and it was like holding a dead mouse, still warm.

The trouble must be that in his concern with the actions of the body Secretary Udall has overlooked the workings of the spirit. If he will think a moment about the unique spirit of my fellow North Dakotans, he must consider: (A) Their innate sense of courtesy; highly literate as they are, they know that politicians have to shake thousands of hands and they have seen pictures of Estes Kefauver's right hand all bandaged up; they *favored* Mr. Udall, that's what they did. (B) Their prevailing political ethos; North Dakota is normally a dedicated Republican state; What did he expect from them—a bear hug?

As to the harder shake of the women, as I analyze this aspect of the problem two solutions suggest themselves. One, the women were brides from the Eastern states, acquired when the men

253

went to Washington to protest against wheat loans and subsidies as corruptive influences. Or, two, the women pressed a little harder because Mr. Udall *is* strapping, crew-cut *and* only forty-two.

I will limit my findings to the above considerations and, because we North Dakotans are modest as well as courteous, refrain from giving prominence to the unspoken truth, known to all my kin and comrades, that the state simply happens to be thronging with unacknowledged Jeffersons, Napoleons and Churchills.

January 1963
The New York newspaper strike and lockout has gone on for a month now, and the climate has subtly but surely changed, both the general, community climate and one's internal, personal weather. After a week or so, with no newspaper for breakfast or the subway ride, it was almost exhilarating. People kept telling each other they didn't really miss the papers and how much more time they seemed to have each day for work, gossip and reading those books they'd been wanting to get to. The public at large, if there is such a thing, took it all with amazing patience and good nature.

Radio and TV news people rather enjoyed putting on the extra news programs and had a little fun doing broadcast "reviews" of the performances of newspaper TV critics who were reading their stuff over the air—the man-bites-dog gambit. Some newspaper men got temporary jobs in broadcasting and felt a bit exhilarated, too. Everybody concerned had something of the feeling we all had as school kids when the regular teacher fell ill and a substitute showed up, after a nice delay; it was work, but the rules were off, and the general disorder was exciting.

But not anymore; there is a general air of grimness in New York now. With those immediately concerned nerves are strained, friendships have been affected, pocketbooks are really pinched; a certain alarm and, indeed, bitterness is developing among other newspaper unions whose members aren't working. Overworked radio and TV news people are showing the strain. It was fun, reading the little news flysheets that enterprising promoters distributed on corners, in waiting rooms and restaurants; *The Harvard Crimson* was a pleasant change, for a day; it was interesting for awhile reading more than a New Yorker needed to know about Newark and Philadelphia, in those papers; but then you began to feel that old friends had just dropped out of your life —like Walter Kerr or Lippmann in the *Tribune,* or Reston in the *Times,* or Harriet Van Horne in the *Telegram,* and many others.

Newspaper reading is a habit, so we all began to acquire new habits almost without realizing it. Mine began as a surprise. For days there was no paper when, in the morning, I pulled on the rope that makes the creaky old dumbwaiter in my brownstone building rise rumbling from the street level. Then one morning I heaved it up and there, in the grimy box, was a fresh but sedate morning paper, the *Christian Science Monitor.* It was a little like meeting a genteel old lady in freshly starched lace coming out a dark, brick alleyway. I don't know why my newsdealer around the corner figured his customers were the *Monitor* type, but he's been sending it each morning and I've learned to be grateful.

Of course, the *Monitor* ought to come in the evening. It's a fireside-in-the-study sort of newspaper; you can't skim through it at the breakfast table or on a bus or commuter's train; it's just not skimmable. You've got to *read* it. Because it isn't just a newspaper, it's also a lecture, a tract, a daily seminar in international affairs, a sermon, a call to high-mindedness. It's homework, that's what it is, and you can't do homework while hanging from a strap in a subway train.

But what a relaxing change it is to burrow through the *Monitor* and leave behind the sweaty world of crime and denunciations and peephole gossip. To be sure, you don't know *what* has happened in many realms of action, reading the *Monitor,* but you find out *why* it happened and what it means, and you just work backwards from there. You get the news behind the news before you get the news in front of the background, if I make myself clear. In a way this is comforting; nothing to excite your nerves, much to excite your deeper thoughts. The *Monitor* uses words like "mankind," "fellow men," the "conscience of humanity" quite a bit; nobody dies in the *Christian Science Monitor,* they "pass." The book-review section naturally deals with the new "Mother Goose" and the new "Hunting of the Snark." The essay still lives in the *Monitor,* with memories of farm life, speculation on "Ways of Regarding Moonlight." If a play or a book is a hit, the word "hit" is placed in decorous quotation marks; if you want to catch up on the latest in stamp issues or in porcelain design, as well as the meaning of the Skybolt affair with Britain, or the status of the House Rules Committee—well, the *Monitor* serves you well.

The *Monitor* takes note of the world's ugliness, sin and danger, but only briefly, as if to say "all this shall pass" and order, sanity and goodness shall prevail; well, that's not a total point of view, perhaps, but it's a point of view, a belief, and I don't think I'm the worse for this immersion; I think maybe I'm a little better.

I view music with alarm. As the man said about art, I don't know anything about music but I know what I don't like, and what I don't like is music to eat by, drink by, fly by, ride by, stand-in-line by and think by. I grant that music in practically any form hath charms for most anybody at some time in his day, night or life, but music, especially canned music, is not to be taken just anytime, nor is it something to be forced on people. A love song on the radio before breakfast, that's like a drink of creme de menthe upon getting out of bed; if you can take either you have a very strong palate—or none at all.

Eardrums, like taste buds, can be ruined by overexposure, and sometimes one feels that Americans are going to be driven deaf—deaf to the subtler tones, deaf to the distinctions in sound.

I got to brooding about this when I heard that the sound system that wires White House offices for such things as Presidential speeches also pipes over music from time to time, for the policy thinker. Well, maybe they *think* they think better to the sound of music, or maybe they just don't dare say anything about it. Where routine, manual work is done by large numbers of people, such as addressing envelopes, it's possible that soft, piped-in music makes the day and the work pass more easily.

But I have yet to be convinced that a musical background helps the thinking process, in spite of one son who, while in his teens, protested that he did his homework better with Elvis Presley caterwauling out of the record player beside him on the floor. No doubt he had the majority of teenagers on his side of the argument; at any rate, I lost it.

But that's voluntary, that's self-torture, and this is a free country—or was free, until we gave it to the teenagers and they began selling it back to us, bit by bit, at holdup prices.

The real point of this mournful monologue is to fuss at big institutions that drown us in music at their pleasure, not ours.

Airplanes pour it over you as they warm up the engines or taxi to the ramp. In some cities streetcars play you music while you're trying to read or re-fight in your own mind the argument you just lost with your wife. In West Palm Beach, they tell me, street-corner loudspeakers give you music.

Or you go in a busy cafeteria for lunch. Dishes are crashing, cash registers are banging, people talking in a mass cacophony, and over, or under, it all music from a loudspeaker. Do they think the music will make the other sounds tiptoe away? All it does is make the customers talk louder, the waitresses scream orders louder.

Of course, I could be in a minority of one on all this—that is, wrong—since the majority vote makes right, if not might. Maybe other people *like* to have music coming at them no matter where they are or what they're doing; but it does make one wonder if silence is no longer tolerable to Americans, especially those massed in the cities.

Do we love music so much or do we just hate silence? Are we afraid to be alone with our thoughts? We seem to have arrived at the point where we need to be distracted even from our distractions.

No doubt I will be told that this is what the public wants. If forced into a corner, I will cling to one specific argument: music in elevators. I dare anybody to prove *that* resulted from any petition by the general citizenry. *That* one is the result of pure conspiracy.

Silence used to be negative and sound positive; people thought up sounds, paid for sounds, organized sounds; silence was just the vacuum between sounds. But you get a good thing going and everybody wants in the act until the *re*-active sets in.

This has now reached the point where a student at the University of Detroit has fixed the juke box in the student union recreation room; you put in a dime and you get a stretch of silence as long as the average recording. The minority, anyway, have had so much of somethings, like sound, that they are forced to pay for nothings, like silence. Rather, nothing has become something, and something rare and precious. This kind of reverse existence has been coming for some time; here's the federal government willing to pay money to the states *not* to permit billboards on the new federal highways. We know people willing to pay more money for *less* automobile.

Obviously the abundant life has become overabundant and

people are choking on it; they want more of less. We know a woman who lost every item she possessed in the sinking of the *Andrea Doria;* she said that when she stepped ashore without even her purse she had a marvelous sensation of freedom.

Well, the eternal verity we intended to doubt was that a rose by any other name would smell as sweet. We think that names, identifications, categories for things change their essence for human beings. This is why we opposed the move in Congress to make the rose the official flower of the United States. Official status is too heavy a burden for a delicate thing like a rose to bear; it would change the rose, including its smell, because it would change all of us in our relations with the rose. We're against the present move to make the marigold the national flower for the same reason; like a lot of couples we know, both the nation and the marigold are doing all right as they are; you tie them together with proclamations, titles and documents and neither will be quite the same again.

Official positions, even titles alone, change people especially. People are wrong when they say about an old friend who's acquired an imposing title or office, "Why, he hasn't changed a bit." He *has* changed, and he's making a big effort to act as if he hasn't because he *knows* he has. Furthermore, the people who say that have changed in *their* feelings toward *him,* or they wouldn't even say it.

We can remember chewing the fat in a relaxed manner with Harry Truman when he was a Senator. When he became President, we couldn't relax for a second in his presence. Titles have an existence of their own. You go and make the marigold the official national flower and you watch—very soon all kinds of ordinary people who never paid any attention to marigolds will have them in their houses because they think they ought to; and all kinds of sophisticated people, however much they loved marigolds before, won't be seen dead with one.

Recently we had to help pick the so-called ten outstanding young men of the year; it was awful deciding between so many equally remarkable people, and awful knowing that whomever we put the finger on would never be quite the same as long as he lived.

Do you suppose that Miss Universe believes she really *is* the most beautiful girl in the cosmos? We would suppose that she does, not in her reason, but somewhere down deep in her feelings she really does. Girls, like flowers, should be untitled, forever unofficial. But if there *has* to be a national flower, let it be the dandelion. The dandelion can take it.

This is about people in their relationship to animals, a relationship that has always interested and sometimes astounded me. Americans are fairly like the English about animals, although maybe not so highly organized to defend them. In England, so I've been told, the Society for the Prevention of Cruelty to Animals gets more financial support than the society for the prevention of cruelty to children—and in some areas of British life children get a pretty rough deal.

What put me on to the matter today was a visit from an American couple who are the only people I've ever known about who hire a yacht each year solely to have their ten-year-old pet cat with them.

Each year this middle-aged American couple go in the winter to spend six months on an island at the southern end of the West Indies. The authorities that be on that particular island don't allow pets to come in without a long period of holding them in quarantine—the British system. So my two friends fly to *another* island first, one of different nationality, hire a yacht with crew, sail two or three days, then, in the dark of night, have their pet cat taken ashore in a rowboat to *their* island. In the morning they land at the normal dock and pick up the pussy at their leisure. Been doing this now for years. They just feel that any law which injures a loving relationship is bad law.

People who have a passionate devotion to their cats or dogs will spend just as much for the pets' welfare as for their children's welfare, though such people don't always have children; and so a shrewd animal doctor will start up his practice in a wealthy neighborhood, just as will a shrewd people doctor. There is a Park Avenue veterinarian, for example, who no longer sees the furry or hairy patients in his offices; he's learned that many cats and dogs are unhappy being treated in strange surroundings, which makes their owners equally unhappy, so now he makes only house calls. In human medical practice Parkinson's law, of course, applies—that is, as many illnesses or apparent illnesses will appear as there are medicines or doctors to treat such illnesses. This also seems to be true with the illnesses of pets, although their owners, not the pets themselves, detect the sicknesses in their rapidly growing number and variety.

Animal doctors become just as fascinated with the behavior of the pets' owners as with the pets themselves. One steady patient of this New York vet is a beautiful old cat which is accompanying its owners to Europe this summer. They can't bear the thought of their cat riding in the baggage compartment of a ship or plane, so they bought a jet plane seat for the cat; then they thought—kitty is a very large, long kitty, so maybe she will feel a little cramped in one seat. They bought two adjoining seats for her—first class, of course. A mutual friend privately remarked, "If they'd buy just *one* seat for me, I'd *hold* the creature all the way over and back."

There is an old lady on Park Avenue whose treasures are a beautifully matched pair of lovable dachshunds. Each evening she takes them out for a walk between her apartment on 72nd Street and the traffic light on 64th Street. But it isn't quite that simple. *Her* dogs will only walk north; they refuse to walk south. So as she leaves her apartment she rings for the doorman to summon a taxi. She then loads the two dogs into the taxi, drives to 64th Street, gets out, pays the driver and takes the dachshunds for their evening constitutional straight north back to 72nd Street.

It is this kind of story—it's a true one—that makes me think the veterinarian in New Mexico who claims that people make pets neurotic is wrong; pets make people neurotic. This vet said that when the owner jumps and rushes to the door when the bell rings, his dog will learn to do the same. Happened the other way around with me and *my* dog. I learned to rush to the door because I had learned that if I didn't, my dog would beat me to it and take another chunk out of the door sill or the mailman's shinbone. If I'm neurotic, I claim my neurotic pets made me that way. Thousands of psychiatrists are working on the wrong set of living creatures.

If it is true that criticism is the healthiest thing in the world for the institution being criticized, television should be roaring with intellectual, spiritual, and esthetic health. God knows it is the national whipping boy. For nearly two hundred years in this country every living soul from moron to Ph.D. has had full freedom to claim authority for three things—religion, government, and the weather. Doubt anybody's right to give vent on any of the three and you were not only un-Voltairian but un-American.

A fourth institution has now been added to this open-stakes rat race.

All right, maybe none of the other three invited as much criticism as TV, but—oh, brother—television could do with a sharp drop in the quantity of criticism and a sharp rise in its quality. How many writers who haven't read a play since Booth Tarkington's *Seventeen* are posing as critics of TV drama? How many lady journalists who never covered the city council are telling TV news departments how they should cover the national conventions? How many boy graduates who can't tell a test tube from a peavey hook are instructing TV networks in the right and the wrong of their science programs? How many nice guys who can just whistle the first bar of four popular refrains are reacting quite positively in print to the operas and musical comedies on the little screen?

Could the Broadway stage survive this kind of monitoring? Could the opera companies, the ballets, the art galleries? Indeed, I may as well add, could the daily press, if it were subject to this kind of capricious, hailstorm attention from, say, TV and radio? Well, sure, they would all survive, but in somewhat the same state of furious, traumatic confusion TV survives in. I happen to think a shocking percentage of TV fare is lousy. I think that is partly due to TV's confusion as to just what it is and where it ought to be going, and I also happen to think *that* is partly due to the fantastically irresponsible, inconsistent pulling and hauling it is getting from the printed press. Not wholly due, but partly.

I don't think anybody who hasn't inhabited the TV bull's-eye for a time can imbibe the full flavor of this. About one review in four of a carefully constructed TV show will make real sense and teach you something you should have known, whether it's a favorable or unfavorable review. The others, even the favorable others, read the way a dog's breakfast looks. They will often indicate that: (a) the reviewer didn't have even an elementary knowledge of the subject matter, or (b) saw only part of the show, or (c) wasn't listening if he was looking or vice versa, or (d) was so preoccupied in the egocentric exercise of analyzing his own reactions that he failed to follow the objective reality in front of him, or (e) got the program confused with another program on another network.

The printed press has been pretty good to me, on the whole,

and since it occasionally makes constructive suggestions about my professional behavior, let me return the favor—just for the hell of it, or maybe for the togetherness of it. (A CBS colleague recently pointed out that I used that word in a book published years ago and I hope he drops dead.)

My first suggestion, editors, is this: break it up. Get your regular drama critic to review the drama on TV; get your Washington correspondent to review the political panels, debates, conventions, etc.; get your school-page editor to review educational programs, your church editor the religious shows, your music man the musical shows, your science man the science shows, and so on; and if you keep a tame historian in your stable, turn him loose on the Westerns—with both guns. You can't afford this switch? Funny —that's just what TV executives say about their failure to break up present program patterns.

In case you don't follow that suggestion, I have a second: straighten out your ground rules. They are quite unfair as they stand. I mean that a critic ought not apply the same rules of evaluation to a nonfiction program as to a fiction program. With a drama, an opera, a Western, or what not, the critic is fully entitled to judge it on the basis of what the little screen shows him and on absolutely nothing else—because in the unreal world the producer, author, director and performers have one hundred per cent control over the material. If the final result is bad, it's their doing entirely. But when TV produces a news show, a basic research science show or puts on a living event like a political convention, the producers, etc., have only partial control over the material. Here, I claim the critic has got to get backstage or at least make a few phone calls, much like a reporter investigating a news story, and find out exactly why this was done and that not done. They would learn a very great deal and their reviews would make a very great deal more sense. Rarely have I known a critic to point out a flaw in a nonfiction program which was not realized and lamented by the producing staff before the program ever took air, but which stayed in because it had to stay in.

Excuse me now, I have to get to work on a radio news analysis, and I can't make up my mind whether to explain de Gaulle, the evils of not cutting taxes, or the trouble with Detroit. Honestly, people just don't realize how many things guys like me have to know all about.

I wish I could think that the quality of my output in my

field were as high as the quantity. When I think of the millions of words I have uttered into the electric microphone in nearly twenty-five years of uttering, when I think of how few of them I should want to preserve, I am appalled.

This produces in one a craving to be brief.

First, I want to discuss—briefly—television news and public affairs. The fact that I am already one of the old-timers in it is testament to its youth as the newest form of journalism. It is also, in some ways, the most powerful form, for good or ill. It is also the most personal form of journalism there ever was. And at the risk of appearing to plead for sympathy, let me say that it is also probably the most difficult kind of journalism to do well.

I think we are all getting better at it. We have bigger staffs to deploy, more money to spend, we are developing specialists and our own techniques. The sense of ever-present responsibility, rather frightening responsibility, is sharpened, not dulled with time.

But we still make some ghastly blunders, and we never quite operate at the level of quality we feel we can somehow attain.

There is one sense in which we are not doing as well in television, I fear, as we did in the best days of radio. In those days we had not had time to unlearn, with the help of sponsors, executives and other eager helpers, the basic lesson of all human communication, and that is that in the end as in the beginning, is the *word*.

TV is not radio with pictures; in terms of special events and some documentaries it's a lot more than that. In terms of news programs and many documentaries, it's often less than that. It has the speed of radio—almost; it has the accuracy; but it does not have the comprehensiveness, the originality or the style. Because it has downgraded the word and the place of those with the gift of words. The man who wrote and spoke with refinement was the man who thought with refinement. The performer with the fastidious mind has been replaced, in considerable degree, by the performer with the chummy voice, the friendly face or the trick manner of speaking. The daily and weekly audiences observe a lot of character actors; they observe rather few minds of character in action.

When TV began to forge ahead of radio and take the great audience with it, it failed to bring along the commentator as such; and there were many such, men of world experience, of disciplined, objective minds, men trusted by millions of Americans whose view of the world had been formed in considerable degree by such men.

They cannot, of course, compete in the ratings with Lucy or with the Billies from the Hills of Beverly. But whoever before in all time thought that the criterion for quality, value, art, intellect, must be the sheer numbers attracted at a given moment?

I do not, in any case, believe in the weary argument that the people are given what they want. How people can know what they want unless they have alternative choices presented, and presented constantly, I have no idea. As Shaw said, "People better get what they want or they will end up wanting what they get."

There is constant concern in television that the least-informed in the audience be able to understand. I wish there could be at least equal concern that the best-informed be interested. I would like to see a short sentence engraved on the desk of every television executive, on both the informal and the entertainment sides of the business: "The lowest common denominator is commonness."

That phrase, "the public," has frozen our thinking. The public are only people, and the people are only persons, no two alike anywhere. I wish this industry I inhabit could begin thinking in terms of persons, not publics; perhaps the fiercely competitive economics of the industry forever prevents this, but I'm free to dream—on local option time, at least.

March 16, 1964

In the last four months the entire nation has witnessed on television the assassination of a President, the murder of his presumed assassin, a jailbreak by criminals in the courthouse where the murderer was being tried and the sentencing of the murderer in the courtroom. The murder and the act of sentencing by the jury were witnessed "live" as they occurred, and the other two events shortly after they occurred. On March 10th the television tube was linked to the computer machine, and within minutes after the polls closed in New Hampshire, "electronic journalism," to use an awkward phrase I once invented in a regretted moment, forecast—nay, announced—the victory of Ambassador Lodge to the nation. People sitting in their parlors in Anchorage, Alaska, or sunbathing beside a radio set in San Diego knew what the New Hampshire voters had done before some of those voters, trudging home from the polling places, were aware of it.

It is not surprising that responsible persons engaged in broadcasting news are surveying their accomplishments with wonder, pride—and some uneasiness. It is time to begin some hard thinking about the real nature and the possible consequences of instantaneous news. I do not pretend to comprehend the full meaning of what is happening in this area of America's "graphic revolution," but it seems clear that what we are confronted with is not merely news by a different medium, but news that, in a certain sense and degree, is itself transformed by the medium. Not only do the individuals who are the subjects of news by television behave differently because of the medium, but the public receiving this news reacts differently.

It is no secret by now that many of the civil rights demonstrations in American streets took the particular form they did take because of the presence of the television cameras. The behavior of both police and protestors was affected. Indeed, there were cases in which protest organizers apprised television stations in advance of their secret plans in order to have full coverage of their actions. When Oswald was shot in the Dallas police department, the chief of police was accommodating reporters and cameramen who insisted on a look at Oswald.

To judge what *could* happen with both the actors in a news event and the receiving public, let us imagine that the full Ruby trial had been witnessed on television. The natural dramatics of the trial would have been intensified, and the whole nation would today be fiercely arguing the justice of the verdict. Judge Brown would have become an object of the utmost contention, not only by practitioners of the law, but by housewives, businessmen, taxi drivers and school children. The concept underlying the principle of open trial in this free society was not that the public should be present, but that representatives of the public be present, as warranty against the secret trial.

We are not likely to see a general practice of televising courtroom trials; the American Bar Association is on record against it and many television officials themselves are uneasy at the prospect. There is much more room for argument, however, when it comes to legislative and quasi-judicial proceedings, such as a Senate hearing. But what is supposed to be a rule, or at least a conjecture, in the realm of physics will still hold true: an object observed alters.

In the matter of television's early and uncannily accurate forecasts of election results, the luxury of discussion over hypotheses may be of very short duration. A hard question of public policy is inescapably approaching. Suppose that in the early evening of next November 3rd the computers discover and television announces that Mr. Johnson or the Republican candidate has been elected President, no matter the votes yet uncounted? Millions of people on the West Coast will have not yet cast their votes. Will supporters of the announced victor then stay home, changing their states' electoral vote and record in history? Will supporters of the defeated man stay home? Just what will happen?

Television is clearly much more than a mirror of events and social forces; it is social force in itself. It not only reports news; it creates and shapes the news.

A Square in a Round World

YOU CAN GO HOME AGAIN

The Great Northern's *Empire Builder* train was just pulling away from the depot in Minot this warm Saturday night of the best Indian-summer October that North Dakota has known in many years. The old folks said it was surely the best; the hunters up from Minneapolis and Omaha were not very happy, since the mallards and the Canadas fly high and flare quickly when the dawn sky upon the prairie is blue and transparent.

I had time to get seated in the club car, turn to the window and wave quickly as they all lifted their hands in the pool of light under the street lamp by the parking place: Bill Francis, who sold the *Velva Journal* six years ago to take it easy; "Aunt Jessey," his "new" wife, who had been Mrs. Beebe in the drayage office on Main Street; Jim Morley and Hazel, his wife, who had been my mother's "hired girl" in those days so long ago; John Kramer, proprietor of the Texaco station on U.S. 52, the Minot-Velva highway, who had stayed when I had moved away, and had grown up to marry Helen, angel of blue and silver, who had somehow, incomprehensibly, grown up too. That morning we had been lying in the weeds near a slough, John and I, waiting for the ducks. His son, Mike, was sitting close by, fingering his 20-gauge, whistling a song, his grave, little-boy's face framed in a sheepskin parka. His face was Helen's face precisely as memory had always insisted.

I had been watching Mike all that week in Velva. He appeared and reappeared on his dusty bicycle; he knew all the same short cuts on foot; he, too, rejoiced in the juice of the cactus berries on the way home from the afternoon hills; he, too, haunted the town library—"a book a day this summer—most of them kids, they don't read!" A fleeting sensation had come over me that this boy was I, that I had never really gone away. Mike is twelve. When we had moved away I was twelve. That was thirty years ago.

(I would never dare advise you, Mike, whether or not to move away when you are older. I understand too little of the bearing of place and time on human happiness or discontent, and now that I have been back and watched and listened and talked with all of you, my certainties number less than ever.)

The eastbound *Empire Builder* pulled away and the faces under the street lamp vanished at once. I knew in my heart I would never see them again. I asked the steward for a drink. My ears adjusted to a conversation behind me. This is what I heard:

"Why, I'm on my way to my old home town in northern Wisconsin. Haven't seen the place in forty-eight years. I wanta see the old place and I wanta see what Agnes looks like now."

It was a heavy businessman type in a gaudy sport shirt, embellished with one of those bright cords instead of a necktie, fastened in front with a gadget clasp. He was talking to a middle-aged couple he had obviously just met that moment at the bar.

He went on, "My wife wouldn't come along. She said she didn't know what had got in me. She said she wasn't going to go and try to beat on a dead horse."

The woman by the bar said, "Well, I imagine you'll find it pretty changed."

The man said, "Yeah, I guess so, I guess I will."

I had an impulse to say something to him, thought better of it and went back to my duplex roomette. The Great Northern roadbed is smooth over those prairies, but sleep did not come until I got up and swallowed a sedative. Then I blanked out and awakened Sunday morning at the Minneapolis station, which was full of college football players in sport jackets, looking weary and stiff in the early light.

It is something not lightly undertaken, a return from middle age to the mystic scenes of your childhood: it is an anxious pilgrimage for anyone, but harder, I think, for those of us whose memories were cradled in North Dakota. Men lived so close to God's will in those prairie places and in those days that we remember, we very many who went away. It was a trial of the human spirit just to live there, and a triumph of faith and fortitude for those who stayed on through the terrible blasting of the summer winds, the merciless suns, through the frozen darkness of the winters when the deathly mourn of the coyote seemed at times the only signal of life.

The memories of a Dakota child are laced with these black threads and for some the binding is too tight, too painful ever to be unstitched. One of my family says, "I can never go back. I cannot go a mile west of the Red River anymore. I glimpse those prairies and I get sick."

All this I know and have always known. I remember sickness and inward weeping in my father's Model T as it jolted along the rutted prairie roads that led nowhere save to another dusty farm under another clump of dying cottonwoods. In stark clarity I remember running away from home at the age of four, crossing the Soo Line tracks, trudging up South Hill and then suddenly confronting the sky and the plains; I was lost, alone in the eternity of nothingness. I remember studying the picture books of the seaside places, the mountains and the crowded cities. Somewhere they existed. I remember tracing the meaningless rectangle of Dakota in schoolbook maps and thinking: Why are we here on the cold, flat top of our country? What am I doing here?

But a child's heart is not made for desolation; it is made for warmth and love, and these it will always find, however hidden in the most barren places. These thirty years my memories have been also laced with many golden threads. I do not know if the psychologists are right, that we tend to remember the sweet and to forget the harsh, but for me in these thirty years the golden threads have outlasted the black. They are composed of many things—shade and the cool grass of our yard, pleasant faces

269

that never die, the creak of saddles and the smell of horses, the nectar of cactus berries and the stain of plums, the secret, devilish gang-thrill on Halloween, the cold, dripping joy of the ice wagon in the hot summer street, the leafy path to the swimming hole, the mad joy of the circus parade down Main Street, the heady drug of printer's ink in the *Journal* shop, the girl of silver and blue, the stately gravity of the Chautauqua lecturer who made me feel so wise and grave on the walk home with Father. What man does not remember and cherish such things? We are all alike, we graying American men who were boys in the small towns of our country. We have a kind of inverted snobbery of recollection and we are sometimes bores about it, but that's the way it is.

For me the river was the source and the key. A true river ran around the edges of our town of Velva. (We laughed at the river's name—the Mouse—but we liked the name of the town. A pleasant word, though what it means we have no idea. Old Oscar Anderson, retired jeweler and keeper of the weather, says that there is no other such place name in all the world, save a small river in northeastern Siberia.) It was the river and the trees that made our town an oasis in the dun-colored desert that surrounded all.

The river. Perhaps I have learned something about its meaning for me. Three or four years ago in a dozing and inward mood I found my feelings—not thoughts, but feelings—slipping slowly down the staircase of my emotional existence. They went down and down, without effort, past my earliest room, past Mother and the first visual recollections, and they stopped at the river. I am a rational man and I do not much believe in "mystic experiences." I asked a psychiatrist if he could explain this. Was this the escapist desire to "return to the womb?" Was it just that the shady and delicious river was an early solace and refuge for a sometimes lonely child? "Not exactly," he said. "But you had a true experience not many have. It is what we call the 'oceanic feeling.' All we know is that human life—all life—traces back to the water. I won't laugh at your saying you felt as if you had touched your origin. We don't know enough about it, but maybe you did."

I traveled back to the little town on an Indian-summer day —out of curiosity, I suppose, more than anything else. Just to see it again, wondering about the effect of the visit on me, how they would receive me and how life had altered there in these thirty years.

There is still only one train a day from Minot to Velva, so I hired a Studebaker and found U.S. 52 by instinct at once. I drove down this valley road, unable to see the river on the left for the iron grating of leafless scrub oak that screened it. My first discovery was that the great hills which had so protected and imprisoned my childhood were not hills at all, but only a sloping escarpment rising from the river. They were not rugged and majestic; they were low and rolling and dimpled, a pleasant windbreak, nothing more. I laughed out loud before I quite realized what I was laughing at. My nightmare had just been abolished. I had it often as a child, and it had come back once in a great while up to a few years ago. It was always the same: immense, fat, tan-colored clouds were rolling remorselessly over me, strangling and crushing, and I always woke out of this dream sick and sweating. It was the hills, nothing more; I knew it for the first time and for certain.

A sign said, KREBSBACH FARM EQUIPMENT, MINOT-VELVA, and I began to breathe a little harder. I found myself slowing the car. A pickup truck passed, carrying a heavy-headed bull, then a trailor with a Wisconsin plate. Another sign said, HEDSTRAND'S MARKET, where watermelons were piled on a roadside platform. I had forgotten that watermelons were spherical, and for an instant I could feel the slippery weight of them when we had "hooked" them by night from Doc Ritchie's garden and cached them in the willows by the coulee. The telephone wires faithfully followed the wind of the road, slim mourning doves perched upon them as always. At slow speed it was awkward to keep the rhythm of the Burma Shave sign, something about "Old Mac-Donald needed charm ... Hello, Hollywood ... Good-by, farm." A car passed with a big screen protecting the radiator grille. The newest cars were coated with dust. I had forgotten about the dust and the hot-weather bugs. But the road was hard-topped, not gravel any more.

———

Another sign said, VELVA 5 MILES, and my hands were sweaty on the wheel. A small uproar began in the back of my mind: "Don't do it, don't do it. Let it stay as it was. You'll expose the negative, destroy a wonderful film of memories. Get the hell out

271

of here before it's too late." The front of my mind said, "It's all right. I'll just slip in a side road and drive around a little for a look. If it's too tough, I can slip out again, and call up Bill and say I'm sick or called back East at once."

But there wasn't any side road in. There never was. You have to keep going. The valley opened out a little and there were the red, high-shouldered grain elevators; there was the little yellow depot, just the way it was. South Hill was wrong, somehow. Where was the water tank and what was that radio antenna doing, sticking up there? The road turned in, under a trestle that didn't belong there, and Main Street was right in front of me. All of it, the whole two blocks of it, absolutely, fantastically the same. J. C. Penney—that was the Muus Bros. General Store. Barbershop—right where it was, downstairs. Ahead was Father's sandstone bank, standing stark and solid.

I never had a chance. The man leaning on the red-brick office front was Bill Francis. I hadn't seen him in 25 years, yet I'd know that rosy, smiling face anywhere, anytime. He stepped off the curb, put his head in the car and said, "Daggone, Bud, you haven't changed. Drive on down and stop by the lumber yard. I'll catch up. Aunt Jessey's got dinner—lunch waiting."

I braked by the Soo Lumber Yard, glanced about, and the swarm started, a jumble of unrelated things. The long, high boarding of the lumber yard was still a faded gray, shelter from the north wind in winter on the way home, sun reflector in summer to be quickly passed...the *Velva Journal* didn't belong there in that white frame shack, that should be F.X.A. Perrin's Harness Shop...the Methodist church and that little house beside it, that was where freckled Wes had lived, the comrade of my hopes and dreams...there had been a weedy open lot for short cuts there where those two modern brick buildings stood, the new city hall and the medical clinic.

The streets were narrower; the houses were smaller. I could see the whole pattern of the squares. I had never noticed that as a child; then, each corner, each backyard was its own complete world, unrelated to all the rest.

But the trees. It was strange—the trees seemed exactly the same height and thickness.

Bill honked and motioned behind me. His new car was pink and cream, and the lettering on it said, *La Femme*. I followed him west, one block, two blocks. We were crossing our street, but I couldn't make myself turn to look. We stopped at the

Beebe house, where Bill now lived. The screened porch was gone, replaced by a big picture window.

I almost called her Mrs. Beebe when she greeted me, instead of Mrs. Francis. The hair had been jet black when she sat at the desk in Ira Beebe's drayage office. Now it was white. The face was still as strong and the mouth as firm, but you identify by the eyes. They reveal the spirit and the essence, and it is the essence, the being itself, the *atmosphere* of each person that is reawakened.

Then it all comes back. (Wasn't it she who had marched into Wasson's meat market that day and said, "Aren't you men ashamed to be sitting here when the President of the United States is about to go through on the train?" Abashed, they had quickly stirred, but it turned out to be the president of the railroad.)

Aunt Jessey had run the drayage front office while Ira was out with his powerful, big-buttocked teams. Ethel Francis had run the *Journal's* front office while Bill was out collecting the news items and the printing jobs. In the late '40s, truck years by then, Ira had tried to get to a blizzard-bound farmer and his heart couldn't stand it. Ethel died the same year. Bill needed somebody to take care of him, and Aunt Jessey needed somebody to take care of, and I could scent happiness in this old house the moment I stepped past the vestibule.

(Aunt Jessey, I was in your house two days, the big, spotless house you manage by yourself, before I realized you can't read a line anymore, that you couldn't make out my features at the supper table. I have met a few great women in my life around the world. Now I think of you among them.)

At lunch Aunt Jessey said, "I think you'll find more familiar names up on the hill at the cemetery than anywhere else. Why, we hardly know half the people in town, any more, ourselves."

Right there began my re-education in the modern truth of the American small town, where nothing supposedly ever changes and everybody knows all about everybody else.

Bill and I walked around the corner to see Oscar and Gertrude Anderson, who were leaving on the afternoon train to see their son, Harry, at Wichita. Harry had been a quiet and studious boy; now he was a surgeon of wide distinction. They were just putting white cloths over their furniture as they had done

273

every year, and they hadn't expected to see me. Now it was almost as if a long-lost son had come home. Mrs. Anderson cried a little and laughed a lot, not over me, but over the memories my appearance evoked, the heartaches, the foolishness, the triumphs of those early days and those early young couples—the banker, the doctor, the lawyer, the editor, the merchants.

"It was so awful here, then—think of it, from Berlin I came as a bride, to *here!* But so wonderful. Such wonderful people there were—the Aakers, the Sevareids, the Thorpes, the Wedges. So hard, so hard it was, and still I love to think of those days. Ach. Bill, why have we all worked so hard all the time? Why didn't we have more fun, more travel? And now we are old! Oscar! Get the little sign Bill sent us from Michigan that time!"

Oscar brought the little sign which said, "Vy is it we get so soon oldt and so late schmardt?"

Then Mrs. Anderson reversed her values. "Oscar had to work so hard at the jewelry store, till midnight every night on the watches. So many years we scrimped and saved, to pay for the house, to buy the clothes and get Harry and Frieda a decent education. But these new ones. It seems so easy for them. Right away a clerk. New car, right away, house paid for so quickly. They do not seem afraid of debt anymore."

Out the window I could see the kids running home from school. Their clothes were bright and new-looking, exactly in the mode of Minneapolis or New York or anyplace else. Two carloads of high-school boys were racing each other in their hot rods.

"Maybe it's better this way," I said.

"I suppose," she answered. "Maybe you are right. We are getting old that's all."

The mind dwells in time. Is the small town only for the young? I was thinking. Is this all that it brings in the end—memories and the axis of Velva-Wichita or Velva-Los Angeles, wherever the grown children now pursue their lives?

Oscar snapped his fingers and hurried out of the room, and it was as if his wife had read my thoughts. "Every day for thirty years he has checked the weather for the government. It is part of his life. Sometimes we think of going away to live, but you know Oscar helped to build this town. Every tree has a meaning for him."

Oscar came back with a triumphal look. "Well, think of that!" he said, "Eighty-six degrees, and last night it was thirty-six. Fifty-degree change in only twelve hours!"

At supper it was talk of who was where, who had died, married, divorced, become rich, gone bankrupt, vanished, ended in the old-folks home or in prison. I could find in it all no pattern, no unfolding of personal life that could be attributed to the town itself, to any of the influences for which we credit or blame the small towns of our country.

The girl who had married, at twenty-one, the old man of seventy-one produced the hushed talk I remembered in the parlor? She had been a devoted wife until he died, and was now a devoted wife to another husband. The little roughneck who had led us in the Halloween backhouse raids and first told me of shameful things? He was middle-aged, pleasant, with several children. That saintly couple who read to their children each evening and had them lined up in church each Sunday? One of those children had vanished. One was in prison. The girl got into repeated troubles, then drifted away.

With a few I could have predicted, from the essence that even a child seems to understand. I would have known that Tubby Anderson, good-natured town bully, could never grow old. I remembered that he was older; he would duck me and my comrades at the swimming hole, then laugh our terror away and take us for a wild ride in his Overland wreck. He drove and drank like crazy. He never grew up; he just quit the effort when he was forty-six, and died.

And of Helen I would have known. She and her husband came in through the kitchen, laughing; he was one of the nephews Aunt Jessey had raised. Helen's children were beautiful, as I had known they would be. Her coloring was darker, her figure was wider, but it was the eyes, again, even through the half-rimmed glasses they all seemed to wear. The peace and serenity had not abated. She had stayed and she was happy, as she had been fashioned from childhood always to be. Place never had anything to do with it.

Eventually the evening broke up, and I mounted the stairs. In odd corners, mementoes of childhood in the twenties lay about: the sewing machine with the treadle; the ivory-shell dressing set on the bureau; the old box camera with the yellow eye; the claw-footed bathtub with the spigot that spouted a thin, hard stream.

A wartime siren began wailing; it was the ten-o'clock curfew (all kids under sixteen off the streets) but no longer a bell. I crawled into the wide bed and suddenly ached with exhaustion.

I listened to the night country noises and incomprehensibly, for no certain reason, just at the moment of passing to sleep, tears came in a silent flood.

In the morning I explored, on foot, alone, as often in the intervening years I had dreamed of doing. In the reveries I saw but was unseen and could go away at will like a ghost. Now I pushed along the riverbank, feeling an awkward Gulliver, very conscious of the stare of a plowing farmer, of the dust gathering on my Madison Avenue shoes, the burrs adhering to my tailored jacket. I stumbled heavily in tangles of dead "wild cucumber" vines, striving for the old path to our swimming hole, and at that moment realized middle age. The river was a wide ditch no more. The mudbanks of the swimming hole had caved in. The place did not seem desolate; it merely seemed *old;* it had grown old, along with me.

I tasted the ripe thorn apples as I had always done on the evening way home from Clay Banks upstream, our rendezvous for battling the Sioux with weedy spears; but I had lost the knack of spitting out the pulpy seeds and swallowing the tangy skin. The murmuring "rapids," soul's solace and heart's delight, were still in place, but the rocks seemed larger, not smaller, for the river was very low. I had known the feel of each single rock under bare feet; I had known their attitudes and characters, which one was slippery, which loose and mocking, which rough and steady and trusting. I found myself staring across the stream, thinking, there should be a great clump of bushes there, and then it came back, even for a flickering moment the anguish of it: I had aimlessly fired a BB pellet into the bush and a flock of sparrows flew out of it. I heard no stir of sound, but something had pulled and drawn me, and I had rushed, slipping and floundering across the rocks; there, in the brush, lay a sparrow, its beak torn to one side. I had put it out of its misery, placing the muzzle on its head, and then gone trembling home.

It was literally true that not a sparrow falleth but He knows, and I promised Him that night never to injure anything again if He would forgive. (I have broken the promise.)

Our island was no more an island, but joined to the bank by a seam of low-water mud. Above the island we had dug our cave and curtained the entrance with gunny sacking. I scrambled down to see the place and found: one new cave, entrance covered with gunny sacking. I parted the curtaining, expecting to find a spirit lamp inside—and found one. It was in this moment, I think, with these symbolic findings that childhood is permanent, forever and ever the same, that a sense of comfort began to grow within me, the tinge of embarrassment and fear about this visit began to die away. It was going to be all right.

North Hill sloped upward, a mere pedestal now for Swedlund's barn, which hung, enormous, dominating the whole village like a French château above its fiefhold. There I had known the wild fright of a runaway horse bolting back into the barn as I crouched over its mane. And there I had seen human cruelty for the first time in my life.

Gordon, the teller of wondrous tales, and I had wandered into the farmyard with Fanny, the mongrel he loved, and Fanny had chased some chickens. A hired hand calmly picked Fanny up by the scruff, put a bullet through her head, let her fall and rolled a cigarette. We had carried Fanny down the slope and buried her in the weed patch, just there, across from our island.

I walked across North Bridge, the prairie at my back, the tree-lined streets before me, and felt for a moment, faintly, the joy this passage had brought me at each re-entry into the oasis with its familiar shapes and smells and sounds, its thousand secret delights, cool water and shade, and home and safety. I understood then why I had loved it so and loved its memory always: it was, simply, *home*—and *all* of it home, not just the house, but all the town. That is why childhood in the small towns is different from childhood in the city. Everything is home.

Through a fringe of trees I could see that the old "haunted house" was gone, replaced by a row of bright-painted trailer homes, unsuited for haunting by ghost or child. Nearby, a Model A roadster was foundering in the weeds, only a few yards from the spot where the old red Maxwell with the bulbous rubber horn had vegetated so long. There were two short streets of homes behind our street, where once there were woods and where the country and freedom had begun.

This was our street now, the nicest street in town. Here I had known every blade and branch and cornice, but now it was as it is in a dream. You know you are in the place you seek, but everything has been subtly altered; the light is different, positions and proportions have been changed to fool and mock you. I had to stop, close my eyes and arrange it all in proper order. Then I could tick them off: the Gilbertson house here, minus the dogs and cats and chickens; Skarison's; Walter Johnson's (he barbered now at the swank new Minot hotel, by appointment only). This must be the Andy Andersons'. He had been in the ill-fated bank with Father. And there I had been sent to sleep that spring night of mystery and foreboding and had been awakened by brother Paul shouting, "Hey, it's a girl and it weighs nine pounds!" He had stolen the line from a Charles Ray movie of the week before, and thus I learned of our beautiful baby sister.

Then the big brown bungalow my father had built for us. The screened porch had been glassed in; otherwise everything, the spiraea bushes, the box-elder trees, all was as before. All the other houses were white; ours was still brown, and I acquired another revelation in my pilgrim's progress of self-discovery. I knew now why I loved the touch and feel of wood, and why brown pleased and comforted me above all other colors. I knocked, to pay my respects to the Widow Leben, who lives there now alone. There was no answer. Perhaps I had knocked too faintly, for I was intensely relieved when she did not appear. I was afraid to go in; I never did go in.

I knew the old short cut to school, though August Peterson's red shack was gone, his iron pump alone remaining, stark, incongruous in the midst of new "ranch-style" homes with picture windows; but at the school I was bewildered and lost. The great cottonwoods were all cut down, the streets filled in to the sidewalk level. Ticky Tillapaugh's rambling house had been cut in half to make room for the new ranch-style house of the present banker, and the new high school (1928) had been constructed right across the front of our old red-brick schoolhouse with the white belfry. (No bell rope now to swing out upon in summer's idleness; no bell rope to hide away the day before school opens.)

But the old schoolhouse was exactly the same. The same smell of sweeping compound and oil; the same little "cloakrooms" where the mittens hung and the brown-paper luncheon sacks rested on the shelves above. The same desks, scarified now by fifty years of small boys' knives, were bolted to the floor. The first-grade room was still the first-grade room, only now the tots sat on tiny chairs, grouped around the teacher in the modern intimate manner. The rear of the new high school blanked out one wall of windows in the second-grade room, the very windows through which, in a seven-year-old's dream, I had once airily floated, to the consternation of Miss West with the bulging, omniscient black eyes.

Omniscient, indestructible Miss West still teaches there, the eighth grade now. She still has eyes in the back of her head, according to Mike. But a new hypothesis, no doubt prompted by the modern scientific spirit, has won favor among some of the kids: the amazing range of her vision is due to the big glassed picture of the Ruins of Athens—it treacherously mirrors what is going on behind her back. The mystery of fifty years, I suspect, has been solved.

I poked about Main Street for a time. Bill Francis' old drum press and the linotype on which he had let me cast my very own name in eternal metal were still in the *Journal* office. The paper seemed much the same, just more pictures and a new slogan over the title: "The only newspaper in the world that gives a darn about Velva and the people living hereabouts." The funeral parlor was now in the basement of the furniture store, no longer in the back, from which a man strange to us used to emerge, bribe one of us to buy him a bottle of vanilla from Welo's store, then drink it in the semidark beside the occasional corpse.

There was an aluminum door on the old sandstone bank, as incongruous as a nickel-plated grille on a Model T. Our bulldog Teddy used to know how to press the lip of the latch on the old door with his paw, and shoulder inside in search of Father. A boarded-up lot was all that remained of Art Smith's hardware store; the opera house, over Welo's, was now converted to ten apartments, the scenery removed to the high-school auditorium; the "racket store" of Old Man Oslie, he with the long white beard who sold the penny jawbreakers, this was gone, but Main Street had a television shop. Imler's pool hall (so respectable even young Mike was allowed to play there) had replaced Andy Leberg's place, where the itinerant, snuff-chewing IWWs had once hung out in harvest time, talking Socialism until Andy would push them out in desperate defense of the Republican Party. They had CinemaScope at the Iris Theater and no "player piano."

George Skarison came out of Welo's to see me, wearing his groceryman's apron; one of the Muus brothers defied me to remember his name and it came back almost at once; Vida Mae popped out of the Christenson store; Clifford Dittmer, who used to deliver our milk with his father's team, walked the street as chief constable, resplendent in blue uniform and badge in the city fashion. He was famous now—he had been a guard at Alcatraz and had shot a celebrated prisoner as he tried to escape by swimming. Clifford had no one in jail at the moment; he rarely did.

I stopped at the post office, where the wall of little boxes with the dial locks stood at right angles now. Ruth Cavanaugh, the postmistress, said, "No, we never have started home delivery. Folks seem to like to drop in at the post office, looking for mail. Sometimes even when they know the train hasn't been through. They like an excuse to come downtown."

I was passing the café and a voice inside rang out, "What's so funny about the town, Eric!" My heart sank. I should have known; someone would resent me. He pushed through the screen door, a stranger, a middle-aged Scandinavian farmer with a lean, sardonic face and glinting eyes. He was drunk, at high noon. I tried to walk along, to save what face I could, but he stumbled beside me, pawing at my shoulder and talking fast. After a moment the meaning came clear, through my panic and pain—he was quoting from my books, whole passages of the love and loneliness of the prairie boy. He was trying to communicate, to share what men cannot share in speech; an instinct told me he had got himself drunk to find the courage. But I am mute with drunks, whatever the communication, and there was nothing I could say. Constable Dittmer took the farmer by the arm, gently, and ushered him into his car.

I walked westward toward the Beebe house and an older man caught up with me to say, "I'm Oscar Christenson, Bud: you wouldn't know me. Well, I only wanted to say—you know that bank failure and how it was with everyone, I wanted to say your father did so much for me. He and Andy Anderson, they carried me on their books a long time. I guess they carried a lot of us, more than we knew at the time." Now I was mute with a perfectly sober and dignified man, but I was thinking: You have given me a thing I came here to find; pray God you told him this; it was a weight in his heart to the day of his death.

I lay in the old house that second night and made an important discovery. I could run through the film exposed this day of 1955 and see it all, the hills, the rapids, the bridge and the house and the streets, all of it as it *is,* in black and white, exact,

280

life-size, no more, no less. Then I could run off the old, eternal negative, larger than life, in its full color and glory—the same scenes and trees and faces—and there was no fading or blur of double exposure. I had both reels now, sealed in separate cans, and I knew I could keep them both, as long as I lived.

I thought of something Aunt Jessey said at supper about the long light of summer and the long darkness of these northern winters. I was thinking that this answered the old, troubling question of why the old film had always shown the green and summer scenes, only a few brief, bright scenes of snow, and nothing of this late autumn time of bare ground and barren trees. I slid into sleep with a phrase distantly sounding: You *can* go home again.

My home town has changed in these thirty years of the American story. It is changing now, will go on changing as America changes. Its biography, I suspect, would read much the same as that of all other home towns. Depression and war and prosperity have all left their marks; modern science, modern tastes, manners, philosophies, fears and ambitions have touched my town as indelibly as they have touched New York or Panama City.

Sights have changed: there is a new precision about street and home, a clearing away of chicken yards, cow barns, pigeon-crested cupolas, weed lots and coulees, the dim and secret adult-free rendezvous of boys. An intricate metal "jungle gym" is a common backyard sight, the sack swing uncommon. There are wide expanses of clear windows designed to let in the parlor light, fewer ornamental windows of colored glass designed to keep it out. Attic and screen porch are slowly vanishing and lovely shades of pastel are painted upon new houses, tints that once would have embarrassed farmer and merchant alike.

Sounds have changed; I heard not once the clopping of a horse's hoofs, nor the mourn of a coyote. I heard instead the shriek of brakes, the heavy throbbing of the once-a-day Braniff airliner into Minot, the shattering sirens born of war, the honk of a diesel locomotive which surely cannot call to faraway places the heart of a wakeful boy like the old steam whistle in the night. You can walk down the streets of my town now and hear from open windows the intimate voices of the Washington commentators in casual converse on the great affairs of state; but you cannot hear on Sunday morning the singing in Norwegian of the Lutheran hymns; the old country seems now part of a world left long behind and the old-country accents grow fainter in the speech of my Velva neighbors.

The people have not changed, but the *kinds* of people have changed: there is no longer an official, certified town drunk, no longer a "Crazy John," spitting his worst epithet, "rotten chicken legs," as you hurriedly passed him by. People so sick are now sent to places of proper care. No longer is there an official town joker, like the druggist MacKnight, who would spot a customer in the front of the store, have him called to the phone, then slip to the phone behind the prescription case, and imitate the man's wife to perfection with orders to bring home more bread and sausage and Cream of Wheat. No longer anyone like the early attorney, J. L. Lee, who sent fabulous dispatches to that fabulous tabloid, the *Chicago Blade,* such as his story of the wild man captured on the prairie and chained to the wall in the drugstore basement. (This, surely, was Velva's first notoriety; inquiries came from anthropologists all over the world.)

No, the "characters" are vanishing in Velva, just as they are vanishing in our cities, in business, in politics. The "well-rounded, socially integrated" personality that the progressive schoolteachers are so obsessed with is increasing rapidly, and I am not at all sure that this is good. Maybe we need more personalities with knobs and handles and rugged lumps of individuality. They may not make life more smooth; more interesting they surely make it.

They eat differently in Velva now; there are frozen fruits and sea food and exotic delicacies we only read about in novels in those meat-and-potato days. They dress differently. The hard white collars of the businessmen are gone with the shiny alpaca coats. There are comfortable tweeds now, and casual blazers with a touch in their colors of California, which seems so close in time and distance.

It is distance and time that have changed the most and worked the deepest changes in Velva's life. The telephone, the car, the smooth highway, radio and television are consolidating the entities of our country. The county seat of Towner now seems no closer than the state capital of Bismarck; the voices and concerns of Presidents, French premiers and Moroccan pashas are no farther away than the portable radio on Aunt Jessey's kitchen table. The national news magazines are stacked each week in

Harold Anderson's drugstore beside the new soda fountain, and the excellent *Minot Daily News* smells hot from the press each afternoon.

Consolidation. The nearby hamlets of Sawyer and Logan and Voltaire had their own separate banks and papers and schools in my days of dusty buggies and Model Ts marooned in the snowdrifts. Now these hamlets are dying. A bright yellow bus takes the Voltaire kids to Velva each day for high school. Velva has grown—from 800 to 1,300—because the miners from the Truax coal mine can commute to their labors each morning and the nearby farmers can live in town if they choose. Minot has tripled in size to 30,000. Once the "Magic City" was a distant and splendid Baghdad, visited on special occasions long prepared for. Now it is a twenty-five minute commuter's jump away. So P. W. Miller and Jay Louis Monicken run their businesses in Minot but live on in their old family homes in Velva. So Ray Michelson's two girls on his farm to the west drive up each morning to their jobs as maids in Minot homes. Aunt Jessey said, "Why, Saturday night I counted sixty-five cars just between here and Sawyer, all going up to the show in Minot."

The hills are prison battlements no longer; the prairies no heart-sinking barrier, but a passageway free as the swelling ocean, inviting you to sail home and away at your whim and your leisure. (John and Helen made an easy little jaunt of 700 miles that weekend to see their eldest daughter in Wyoming.)

Consolidation. Art Kumm's bank serves a big region now; its assets are $2,000,000 to $3,000,000 instead of the $200,000 or $300,000 in my father's day. Eighteen farms near Velva are under three ownerships now. They calculate in sections; "acres," is an almost forgotten term. Aunt Jessey owns a couple of farms, and she knows they are much better run. "It's no longer all take out and no put in," she said. "Folks strip farm now; they know all about fertilizers. They care for it and they'll hand on the land in good shape." The farmers gripe about their cash income, and not without reason at the moment, but they will admit that life is good compared with those days of drought and foreclosure, manure banked against the house for warmth, the hand pump frozen at 30 below and the fitful kerosene lamp on the kitchen table. Electrification has done much of this, eased back-breaking chores that made their wives old as parchment at forty, brought life and music and the sound of human voices into their parlors at night.

And light upon the prairie. "From the hilltop," said Aunt Jessey, "the farms look like stars at night."

Many politicians deplore the passing of the old family-size farm, but I am not so sure. I saw around Velva a release from what was like slavery to the tyrannical soil, release from the ignorance that darkens the soul and from the loneliness that corrodes it. In this generation my Velva friends have rejoined the general American society that their pioneering fathers left behind when they first made the barren trek in the days of the wheat rush. As I sit here in Washington writing this, I can feel their nearness. I never felt it before save in my dreams.

But now I must ask myself: Are they nearer to one another? And the answer is no; yet I am certain that this is good. The shrinking of time and distance has made contrast and relief available to their daily lives. They do not know one another quite so well because they are not so much obliged to. I know that democracy rests upon social discipline, which in turn rests upon personal discipline; passions checked, hard words withheld, civic tasks accepted, work well done, accountings honestly rendered. The old-fashioned small town was this discipline in its starkest, most primitive form; without this discipline the small town would have blown itself apart.

For personal and social neuroses festered under this hard scab of conformity. There was no place to go, no place to let off steam; few dared to voice unorthodox ideas, read strange books, admire esoteric art or publicly write or speak of their dreams and their soul's longings. The world was not "too much with us," the world was too little with us and we were too much with one another.

The door to the world stands open now, inviting them to leave anytime they wish. It is the simple fact of the open door that makes all the difference; with its opening the stale air rushed out. So, of course, the people themselves do not have to leave, because, as the stale air went out, the fresh air came in.

Human nature is everywhere the same. He who is not forced to help his neighbor for his own existence will not only give him help, but his true good will as well. Minot and its hospital are now close at hand, but the people of Velva put their purses together, built their own clinic and homes for the two young doctors they persuaded to come and live among them. Velva has no organized charity, but when a farmer falls ill, his neighbors get in his crop; if a townsman has a financial catastrophe his personal friends raise a fund to help him out. When Bill's wife, Ethel, lay dying so long in the Minot hospital and nurses were not available, Helen and others took their turns driving up there just to sit with her so she would know in her gathering dark that friends were at hand.

It is personal freedom that makes us better persons, and they are freer in Velva now. There is no real freedom without privacy, and a resident of my home town can be a private person much more than he could before. People are able to draw at least a little apart from one another. In drawing apart, they gave their best human instincts room for expansion.

Yet youth must leave the small towns of our country, and youth does leave. Tony Swedlund complained, "We always export our brains." How can it go otherwise? Hungry young brains must have food to work on and Velva cannot provide it; it has not the industries, the laboratories, the law courts and colleges for young brains to flourish and ambitions come true. This is what sends them away, this more than the faint, remaining staleness in the air they breathe. How many would stay were the opportunities there I cannot say. Perhaps not many. Yet the two boys roughly of my own age who stayed, Jay Louis Monicken and Vendler Johnson, are there because for them opportunity *was* there, in the businesses they inherited. Last summer Stephen Johns (does he remember our fist fight under the cottonwood at recess time?) drove back to the old home town from California. Vendler's sister, Evelyn (does she remember the May basket I hung on her door?), said to Stephen, "Here we are, Vendler and I, the only ones still in Velva. Are we the failures?" And Stephen said, "You are the lucky ones. You had the means to stay. The rest of us did not."

Perhaps, though I am not sure of this in my heart. It does not really matter. For Velva is small, the world calls, the gate is open and they are young; go they must and always will.

This is what my home town and yours really are in the American story and system; not stagnant plants at all, but seedbeds, ceaselessly renewing themselves, their seed constantly renewing the nation. They are not quiet, fixed and static, but vital as life itself, pulsating with the lives that come to them and the lives they give away.

So we have gone away, nearly all of us. But few of us can stay away. Unbidden, as age grows upon us, the heart creeps back, again and again; it seeks once more the river and the tree, the old board wall and the barn, just once more.

Evelyn looked across the sleeping form of her child on the couch to the window giving on the spacious yard and said, "That big old oak over there. When Marjorie and Norma and I were little we swore a secret pledge; when we became forty years old, wherever we were in the world, we would come back and meet one another under that tree. I wonder where they were on their fortieth birthdays."

Dear Evelyn, they were there, under the tree. They never left it. After all, I've lived all my life in the house right across the street and I'm sure I would have noticed it if they had ever gone away.

WARNING TO YOUNG MEN

Young man, do you aspire to success in your chosen field? Do you yearn to be a credit to your community and your country? Then, sir, do as I say, not as I did. Or, to put it more accurately, do as I didn't.

I warn not of alcohol, low companions and gambling—I have found considerable pleasure and instruction in alcohol and low companions and would have enjoyed gambling, too, except that I loathe releasing a dollar, a trait inherited from Norwegian forebears who make their Scotch cousins look like spendthrifts.

No, I warn of Stupidity, Timidity, Bad Luck and Bad Timing. All you have to do is avoid these four elements in your life and the rest is easy, especially in my trade—journalism. Avoid them, and you, too, can be a scoop artist, like the embattled brotherhood of the Alsops, and live to write a book on How I Did It. Avoid them and you will avoid ending up in contrite middle age, writing a short confessional for the good of your guilty soul on how you didn't do it, how you missed this big one, fumbled that one and bumped into the third, said, "Pardon me," and walked on.

I am not sure, now that I search the recesses of unhappy memory, just when the habit of stupidity began with me. But timidity I know had me in its grip as early as the age of seventeen, when I was the solemn editor of the *Central High School News* in Minneapolis and knew that the American press and the epoch awaited another Richard Harding Davis.

Jack Dempsey, ex-champ, the Manassa Mauler, was in town at the Nicollet Hotel. With a cigarette dangling from my lip, I casually announced to the awe-struck news staff my intention to interview the great man. I had got no farther than the streetcar stop outside the school when I began to feel awfully alone. Johnny Lang, who played end on the touchball team in my block, ambled by. "Hey, Johnny," I said, "come on downtown with me. You won't be sorry. I'll pay your fare."

We rode downtown and walked into the overpoweringly elegant hostelry. With quavering voice I inquired the number of the champ's room, and we rode up the elevator in stricken silence. Halfway down the corridor to his room I stopped. "Maybe he isn't there," I said to Johnny. "Maybe he's asleep. Maybe he's in a big business conference. He might get mad. He's pretty strong."

Just then a door banged open and out burst the champ himself, with a nameless gentleman. They strode past us as Johnny and I plastered our skinny frames against the wall. The champ was laughing and pretending to cuff Nameless about the head. We followed at a short but respectful distance. The elevator doors opened, they stepped in and the champ said, "Going down, kids?" In utter silence I stood beside the great man all the way down. In utter silence I followed him to the street. As he waited for his cab, I said, "Sir, I—ah—I am from the high-school newspaper and—"

He said, "You want an interview? O.K. Work hard. Live clean. Get a lot of exercise."

I said, "Gee, thanks very much." How I made a story out of this exchange I'm not sure, but journalists, as everyone knows, live by their wits and their adjectives.

By the age of eighteen I was a reporter on the *Minneapolis Journal* and far gone in the habit of bold starts and bashful endings. There was the case of the Fake Waiter and Katharine Hepburn. I was the Fake Waiter. She was Katharine Hepburn, the real one. She failed, that sub-zero morning, to descend from her Pullman car at the station, so I announced to the shivering colleagues, "I'll fix *her*. I got a plan."

Two hours later, when she rang for breakfast from her room in the Curtis Hotel, she was attended by two white-coated waiters, one real. The star was in bed, her beautiful hair spread over a bank of pillows, and she was dictating a family letter to a secretary who scribbled at a desk. I was transfixed by this intimate proximity with glamor. She spoke to me, and I stammered. She requested a dish, and I dropped it. She smiled sweetly and wasn't fooled for a minute. By the time I was escaping through the lobby, she had already bawled out the hotel manager, and I suspect that if the advertising department had got its way, "Richard Harding Davis" would have been fired. As a matter of fact, I did get fired. But that was much later, and it was stupidity, not timidity. I got the Veterans of Foreign Wars mixed up, in a story, with the American Legion. There seemed to be a difference between them—the first were *not* members of the second.

It was stupidity that prevented me from walking right in on a holdup and getting either (a) a conk on the head or (b) a big scoop, and maybe both. Casey Jones, the city editor, had said, "Look, punk, there's nobody around but you. Beat it over to Number Such-and-Such on Hennepin Avenue. Loan company being held up. Guy heard the talk over an open telephone. Cops aren't there yet. This is your big chance, punk. Hennepin Avenue."

I had just been writing a squib with the words "Nicollet Avenue" in it, and I am the sort of writer who dreams over every one of his own words. I promptly dashed to the corresponding number of Nicollet Avenue and consumed fifteen minutes trying to persuade the bewildered manager of a shoe store that he had been held up. By the time I got to the loan company on Hennepin, all was over, including my big eyewitness scoop.

One Saturday night Casey said, "Punk, go over and look in on that dance marathon in the auditorium that the Good People are fussing about." In the auditorium a municipal bureaucrat whispered in my ear that the mayor was about to raid the place. This sweet scoop was mine, all mine. But I needed more dope. I sidled up to a uniformed policeman who hung on the rail, watching the soiled and sordid couples shuffling around in their sleep. "When do you put the muscle on the joint?" I inquired out of the corner of my mouth. One minute later, my money had been not very cheerfully refunded at the box office and I was out in the street. The place was raided, all right, but R. H. Davis, alias The Punk, wasn't there. Rather slowly it dawned on me that the special policemen hired by the marathon management wore uniforms remarkably similar to those of the city police.

But all that was in my extreme youth. As I grew older and exchanged Minneapolis for Paris, and newspapers for radio, I became more and more adept at Stupidity, Timidity, Bad Luck and Bad Timing. As I think back over the remarkable roster of my anti-scoops, I rather incline toward giving first place to my performance on the day France declared war in September of 1939. During the morning hours of that anguished day I played right out of character. I mean I got the only copy through the official censors which stated that France would go to war at five o'clock. André Glarner, who ran a French news agency, telephoned to say that he had heard of my unique status and intended to flash a bulletin, without benefit of censorship, at 1 P.M., the opening minute of my historic broadcast-to-be, saying that CBS had reported the French decision. Now, it is not often that one lone reporter possesses the privilege of exclusive announcement to the world of an event like a great power declaring war. I savored those moments as the studio clock ticked toward 1 P.M. I anticipated in my mind, word for word, the congratulatory telegram that would come from CBS news director Paul White in New York. I tasted various guesses as to the amount of my pay increase, upping it each time.

"Hello, New York . . . Hello, London," I called as the talk-up period began.

Only the short waves of static responded. I called again. I began to holler, a bit hysterically. The French studio engineer poked his head around the door and said, "London says big story, Britain gone to war two hours ago."

"But everybody knows that!" I screamed. "Nobody knows about France! Tell London to call me in!" The engineer popped back. The minutes passed. All the minutes. He popped out again and said, "London says very sorry, but very big story over there. They want you up tonight."

Glarner, I believe, got a world scoop, based on a Sevareid broadcast that was never made. Ed Murrow, they tell me, was quite eloquent from London that day.

My next exploit should be put into Category No. 2—Timidity. The understanding in Paris was that no journalists of any nationality were allowed to go to the front until all arrangements and credentials were in order. Days passed. Occasionally a wire service reported a great battle at the Belfort Gap or some such impressive-sounding place. But the world remained in total ignorance, believing one day that vast armies were drenching the soil in blood, believing the next day that nothing was happening whatsoever.

Over the second or third Pernod, we said to each other, "Are we men or mice?"—"we" being Walter Kerr of the *Herald Tribune;* Geoffrey Cox of the *London Express,* and Chuck Findley, an American newsreel executive. So, on a Sunday morning we trundled off in Cox's tiny car toward the rising sun. At Château-Thierry the military guard said, "They will stop you at Verdun. At Verdun the guard said, "You won't get past Metz." However at Metz they said nothing. Beyond Metz we proceeded as far as daylight, military traffic and Findley's unexpected appendix attack would permit. But it was close enough. We knew. No fighting was going on whatsoever—except for a few lackadaisical artillery exchanges.

We could write the first eyewitness descriptions of what the second great war of the Western Front was really like.

As I was composing mine in my Paris hotel room, Cox phoned to say we were in trouble. General Gamelin had heard about our trip, and a French official had called Cox with threats of punishment. The delay had already lost Cox his first edition of the *Express.* So I wrote my broadcast very carefully, avoiding any proclamations of "first" or "exclusive," but making it perfectly clear to the intelligent listener, I thought, where we had been and what the truth was. It went through censorship, I delivered it and brother Murrow, listening at London, said, "Very, very nice."

Cox phoned again. "It was a hoax," he said. Kenneth Downs, of INS, had heard about our journey as soon as we had regained Paris. The threatening phone call to Cox had been made by a man named Wilson in Downs' office, impersonating a high official.

Three or four days later, Downs, Paul Ward, Edgar Mowrer and Edmond Taylor made essentially the same trip. No timidity there. They hit the story for all it was worth, especially Downs. One week later *Time* magazine carried the pictures of these four and a long story about their daring exploit to bring the truth to the world. Two weeks later *Editor & Publisher* published an account by Downs of how he had studied the "rules," perceived a loophole and organized their historic trip. Of our trip no mention anywhere.

Except in the French High Command. General Gamelin was sore. We did get in trouble—in fact, we were almost expelled from France. Downs and company escaped scot-free, on the grounds, apparently, that they had merely followed our wicked example.

In the months of the "phony war" that followed I must not have been myself—I didn't get beat on anything big, an unnerving sensation for one so conditioned as I. Well, there was the time I got sick and couldn't make that famous taxi ride through the Siegfried Line from Luxembourg, along with Walter Kerr, and Bob Casey of the *Chicago Daily News*. And there was that Christmas Eve in a Maginot Line fortress when an engineer in Paris or New York considered that cutting through to the Mannerheim Line in Finland produced enough fortress talk, so that William L. White spoke his famous "There Shall Be No Night" piece to millions of radio listeners in America and I spoke graphically to myself. But those I put down to Bad Luck.

Indeed, that winter I managed to argue my way into a French concentration camp for Central European refugees and reported the story. In the spring I beat the world with the news of the German tank breakthrough at Sedan, which sealed the fate of France, by means of a prearranged cable code with New York. Though, of course, CBS didn't dare credit me by name in the justified fear that I would end up in a French Army guardhouse. And around June 10, 1940, I'm pretty sure I got the first definite word out that the French government and army had abandoned Paris. That was one of those "last broadcasts from;" when the tide of war turned, the style changed to "first broadcasts from," as reporters foot-raced one another into places like Kokokooma Village, Somewhere in the Pacific.

A bit later in June of 1940, with the capitulation of France at Bordeaux, I found my old stride again. I burst with anti-pride over that one. Timidity lifted me to the very heights.

BACKGROUND: All news copy from the hundred or so scrambling, exhausted journalists had to go by automobile courier, once every couple of hours, to a press wireless transmitter far out of the city, where it piled up in great gluts.

PLOT: Sevareid finds out that the Germans have not yet reached the mid-France radio transmitter used by Bordeaux Radio studios at the edge of Bordeaux. He will simply arrange to use the studio microphones on demand and have his graphic description of the denouement, when it comes, beamed to the Western Hemisphere. CBS, New York, monitoring around the clock, will pick it up.

ACTION: Sevareid slips quietly into office of the French radio director in the middle of Bordeaux to make above arrangements. Sevareid hears polite cough, looks around and finds NBC correspondent, suspecting plot afoot, has followed him into the office. Sevareid requests competition to leave. Competition grins. Competition is about half Sevareid's size. Sevareid does nothing about it. Broadcast arrangement made.

CLIMAX: Word comes to regiment of journalists that Pétain is premier, with list of new cabinet. This is It. Press journalists, discovering press wireless courier has just left, go insane, not being aware of Bordeaux Radio. Sevareid drives frantically to radio studio, dashes up stairs to microphone as NBC half-pint strolls down wearing same grin.

"What did you say on the air?" demands insane Sevareid.

"Why," says he, "I said this means continued resistance. Look at all the generals and admirals in the new cabinet."

Sevareid screams "Hah!" of maniacal joy, rushes to microphone and blurts out news to world that France will capitulate.

Get it first, but get it right," says the motto of a great news agency. I got it right, but NBC with its flash on the cabinet change, got it first, and there went the bubbles out of *that* champagne.

To complete the story of this historic semi-anti-scoop, let me add that *The New York Times,* the newspaper of record chiefly consulted by historians, printed the account of my broadcast. I had said that the new Pétain cabinet would *not* mean continued resistance. The *Times* story, imperishable, on file for all posterity, had me saying that the new cabinet would *now* mean continued resistance.

Well, I had been overseas three years, long enough to prove the old saying that you can take the boy out of the country, but you can't take the country out of the boy. I recrossed the Atlantic, and Timidity, Stupidity, Bad Luck and Bad Timing followed me like a school of sharks. I flew to Mexico City to cover the inaugural of President Camacho. Arriving at the American Embassy one night I found a fearful anti-Yankee riot going on in protest against the visit of Vice-President-elect Wallace. Wallace's entourage, including all other American reporters, was still miles away. What a gift!

I scribbled out a series of telegram "takes," handed them to my driver, Luiz—his card read INGLIS AESPINKING DRIVER—shooed him off to the telegraph office and relaxed with the embassy's best Scotch. I called New York the next day to be told that the riot was the headline story of the day—the other reporters having eventually reached the scene—and to be asked, "Why didn't you file it?" I never did learn the answer to that one. My Spanish and the torrent of INGLIS that Luiz spank to me didn't coincide closely enough.

———————

Onward and upward. I did chores around Washington for a couple of years, covered the 1941 Army maneuvers—ignoring another reporter's advice to "go see a colonel at headquarters named Eisenhower"—and in 1943 flew off to China. The China experience, I claim, was strictly Bad Timing. It was a tremendous story—the bitter feud between Stilwell and Chiang and between Stilwell and Chennault; the fantastic inflation and the wastage of American war goods; the reeking corruption; the strength of the Communists; and particularly the incompetence and idleness of almost the entire Nationalist army. It was the complete reverse of the picture instilled in the minds of the American people by Madame Chiang and others. It amounted to a sensational shocker, but the truth had to come out if America was to be prepared for the almost inevitable collapse. I wrote my broadcast scripts and magazine articles in India, and took them back to Washington personally in a file sealed by General Stratemeyer. All of it was stopped, censored cold by the Department of State. A few months later, when Stilwell came home, the whole story erupted with a roar that was not stilled for years. I had timed it all wrong. No copybook maxim in journalism had ever warned me about being too *early* with a story.

Back to the war again, in North Africa and Italy. My genius for the anti-scoop remained unimpaired by past successes. Some Army boys and I lugged a mile of wire to the edge of Vesuvius' crater and made the first recording of that famous volcanic mountain in eruption. Message from New York two days later: "Sorry, static washed it out." Pure Bad Luck. Well, I had a *little* luck— an hour after we had left the crater's edge the section we had been standing on fell in.

Now, you will be thinking that somewhere the universal law of compensation would have to set in. And you are correct. Obviously, according to the laws of nature, a fellow who half kills himself in order to miss is going to fall into the rainbow's pot of gold someday when he's not even trying. Consider the case of the great breakout of American and British forces from the Anzio beachhead. That evening the following exchange of cables took place between New York and Italy. From CBS news director Paul White:

> CONGRATULATIONS YOU DID IT AGAIN YOUR STORY UPJOINING SOUTHERN ETANZIO FORCES UPPICKED EVERY PRESS ASSOCIATION WIDELY FRONTPAGED STOP IF YOU MANAGE TO FIND ANYTHING SUFFICIENTLY POTABLE THEN BLOW YOURSELF BURDETT AND FOWLE LARGE EVENING OUR ACCOUNTING DEPARTMENT LATER UNBLINKINGLY APPROVE EXPENSE ITEM AMID RESPECTFUL SILENCE.

From me to Paul White:

> HOPE UNTOO MUCH PUBLICITY THIS BEAT WHICH DUE ENTIRELY DUMB LUCK HAVING BROADCASTING SPOT SCHEDULED MOMENT ANNOUNCEMENT RELEASED STOP MATTER FACT THEY FORGOT WAKE ME THIS MORNING EYE LAST REPORTER REACH SCENE JUNCTION TWO FORCES STOP ALL OTHERS AWARE MY BEAT NOW SAYING QUOTE WE SHOULD HAVE STOOD IN BED UNQUOTE.

Max Shulman's wise old father was clearly correct in his advice—"Git rich, sleep till noon." But habit won over intelligence again, and there I was, a few months later, working like mad on a ship, recording a sound history of soldiers approaching the invasion beaches of southern France. As prearranged, a speedboat swirled up, the wire recordings were dropped to its deck, the speedboat sped off to a waiting seaplane, which flew off to Rome, where the stuff would presumably be flown to New York. One of the greatest radio documentaries of the war, I figured, as I walked ashore in France. What a job Norman Corwin could do writing the script for material like this! One year later, when the war was over, the recordings arrived in New York. God and the United States Army know why; I don't.

Peace or war, Europe or America—it made no difference to Sevareid, the old reliable. True black and blue, that's me. Reassignment to peacetime Washington didn't break my stride for a minute. A civil servant in my morning car pool related, step by step, the weird story of a State Department fellow who was followed secretly by security agents for weeks and, when the dramatic arrest was made and his briefcase supposedly full of Russia-bound secrets was opened, the agents found his unfinished Ph.D. thesis! I made careful notes on the story, went off to Rio on assignment, forgot about my notes and shortly thereafter Bert Andrews, of the *Herald Tribune,* won the Pulitzer Prize for the same story, episode by episode.

Not that I favor the *Herald Tribune* particularly with my anti-scoops. In the fall of 1957, at the time Sputnik shook the country, I was told most of the findings in the still "secret" Gaither Report. I related them, in two or three broadcasts. No reaction. Weeks later Chalmers Roberts of the *Washington Post* published the findings and won the Raymond Clapper Memorial Award. This couldn't have been Stupidity, Timidity or Bad Timing. It was Bad Luck, Grade A. It just so happened that on those two or three nights every one of the 175,000,000 people in the United States, in a kind of mass instinctive urge, like lemmings entering the sea, had turned off their radios and gone to bed early. There is only one other possible explanation—poltergeists short-circuited every one of the 149,000,000 radio sets in the United States on those nights. But I discount this theory. It would have got in the papers. I think some reporter would have uncovered it. I think he would have won the Pulitzer Prize.

In the 1952 conventions I played 'way over my battered head. Late on the eve of the balloting I heard a cryptic remark from an anti-Stassen Minnesota delegate and figured out that it could have only one meaning; so I grabbed a CBS Radio microphone on the floor and blurted out that after the first roll call Minnesota would rise to change its vote from Stassen to Eisenhower and would thus shove the Eisenhower bandwagon to a one-ballot victory. I don't know why I always think of radio in a crisis; I might have known that most of the audience was following brother Cronkite on TV. I guess I'm the sort of sucker who is forever defending minorities.

Same thing in the Democratic convention that year. I borrowed part of Ed Murrow's radio program on the opening day to make the flat prediction that it was bound to be Stevenson. Predictions are not a reporter's proper business—and are outside CBS news policy—but I knew I was right and why. Murrow made the time for me, saying, "For a guy with your self-doubts, that fanatical look of yours impresses me—go ahead!" *Somebody* must have heard that show. I cling to the thought.

On the Presidential election night somebody somewhere must have had his radio on. But not the TV-radio critics; they never work past the hyphen. It was like this: I got into the CBS election studio early that November night in 1952. At 7:10 P.M. I went on radio and said that Eisenhower had it in the bag. There was no mistaking even those early returns. At about 8:10 P.M. Ed Murrow walked into the studio. "It's all over, brother Ed," said I in a brotherly way. "Too soon, cousin Eric," said he, in a cousinly way. At about 8:45 P.M. brother Ed went on TV and said Eisenhower had it in the bag. The next day every TV-radio critic in the American newspapers—which for some reason were printed in bloodshot red that day—credited brother Ed with bringing the tidings of the Age of Ike.

So now you know the Story of My Life. My secret shame is out, along with that of ex-drunks, ex-addicts, ex-lechers and ex-movie stars, though they managed to expand theirs to book length.

I can write mine now because I, too, am an Ex. I am an ex-scoop artist. I have finally reformed and have found my true path. A mere snatch of conversation overheard has changed my life, like that of so many people you have read about in the *Reader's Digest* and in the works of Norman Vincent Peale.

A couple of reporters were arguing at the National Press Club bar as I was passing. One of them was saying, "Yes, but you have to admit that Lippmann is a great reporter in the sense that he is first with so many new ideas. He gets the 'intellectual scoops,' you might say—the 'think scoops.' "

The "think scoops!" At last I had hit upon my true métier. No more half-killing myself. No more frantic dashes to microphones and telegraph offices. Thinking! Why hadn't I thought of that before? That's what I'm doing now. No more Timidity, Bad Timing or Bad Luck. There is only Stupidity to get in my way.

My obstacles are three-fourths overcome, and nobody can expect everything. And what a fortunate coincidence that I do so much of my best thinking in the late morning, in bed.

MANO A MANO

Málaga, Spain

In near-by Seville, where modern bullfighting was born, an estimated 80 percent of the male population has tried fighting the bulls at one time or another. This makes the crowd in the Seville arena the toughest to please in the whole country. In the whole country an estimated 80 percent (my estimate) of American summer visitors have read Hemingway's *Death in the Afternoon*. This makes us equally authoritative. We are even more impressively expert than the Spanish experts because, I think, there are more expletives in English than in Spanish. We are especially positive in the post-mortems in the Hotel Miramar barroom after the Málaga fights and have been known to upset two waiters and one and a half trays of dry Martinis while demonstrating how the local boy, Manolo Segura, went over the right horn wrong making his kill.

I will not tell the whole story here of how I abandoned the sport of following President Eisenhower's intricate terminological *faena* while he dodged a sharp-horned question, and became an *aficionado* of the real thing; the fact that the stone seats in the bull ring are more comfortable than the folding chairs in the Washington press conference room probably has something to do with it. In any case I have now graduated from the *novillero* class as an observer and can hold my own in any bullfight café, because I have seen the worst fights of the season here and what was possibly the greatest fight of the twentieth century. At least when it was over last Friday and I got to the Miramar saloon, I put the question straight and true to Hemingway and he said, "It was the greatest bullfight I have ever seen in my *life!*" And Ernest has been going to bullfights for nearly forty years. Coming from the man who revolutionized writing by eliminating most of the adjectives, this is a considerable statement.

This has been my first season with the bulls and it has been a very smug one. It began in Mexico City in December, where I learned the basic requirements of *corrida* observing: luck and patience. Eight out of ten bullfights are bad, anywhere. I know Spaniards who have never managed to hit a good one in their lifetime. A good fight is a beautiful, exalting ballet of frail man versus wild beast. A bad fight is not only different in degree, but in kind; it is a travesty, a sordid, cruel mockery. As someone else has remarked, the beauty is the sole justification and when that is absent the affair is a sickness.

The first four fights in that Mexico City *corrida* were horrid and my more sensitive or less patient colleagues, Mark Childs and Roscoe Drummond, fled the arena in a high dudgeon. (They rented it, with driver.) I stayed for the fifth bull, one so beautiful, so perfect in his ceaseless charges that even the *novillero* fighting him was perfect and the berserk crowd forced the judges to grant the bull pardon and turn him back to pasture for breeding purposes.

That was bullfight history and last Friday's affair was bullfight history, partly of course because it was the first completed two-man duel (three bulls apiece) of those celebrated brothers-in-law, Dominguín and Ordóñez. I guess they were fighting it out for the world championship, but I only guess. *Life* magazine, which had reporters and cameramen all over the place, will probably be quite certain; they usually are. They have a way of enthroning and dethroning all champions, from atomic physicists to checker players, at the flip of a page.

According to the crowd, which gave him handfuls of ears and tails plus *two* hoofs, the twenty-seven-year-old Ordóñez won. I think he won, too, but I had just become acquainted with him the day before and I always vote for my friends. When I met him he was butting tennis balls with his head in a swimming pool and everybody knows you can't meet in more intimate circumstances than that.

I may as well go back to the beginning. My plane arrived in Málaga on June eleventh, but I was not on it; I was delayed in Madrid. Ordóñez was on it, coming from a hospital recuperation period, and Hemingway met him at the airport. If I worked for *Life,* I would have been on it; I would have bought the plane. So I got here and went swimming for a few weeks, waiting for the August fiesta in Málaga when the *mano a mano* duel between Ordóñez and Dominguín would crown the week of bullfights. In the interval I got all my news from Pepe, my hotel waiter, since every day around here is a saint's day and the newsstand is always closed.

"Big news," Pepe said one day as he served the salad. "Ordóñez was in the street crowd during the running of the bulls at Pamplona and he was the only man in the crowd to get gored. Hemingway is with him." I began to get nervous about that long-awaited *mano a mano* in Málaga.

Many days later Pepe put down the toothpick container and said, "News! Ordóñez and Dominguín were doing their first *mano a mano* at La Coruña and they never decided it because Dominguín got a bad goring." Later dispatches from Pepe established that the goring was in the thigh or in the groin or in the cheek. The Málaga city fathers began to get nervous about their festival and scalpers' prices for bullfight tickets began to drop.

"What do you think!" Pepe exclaimed a few days later as he uncorked the red wine, "Ordóñez was gored at Palma! A bad one! The radio says it is in the kidneys or in the shin or maybe in the abdomen." Hemingway flew up to Madrid to visit Ordóñez in the hospital.

Well, the Málaga fights started and most of them were terrible. But the Hemingways were there, and on the strength of the fact that Mary Hemingway was born in Minnesota and I was born in North Dakota, two states separated only by a narrow river, and in dry times not separated at all, we became acquainted. Mary is gentle at all times and Ernest is gentle when not passionate about something, and I fell in love with both.

Ernest sat through the bad fights in the front row, resting his beard on the rail. Sometimes a fighter would dedicate a bull to him and teenage Spanish girls would clamber over for his autograph and then ask others who the man was. Usually they thought he was a prophet or perhaps a patron saint of bullfighting who had made it while still alive. More worldly wise teenagers knew, however, that no prophet or saint wore a long-visored baseball cap. Saints don't lose their temper, either, and the thing that makes Ernest really passionate is a knowing remark from somebody about something he knows not. A matador friend of Ernest's missed his sword thrust on one bull and Kenneth Tynan, the junior Delphic Oracle of the New York and London theater critics, announced, "He was four inches off." The reaction from Hemingway was confused by some with the dying bellow of the bull. I think Ernest apologized later to Tynan. I wish he hadn't; I never heard of Tynan apologizing to a playwright for wrecking his play with a careless paragraph.

The date for the great Ordóñez-Dominguín duel was postponed a week. The tension built up. Consider the situation: Dominguín, thirty-three years old, had reigned supreme since he competed the great Manolete to the latter's death in 1947. Antonio Ordóñez, who married Dominguín's sister, was now threatening to dethrone Dominguín. All Spain has been familiar with the stories of the bitterness between the two. So deep was this feeling at one time that when Señora Ordóñez' father died, she did not attend the funeral with her brother. Both men knew what would be at stake in their Málaga meeting. Both would be facing this supreme test as their first fight after the unnerving experience of a bad goring. The genius of a Tex Rickard could not have promoted a better box-office situation.

The day before the great showdown I gladly—nay, feverishly —accepted a luncheon invitation to the Bill Davis estate near Málaga, where Ordóñez was recuperating with the Hemingways and assorted friends. I found Ernest by the pool, swinging a club back and forth—for exercise, I hoped. He was bellowing, but *sotto voce,* about the *Life* magazine man who had come the previous day, spent two hours with Ordóñez without knowing who he was because Ordóñez was in street clothes. I thought I had to defend my professional brethren. I did not tell him about the time I spent an hour with Winchell at a Stork Club table while impatiently waiting for Winchell to arrive for a scheduled interview. But I did tell him about the dinner in London when Dorothy Thompson talked for three hours, then rose to say she had to get ready for an interview with Viscount Cranbourne (I think it was) in the morning. Viscount Cranbourne was the little man with the mustache who had been sitting beside Miss Thompson all evening and who had just departed to get his rest. Ernest whooped and narrowly escaped falling into the pool.

Now, I had read books about bullfighters and I expected to find Ordóñez in prayer and meditation somewhere, somber-eyed with the fear that precedes a great contest with the big bulls. Or I would find him nervously trying to reply to the jokes of well-meaning friends endeavoring to take his mind off the terrible, impending trial.

Ernest said, "That's Antonio, there." That was when the ageless *mystique* about bullfighters vanished for me. Antonio resembled a husky, happy Purdue halfback *after* a winning game. Antonio was receiving tennis balls pitched by an American from the other end of the pool by leaping sideways into the air, whacking the pellet with his head like a soccer player and then falling into the water. He never missed and he shouted with pure joy every time he came up for air. *Dominguin,* I thought, *you've had it.*

Antonio came and sat in a chair. The thigh wound was high up, close to the groin. It was a good 8 inches long, a twisted, jagged red line because bulls jerk when the horn goes in. This wound had been 4 inches deep and I counted some twenty stitches. A small hole was still open, for suppuration, I supposed. By the book he should never be in that unsterilized pool, but "Papa" Hemingway plastered a bandage over the hole in the flesh and we went to lunch.

Antonio ate everything in sight; Antonio drummed the table and sang calypso songs. Only a totally nerveless man can sing so loudly knowing he's off-key and not give a solitary damn. Antonio grabbed a girl and danced a *paso-doble* around the table. Antonio grabbed a child's guitar and did a rock-and-roll solo around the table.

I looked across at Hemingway with glazed and disenchanted eyes. A slow, wide grin spread through the gray beard and Ernest said, "He's not very spooky, is he? Good God, the way we write about bullfighters!" That night I had a bad dream in which Dominguín was trying to get away from a lion, among the trees.

At six the next afternoon I could see Dominguín in my binoculars as the fighters waited with their entourages for the parade across the plaza to salute the *corrida* president. Dominguín was tall, slim, with a proud, sensitive, civilized face, and he was wetting his lips. For a moment I wanted him to win; competing for the crown against a man with no nerve ends comes under the heading of cruel and unusual punishment.

Dominguín was nervous on the first bull, a staccato charging beast that crowded him so closely he once had to retreat. The kill was not clean and Dominguín did not receive even one ear from the crowd. When Ordóñez took two ears on the next bull with the laziest-looking, most graceful capework and the most perfect kill I'd ever seen, I thought Dominguín's nerve must be broken for good. But he hadn't been Number One for ten years for nothing. He ended that round with both ears and the tail, and the tension increased.

I won't detail the rest of this bullfight; it is history. With the next bull Ordóñez took the works—ear, tail and hoof. On the next Dominguín took the works. On the sixth and last animal, Ordóñez again got ears, tail and hoof.

Three hoofs cut in one afternoon. It was paralyzing in its perfection. Neither man missed a sword thrust; all three of Ordóñez' thrusts went to the hilt and no dagger was needed. It was the kind of bullfight *aficionados* all over the Spanish world dream about. It was the theory of bullfighting made manifest. In reality it is not supposed to happen—ever.

Luis Miguel Dominguín is the world's second-greatest bullfighter. He represents, in his slim, sensitive body, the standard theater of bullfighting—human against beast—and when he was lifted like a willow wand on the horns of the fifth bull for what seemed an eternity, classic Greek tragedy seemed to have reached its climax. For a time, to the amateur observer, the husky, sure-footed Ordóñez does not provide the same dramatic contrast. You

301

feel for a moment that he meets the bull on its own terms. Then, as you see him float the big cape along the horns in unbelievably slow tempo; as you see him wind the animal around and around himself with the *muleta* in perfect cadence; as you see him launch himself with the sword upon the beast like a great panther—as your eyes assemble this pageantry, your mind accepts a truth Hemingway discovered long ago.

It is this, I think: that the difference between the great and the master in any sport is more than a difference of degree; it is a difference of kind. The great has learned to do it by thought and training and enormous dedication; the master just does it, from the beginning, and does it to perfection when his natural endowments have reached their full bloom. A great bullfighter like Dominguín is in command of the bull because he knows the bull. Ordoñez, the master, is in command of the bull because he is in command of himself. He knows himself. It is the difference between talent and genius, between what a great man can do for himself and the gods do for him with their touch.

This is why I feel utterly sure that no bullfighter will ever seriously challenge Ordoñez while he remains in his physical prime; and he will stay in his prime for years.

After the fight I found Hemingway in the Miramar bar. "Well?" I said.

"Antonio is the greatest bullfighter alive," he said. "It is quite likely that he is the greatest who ever lived."

"Ernest," I said, "enlighten me. Didn't Antonio do a cross-over to the far horn while patting his hip?"

"He did."

"Isn't that horribly dangerous?"

Hemingway looked at me as if astounded that I could even ask the question.

"Didn't he do a pendulum pass, front to back, while still moving his feet?"

"He did, my friend."

"Why and how, in God's name?"

"Because he has absolute certainty about his own reflexes."

I told Ernest I had to ask him one more question. When Ordoñez was trotting around the ring with his hands full of ears and tail and the hoof and had run over to Hemingway at the fence, what was it that Hemingway had said to him? Had he suggested what Ordoñez then did—escort Dominguín out with him for a triumphal circle of the arena together?

"Hell, no," said Hemingway. "I suggested he throw the hoof to Hutch." Hutch was the young American who had played the tennis-soccer game in the pool with Ordoñez the day before.

"They've been throwing things at each other all week," said Ernest.

"TAKE HEAVEN, TAKE PEACE, TAKE JOY"

Christmas offers us peace in one hand but in the other it carries a sword. The peace it offers is the love we felt in childhood and may still feel again if we have lived our lives as we were instructed in our early days. The sword is our conscience, glittering as sharply as the icicles on the Christmas tree. This is why most of us welcome Christmas and yet we dread its coming.

Christmas is anticipation for the children; it is memory for most adults. It fastens the grip of truth upon us and will not let us go. Implacably it demands of us that we regard our work and what we have made of our lives, our country and our world.

By the glow of the soft lights, by the sound of child voices in song, piercing us with an almost unendurable purity, we are obliged to remember that our first and only commandment was to love, and we have not truly obeyed; that men were so commanded not to improve them, but to save them from themselves, and we have not truly understood.

Of course, we say as the moment of truth approaches, "Christmas is really for the children." Suffer the little children to take this burden from us.

Perhaps, were we to know the realities of our own deepest motivations, we would conclude that this is why we have made of the Christmas occasion an immensely complicated business. It is the sheer busyness of Christmas, not so much its commercialization, that has changed its forms and rituals. Perhaps we have lost not only the art of simplicity but the desire for it as well. But not, I think, in our deepest beings. And as long as we know in our hearts what Christmas *ought* to be, then Christmas *is*.

The sophisticated may belittle the almost assembly-line transaction of the printed Christmas cards that swamp our parlors in piles and windrows. It is impersonal, yes, as compared with the old-fashioned family trek down the street for greetings at the door. But each little square or rectangular printed card is a signal of human recognition, a reassurance from others that we live in part, at least, of their consciousness, however small a part, and so are not alone.

It is possible to work and to walk the streets fifty weeks of the year feeling that one has dropped from the awareness of a host of names and faces, and then at the Christmas season be overwhelmed with gratitude and humility by the fusillade of signals from names out of one's remotest past that one may even have forgotten.

Christmas is a personal renaissance for all of us; it is, for however short a period, a defiance of time and anonymity, a marshaling of forces by all those loose associations, from family outward, that have given each of us our identification and made life tolerable and to some purpose.

For all those of middle and older years it is the past rising in our hearts, demanding review, in pleasure and in pain. And the memories of sharpest pain and keenest delight are the family memories. For those families who find it psychologically impossible to say to one another, "I love you," Christmas is a crisis of inhibited emotion.

Now that I think back in my middle years, it seems to me that it is the painful Christmases, the occasions when the tensely guarded emotional dikes were broken, that I remember more clearly than I recall the smooth and pleasurable times. There came a Christmas in my early teens when for the first time I had my own earned money to spend and spent it on what were for me expensive gifts. Christmas, I knew, meant a financial strain for my father, upon whom misfortunes had fallen heavily. So with the secret, self-serving generosity of the "good" boy I had bought for my stalwart older brother a leatherbound book and a silver-plated cigarette lighter, treasures for him undreamed of. He received them with a stricken look; a necktie was all he had for me in return. After he handed me this he broke into tears. Out of smugness and pride, as much as generosity, I had destroyed his Christmas. I had not yet learned that the head must sometimes govern the heart, that it may not always be better to give than to receive.

It was later, during the thirties, when war was building up in Europe with its implied threat to all Americans, that I first saw Christmas break my father's exterior of stoic reserve. In those days Mme. Schumann-Heink used to sing "Silent Night" each Christmas Eve over a new device known as the radio set, one of which I had bought for my mother. On one of these occasions

she finished the song and then—spontaneously, it seemed to me
—burst into a passionate spoken plea that people love and understand and live in peace.

―――――――――――――

My father was a big man, strong and grave of face, brought
up as a child on an austere Scandinavian family farm, the kind
of life in which revelation of the gentler emotions is expected of
children and poets but not of others. He listened that night to
the heavily accented words of the singer, began to tremble, and
then hurried upstairs to hide what I realized with immense surprise were tears. I think perhaps he knew in his heart what was
coming to the world, and that in his mind's eye he was seeing all
the years of heavy work, his few possessions, his family, including
three sons approaching the age of military service.

These Christmas memories in all their pain come back so
clearly now; they must have lodged deeply and firmly in my
awareness all these years. But if in recollection the pain is only
fleeting, it is because something very important happened in
those moments of emotional crisis. Contacts were made between
brothers and from sons to parents. The close but tenuous stitch-
ing over our hearts was unstitched, however briefly. Of course
there had to be pain in these sudden, unanesthetized surgical
operations, but only by this means could there be health and
healing. By the sword, if necessary, will the heart be opened, as
opened it must be if it is to give as well as to receive.

We cannot live, in our families, in our nations or in our
world, if we cannot open our hearts. I do not know how this
compressed, elbowing and suspicious world is to go in peace if
this cannot be done. I see no ultimate security in any "balance
of power" or "balance of terror" peace. We know instinctively
that in the end only a peace through a balance of kindness will
preserve us.

All of us, in our Christmas selves, want to be kind to one
another, to love one another as we did when we were children.
I do not believe this suppressed yearning can be any different
among the Russian people or the Chinese people or the Cuban
people. The difficulty is that man's institutions have selves of
their own, and these selves cannot love as the person loves. I
have never observed a government committing an act of love directed at another government. Governments are our tribal devices for protecting the in-group from the out-group. They are

unable, in themselves, to break the mold that produced them, to make a jointure instead of perpetuating the separations.

There are new books, like the remarkable *African Genesis*, by Robert Ardrey, that tell us that in these devices of ours for protection, real or false, pure animal instincts are at work, inherited from the primates in the forest; because, by the evidence of science, we come not from a fallen angel, but from a risen ape. But if we are so risen, we have risen to a very considerable height—in the direction, at least, of the angels' habitation. If we cannot change these instincts, including the warring instinct, by an effort of will, we can at least observe and check them. For by Mr. Ardrey's own testimony we are also "nature's first brief experiment in self-awareness"—we alone among animal creatures can see what we are feeling and doing. Somehow our collectivity must not be allowed to amount to less than the sum of our individual selves.

We can see only a relatively few faces in our lives and only a few can see ours; in our immense collectivity we have only words as our instruments for operations within the breast. There are a few words I read every time the Christmas season comes around. I do not know now where I first came upon them. I was once told they were written by one Fra Giovanni in the year 1513. I took this on faith, but was later told they were written by someone still unknown to me only a few years ago. It does not matter. I do not see how anything could be added to or subtracted from these words, which sometimes I think of as the most perfect passage in our language. Let it be my Christmas card to friends and strangers alike.

"There is nothing I can give you which you have not; but there is much that, while I cannot give, you can take. No heaven can come to us unless our hearts find rest in it today. Take heaven. No peace lies in the future which is not hidden in this present instant. Take peace. The gloom of the world is but a shadow; behind it, yet within reach, is joy. Take joy. And so, at this Christmastime, I greet you with the prayer that for you, now and forever, the day breaks and the shadows flee away."

About the Author

Eric Sevareid was born in Velva, North Dakota. For twenty-five years he has been a reporter and commentator for CBS News, working in Washington, Europe, Asia, Africa and Latin America. He writes a syndicated column each week for nearly a hundred American newspapers. He is the author of *Canoeing with the Cree,* a children's book; *Not So Wild a Dream,* a report on the war and his wartime generation; *In One Ear* and *Small Sounds in the Night,* collections of broadcast essays, and was the editor of *Candidates 1960.* Mr. Sevareid has won all of broadcasting's major awards, holds two honorary degrees, and decorations from the Kings of Norway and Belgium.